ON THE EDGE OF COMMITMENT

ON THE EDGE OF COMMITMENT

EDUCATIONAL ATTAINMENT AND
RACE IN THE UNITED STATES

Stephen L. Morgan

STANFORD UNIVERSITY PRESS
STANFORD, CALIFORNIA
2005

Stanford University Press
Stanford, California

Printed in the United States of America on acid-free,
archival-quality paper

Library of Congress Cataloging-in-Publication Data
Morgan, Stephen L. (Stephen Lawrence), 1971–
    On the edge of commitment : educational attainment
and race in the United States / Stephen L. Morgan.
        p.   cm.
    Includes bibliographical references and index.
    ISBN 0-8047-4419-X (hardcover : alk. paper)
    1. Minorities—Education (Higher)—United States.
2. College attendance—United States.   3. Educational equalization—United States.   I. Title.
LC3731.M674 2005
378.1′9829′073—dc22
                                        2004018556

Typeset by G&S Book Services in 10/14 Sabon

Original Printing 2005

Last figure below indicates year of this printing:
14   13   12   11   10   09   08   07   06   05

FOR MY SIGNIFICANT OTHERS

CONTENTS

Tables

Figures

ACKNOWLEDGMENTS

Aage B. Sørensen introduced me to the study of educational attainment in a social stratification course that I took in 1991 as an undergraduate. Commencing with the encouraging comments that he offered on my term paper on educational expectations, his support of my early research was invaluable. Tragically, Aage's February 2000 walk around Fresh Pond kept him away from William James Hall for longer than he anticipated, and he has since passed away. As a result, Aage was unable to read or comment on the vast majority of this manuscript, either in its original form as my 2000 dissertation at Harvard University or in this heavily reworked book.

Even though Aage was the most important figure in my early development as a scholar, he had many competitors for that status. I received training, as both an undergraduate and graduate student, from the entire department of sociology at Harvard. I recognize, with each day I spend teaching my own students now, that the training I received was second to none. And I am therefore grateful to all my teachers between 1990 and 2000.

For this particular project, however, the contributions of several of these professors deserve special mention. The remaining members of my dissertation committee—Christopher Winship, Christopher S. Jencks, and Richard J. Murnane—provided crucial comments on the dissertation in its final stages. And Chris Winship deserves a very special thank you. He has provided constant encouragement and support since I met him in 1995. I have always thought of him as a fabulous teacher and scholar, but I am especially happy now that I can count him among my close friends.

As all graduate students know, among the best teachers you will find are those who know the nuts and bolts of data analysis. For me, these wise sages were Nancy Williamson and Cheri Minton, whose job titles as programmers/analysts do not do them justice. I cannot imagine where my career would have gone had I not met them while an undergraduate, as they taught me the real business of research while instilling in me an obsession with the details of data that make my current research assistants slightly nuts (but, an obsession, which I notice with pleasure they are now beginning to emulate...).

Despite the debt that I owe to all of these mentors, many other colleagues deserve heartfelt thanks as well. Since 2000, I have found an intellectual home at Cornell University. My Cornell colleagues David Grusky and Douglas Heckathorn provided encouraging and helpful comments on some of the core ideas of this book, especially Chapters 3 and 4 when they were in journal article form. Outside of this direct circle of colleagues, I would like to thank a wider group of scholars who may not be aware of their contributions to my work. Through comments on my work in various roles as editors and reviewers, I thank Karl Alexander, Aaron Pallas, and Barbara Schneider for their thoughts on some of the material in Chapter 6. I also received many helpful suggestions from faculty and graduate students when presenting the material in seminars at Arizona, Columbia, Cornell, Harvard, Indiana, Minnesota, Northwestern, Stanford, and UCLA. Charles Ragin's comments at Northwestern, Cecilia Ridgeway's comments at Stanford, and Don Rubin's comments at Harvard were among the most memorable and helpful.

I thank Greg Austic, Erin Jacobs, Mark McKerrow, Rebecca Vichniac, and Wubiao Zhou for working as research assistants on various portions of the book. Erin Jacobs also proofread the entire manuscript (and insisted that I inform readers that she feels that the even-numbered chapters are the best).

At Stanford University Press, I thank Nathan MacBrien, then Pat Katayama, and then Alan Harvey for shepherding the book through the editorial board. Yossi Shavit read the entire manuscript for the press and provided many valuable comments, from which I benefited greatly. Kate Wahl, Carmen Borbon-Wu, Cheryl Hauser, and Judith Hibbard pushed the manuscript through final production.

My professional debts having been noted, I move to the equally important personal ones. To my graduate student friends from William James Hall, I am grateful for your good company. I will always cherish the frequent midnight tea breaks that Susan Dumais and I shared in the fifth floor lounge, and then the 1:00 AM cheeky banter with Karen Chai and Tomas Jimenez in our shared office. Foosball with Ian Dowker and clam chowder with Tracy Marshall made Lowell House survivable.

Finally, I thank my family. My father has served as a sounding board for many of my crazier ideas and, in the process, further convinced me of his wisdom. Sydney (who has forgiven me for my dedication to this book, now that I have explained it to her) and my mother (who has not yet forgiven me for the same dedication, even though I have explained it to her too) deserve thanks for their support. I am quite certain that my mother never expected me to end up as a sociologist just like my father, and neither did I! Her continuing refusal to let father and son talk shop on any regular basis is very healthy for everyone, and I am grateful for her lack of tolerance. Sydney has been a wonderfully supportive partner, and I am overwhelmed with joy that I will be spending my life with her.

The research in this book was first supported by a grant from the American Educational Research Association which received the funds for its "AERA Grants Program" from the National Science Foundation and National Center for Education Statistics (U.S. Department of Education) under NSF grant #RED-9452861. The dissertation write-up of the project was supported by a dissertation completion fellowship from the Spencer Foundation and then an Eliot Fellowship from Harvard University. The subsequent revisions were then supported by funds from the College of Arts and Sciences and from the Center for the Study of Inequality, both of Cornell University. The opinions found within this book are my own and do no not necessarily reflect those of the granting agencies.

ON THE EDGE OF COMMITMENT

INTRODUCTION

CHAPTER ONE

Why Do We Need a New Model of Educational Attainment?

Explanations for patterns of social inequality are only as strong as the models of educational attainment on which they depend. Educational training creates and then uniquely signals many of the skills and habits that determine styles of life and economic well-being. Educational credentials and the social connections they embody facilitate the allocation of individuals to alternative occupational and labor market positions. No convincing causal model of intergenerational mobility can be fashioned without incorporating these mechanisms.

Shifting from one depiction of the structure of inequality to another does not relieve the burden of having to account for differences in educational attainment. Class schemas, prestige hierarchies, and labor markets are similarly incomprehensible without an explanation of how the distribution of educational attainment emerges. Even explanations for patterns of ascriptive inequality are crucially reliant on foundational models of educational processes. The extent of racial and gender discrimination in the labor market, for example, cannot be assessed without taking a position on how and why individuals accumulate alternative educational credentials and skills.

This justification for rigorous modeling of educational attainment, on which generations of social stratification researchers and sociologists of education have relied, is even more compelling now. Over the past three decades, the evolution of postindustrial society has increased the stakes for comprehensively modeling patterns of educational attainment, as these now more strongly predict economic well-being.[1] Between 1979 and 1999, the real wages of high school graduates decreased by 8.9 percent, whereas the real wages of college graduates and advanced degree graduates increased by

3

13.0 and 18.9 percent, respectively (Mishel, Bernstein, and Schmitt 2001: 153). By the late 1990s, levels of labor market inequality in the United States reached levels more extreme even than those observed in the 1930s. And therefore, as educational attainment becomes a stronger predictor of lifetime well-being, understanding why some adolescents carry on to postsecondary education and others do not has become increasingly important.

Unfortunately, it is also becoming clear that current models of educational attainment are insufficiently complete. Consider the capacity to determine the consequences of the growth in labor market inequality for patterns of educational attainment. Over the same time period, policies designed to increase college enrollments have changed only modestly. From a variety of theoretical perspectives, it can be argued that increases in labor market inequality should have variable effects on different groups of prospective college students. The increasing incentives for obtaining college degrees should prompt more students to enter college, but the rate of increase in college enrollments should differ by social background. One would expect the increase to be less pronounced for prospective students from relatively disadvantaged social origins, for these students' relative access to liquid funds to finance a college education has declined as inequality has grown.[2]

Explanatory models of educational attainment in the social sciences are unable to determine whether this prediction is accurate, to say nothing of the underlying mechanism that supposedly generates it. None of the established models, I will argue in this book, can be used to determine whether or not students' beliefs about their future prospects are responsive to changes in incentives, and, if so, how changes in beliefs affect the long sequence of commitment decisions that determine a student's final level of educational attainment. The main goal of this book is to develop the foundation for a new and better model of educational attainment, one that can generate sufficiently complete explanations by specifying and modeling the belief-based mechanisms that have been assumed away in the past.

Before proceeding to development of the model, in this introductory chapter I present the basic facts on college entry and college completion in the United States. I then demarcate the limits of current knowledge and develop two sets of reasons why the social sciences need a new and better model of educational attainment—to resolve empirical puzzles and to guide better policy development and evaluation. I then discuss why sociology as a discipline is well prepared to produce and embrace a new model, and I conclude by justifying the mode of theoretical development that I will pursue in subsequent chapters.

THE BASIC FACTS ON EDUCATIONAL ATTAINMENT IN THE UNITED STATES

Who goes to college, and who graduates? Table 1.1 presents the college entry and graduation patterns of the high school classes of 1982 and 1992, as of 1990 and 2000, respectively. The findings are based on parallel analyses of the two most widely used national surveys sponsored by the U.S. Department of Education, the *High School & Beyond Survey* (*HS&B*) and the *National Education Longitudinal Study* (*NELS*) (U.S. Department of Education 1995, 2002).

In the first column of each panel, the college entry patterns of high school graduates are presented separately for the four largest racial/ethnic groups in the two surveys. For example, for white students of the class of 1982, 53.84 percent of students entered college within one year of graduating from high school, 18.10 percent entered college more than one year after graduating from high school, and the remaining 28.07 percent never entered college (as of 1990, the final year of the measurement window).[3]

In the second column of each panel, bachelor's degree attainment patterns are then tabulated, conditional on the timing of college entry. Again, for white students, 35.79 percent of those who entered college within one year of high school graduation then obtained a bachelor's degree within five years. An additional 16.60 percent obtained a bachelor's degree in more than five years, and the remaining 47.60 percent never obtained a bachelor's degree (again, as of 1990, the final year of the measurement window).

Although there are many patterns within Table 1.1, focus first on the findings common to all groups. Among those students who enter college, many students do not obtain a bachelor's degree. Some of these students enter two-year colleges and never transfer to four-year colleges. Others simply drop out of college after one or more years. Some work part time, obtaining only a few college credits per year, making steady but slow progress toward the credentials they hope to secure at some point in adulthood.[4]

Aside from this pattern, which demonstrates clearly that college entry does not on its own guarantee college graduation, the table shows important racial and ethnic differences in college entry and graduation patterns. Black

TABLE 1.1

College Entry and Completion Rates for the High School Classes
of 1982 and 1992 (by 1990 and 2000, respectively)

	Class of 1982		Class of 1992	
White Students				
Enter College ≤1 Year After High School	53.84		62.71	
Received a Bachelor's Degree ≤5 Years		35.79		41.99
Received a Bachelor's Degree >5 Years		16.60		12.06
No Bachelor's Degree Yet		47.60		45.96
Enter College >1 Year After High School	18.10		19.00	
Received a Bachelor's Degree ≤5 Years		9.44		9.00
Received a Bachelor's Degree >5 Years		10.94		27.26
No Bachelor's Degree Yet		79.61		63.74
Never Entered College	28.07		18.28	
Black Students				
Enter College ≤1 Year After High School	44.35		52.92	
Received a Bachelor's Degree ≤5 Years		18.06		24.75
Received a Bachelor's Degree >5 Years		12.40		9.03
No Bachelor's Degree Yet		69.54		66.21
Enter College >1 Year After High School	18.86		25.72	
Received a Bachelor's Degree ≤5 Years		3.61		1.71
Received a Bachelor's Degree >5 Years		8.64		21.89
No Bachelor's Degree Yet		87.75		76.40
Never Entered College	36.79		21.36	
Hispanic Students				
Enter College ≤1 Year After High School	42.95		52.50	
Received a Bachelor's Degree ≤5 Years		15.39		15.79
Received a Bachelor's Degree >5 Years		14.81		9.85
No Bachelor's Degree Yet		69.80		74.36
Enter College >1 Year After High School	20.24		25.44	
Received a Bachelor's Degree ≤5 Years		2.22		1.42
Received a Bachelor's Degree >5 Years		5.19		29.40
No Bachelor's Degree Yet		92.59		69.18
Never Entered College	36.80		22.06	
Asian Students				
Enter College ≤1 Year After High School	72.67		79.15	
Received a Bachelor's Degree ≤5 Years		39.73		43.20
Received a Bachelor's Degree >5 Years		23.30		16.23
No Bachelor's Degree Yet		36.98		40.57

TABLE 1.1
(*continued*)

	Class of 1982		Class of 1992	
Asian Students (*continued*)				
Enter College >1 Year After High School	16.08		10.81	
Received a Bachelor's Degree ≤5 Years		11.88		23.77
Received a Bachelor's Degree >5 Years		.06		8.23
No Bachelor's Degree Yet		88.06		68.00
Never Entered College	11.24		10.03	

NOTES: Data are drawn from the *High School & Beyond* sophomore cohort 1980 through 1992 waves and the *National Education Longitudinal Study,* 1988 through 2000 waves. The analysis sample includes 9,140 respondents for the class of 1982 and 10,700 respondents for the class of 1992. However, in this table, the entry and graduation patterns of the small "Other" racial/ethnic group are not presented. In subsequent tables in this chapter, these respondents are included.

and Hispanic high school graduates are less likely than white high school graduates to enter college immediately after high school. Asians, in contrast, are much more likely to do so. And, once in college, whites and Asians are similarly likely to receive bachelor's degrees while blacks and Hispanics are much less likely to receive them.

Across all groups, between the classes of 1982 and 1992, college entry and college graduation rates increased notably. This pattern is consistent with other evidence that I will present later, but note the differences in the sampling schemes and measurement instruments of the *NELS* and *HS&B* surveys are substantial enough that one should approach with caution the interpretation of the over-time differences revealed in Table 1.1. For example, although the rate of college entry increased for Hispanic students, the college completion rate appeared to (1) decline for those who entered college immediately but (2) increase for those who entered college more than one year after high school graduation. Although possibly true, the sampling scheme for Hispanics changed between the two surveys (as did the target populations because of immigration patterns), and as a result I will refrain from overinterpreting such changes. Indeed, for much of the empirical analysis in this book, I will focus narrowly on whites and blacks, in part because over-time comparisons are more tricky for other groups, and in part because the classic literature in the sociology of education—which I aim to reinter-

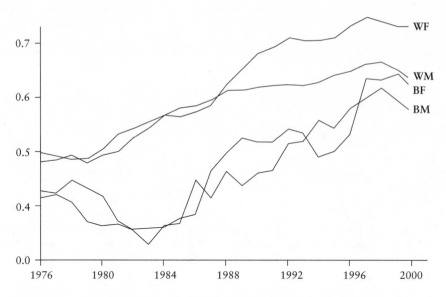

Figure 1.1.   College Entry Rates of Recent High School Graduates, Ages 18–21 (three-year moving average). WM = white males, WF = white females, BM = black males, BF = black females.

SOURCE: *Current Population Surveys*, 1977–2001, October Supplement

pret and extend—is often built around black-white comparisons of educational outcomes.

To further assess changes in college entry rates, consider the next set of findings, based on an analysis of the 1976 through 2000 October *Current Population Surveys*, the data source most commonly used to track changes in college entry rates. Figure 1.1 presents estimates of the college entry rate of recent high school graduates between the ages of 18 and 21, separately for white males, white females, black males, and black females.[5] The trends presented in Figure 1.1 are consistent with the college entry rates of whites and blacks from Table 1.1. But, because many more graduating cohorts of high school seniors are analyzed, additional patterns and more recent trends are revealed as well.

Notice, first, the decline in the college entry rate of blacks in the early 1980s. Immediately after this sharp decline, the rate of college entry among blacks rebounded quickly. By 2000, black males and females were nearly as likely as white males to enter college after graduating from high school. But a new trend emerged in the 1990s. White females began to enter college at a record pace. By 2000, nearly 70 percent of white female high school graduates entered college immediately after graduating from high school.[6]

What predicts college entry and college graduation? Table 1.2 presents the results of nine separate models where the three-category breakdown of college entry (from the first column of each panel of Table 1.1) is specified as the outcome variable. Each of the nine variables listed in Table 1.2 is specified in a separate multinomial logit model as a linear predictor of the probability of entering college within one year of graduating from high school and simultaneously of the probability of entering college more than one year after graduating from high school (both in comparison to not entering college by the end of the measurement window, 1990 and 2000 respectively).

For the discrete change in the predictor variable presented in the relevant cells in columns one and two of the table, the last four columns report the corresponding changes in these estimated probabilities. For example, for the class of 1982, the probability that a student would enter college within one year of high school graduation was .274 higher for students whose fathers were college graduates (that is, those whose father's education was equal to 16 years) than for students whose fathers were only high school graduates. Likewise, the probability that a student would enter college more than one year after high school graduation was .051 lower for students whose fathers were college graduates. This implies that the probability of ever entering college was .223 higher for students whose fathers were college graduates (that is, .274 − .051). And, the simple qualitative conclusion to draw from the estimates is that having a father who is a college graduate increases one's likelihood of entering college and also of entering college immediately after graduating from high school.[7]

The next four rows present similar estimated changes in probabilities for mother's education, father's and mother's occupational prestige, and family income. The designated discrete change for mother's education is again 12 versus 16 years of education. The discrete change for occupational prestige is fixed at the SEI values of 35 and 48, which is close to one standard deviation centered on the mean of occupational prestige.[8] For family income, the designated discrete change is also centered around the observed mean of family income, but it is proportionately much narrower at only $6,000 in 1992 and $4,150 in 1982, an equivalent amount after adjusting for inflation.[9] This dollar amount is roughly equivalent to the combined costs of tu-

TABLE 1.2

Predicted Changes in the Probability of College Entry for the High School Classes of 1982 and 1992

	DISCRETE CHANGE IN PREDICTOR VARIABLE (1982/1992 WHERE APPLICABLE)		ENTER COLLEGE ≤1 YEAR		ENTER COLLEGE >1 YEAR	
	From:	To:	1982	1992	1982	1992
Father's Education	12	16	.274	.258	-.051	-.100
Mother's Education	12	16	.281	.240	-.049	-.091
Father's Occupational Prestige	35	48	.185	.165	-.013	-.060
Mother's Occupational Prestige	35	48	.116	.135	-.003	-.033
Family Income	$21,422/$31,568	$25,572/$37,568	.037	.030	-.008	-.012
Test Score in Sophomore Year	21.23/111.85	38.78/142.74	.224	.214	-.020	-.099
Test Score in Senior Year	25.83/122.95	44.99/154.60	.248	.222	-.032	-.101
Significant Others' Influence in Senior Year	.4	.8	.304	.247	-.069	-.093
Years of Education Expected in Senior Year	13	16	.447	.414	-.027	-.104

NOTES: Numbers of respondents are 9,140 for the class of 1982 and 10,700 for the class of 1992.

ition and fees of $2,300 and living expenses of $3,700 at a typical four-year public university in the 1990s (see Kosters 1999).[10]

The resulting predicted probabilities imply the same basic pattern as for father's education. For example, students from the class of 1992 and from families with $6,000 more income were more likely to enter college immediately (.03 in probability), less likely to enter after one year (−.012), and hence in combination more likely to ever enter college (at .018 in probability, which equals .03 − .012).

For these education, occupational prestige, and family income variables, the predicted probability changes are slightly different for the earlier time period, suggesting a greater increase in the probability of entering college immediately, a smaller decline in the probability of entering college after more than one year, and in combination a greater relative increase in the probability of ever entering college for the class of 1982. One could interpret this small cohort difference as an indication that family background was more predictive of college entry patterns for the earlier cohort, but since the two datasets are slightly different, results differing by this magnitude could have emerged because of study design differences. And yet, no matter what interpretation one gives to these small differences, there is surely no evidence of a large increase in the importance of family background for college entry patterns, as one might hypothesize would result from the generalized increase in inequality in the 1980s and 1990s.

What about the characteristics of students themselves? For the models reported in Table 1.2, test scores in the sophomore and senior years were specified analogously in separate models. The specified discrete changes are equal to one standard deviation on the relevant test, centered around the mean test score. The resulting estimates show that for both cohorts, the probability of entering college immediately after graduating high school was higher by at least .2 for those students who scored one-half of a standard deviation above the mean than for those who scored one-half of a standard deviation below the mean.

In the last two rows of the table, two additional predictor variables were deployed, each of which will be discussed in detail throughout this book, especially in Chapters 2 and 3. Significant others' influence is the proportion of a student's parents, teachers, and peers whom the student felt expected him or her to attend college immediately after high school. Educational expectations are answers to the question "How far in school do you expect to

TABLE 1.3

Predicted Changes in the Probability of College Graduation
for Those Who Entered College Within One Year of
Graduating from High School

	BACHELOR'S DEGREE ≤5 YEARS		BACHELOR'S DEGREE >5 YEARS	
	1982	1992	1982	1992
Father's Education	.191	.219	.053	.034
Mother's Education	.176	.230	.042	.020
Father's Occupational Prestige	.102	.111	.037	.023
Mother's Occupational Prestige	.072	.112	.014	.010
Family Income in Sophomore Year	.022	.033	.008	.005
Test Score in Sophomore Year	.181	.212	.056	.021
Test Score in Senior Year	.199	.219	.066	.026
Significant Others' Influence in Senior Year	.185	.116	.045	.017
Years of Education Expected in Senior Year	.190	.172	.080	.037

NOTES: The discrete changes in the predictor variables are the same as specified for Table 1.2 (even though the modeled respondents are more disproportionately from the upper tails of their distributions). Numbers of respondents are 5,325 for the class of 1982 and 6,918 for the class of 1992.

get?"—which were then converted from levels of educational attainment to a years-completed metric. The last two rows of the table show that the views of students' significant others and their forecasts of their own future behavior are strongly predictive of the probability of entering college.

Table 1.3 repeats the same basic analysis for the college graduation patterns of Table 1.1, but only for those students who entered college within one year after high school graduation. Virtually all of the patterns are the same, except that there is no estimated movement out of the category "Obtain bachelor's degree in more than five years" in the way that there was movement in the models of Table 1.2 out of the category "Enter college after more than one year after high school graduation." That is to say, empirical support for shifts toward faster bachelor's degree completion (as opposed to slower bachelor's degree completion) was not as strong as evidence for shifts toward immediate college entry (as opposed to delayed college entry).

What should one make of these predicted probabilities? They indicate that social advantages, conceptualized as family background, are predictive of eventual patterns of educational attainment. Likewise, test scores, which to some extent reflect the quality of education one's family background can command, are also predictive. Moreover, students whom others think will go to college seem to be more likely to do so. And finally, students' beliefs about their own future attainments are predictive as well.

One can attempt to partial out the bivariate relationships in Tables 1.2 and 1.3 across each of the predictor variables, using variants of regression analysis. Mathematically and computationally, this is accomplished easily, as one need only estimate additional models, including more than one predictor variable in each model. But, unless one completely misconstrues what regression models can accomplish, these additional models will not reveal much new information in this context. The variables in Tables 1.2 and 1.3 will not magically control for each other, somehow turning survey data into experimental data.

In the past two decades, progress has been made in identifying additional variables that also predict educational attainment patterns, such as family disruptions, wealth, and neighborhood and school characteristics. It is unclear how much new information these additional associations reveal, as they tend to be associated with the basic family background variables of Tables 1.2 and 1.3. Nonetheless, the empirically oriented literature has succeeded in developing a rich portrait of the many characteristics of students and their families and communities that predict patterns of educational attainment. This progress does not, of course, mean that the modeling of educational attainment has been without substantial limitations, as I discuss next.

INSUFFICIENT EXPLANATORY POWER

A main limitation of current knowledge about college entry and graduation patterns is that we cannot determine the causal primacy of the many variables that we know predict educational attainment. Even holding aside the thorny question of what types of causal effects we should be attempting to estimate, consider the complexity beneath the results presented earlier in Tables 1.2 and 1.3. There are 511 distinct regression models that one could fit using the 9 separate variables (that is, 9 one-variable models, 36 two-variable models, 84 three-variable models, and so on). The task taken on by sociologists of education who have analyzed similar survey data has been to figure out which of these many mathematically possible regression models yield coefficient values that are theoretically meaningful. In the process, researchers have learned a great deal about how regression models function when used to analyze survey data, but few conclusions other than the simple descriptive claims from the last section have achieved a consensus.

I will return to some direct discussion of this predicament later at the end of this chapter, as I motivate the style of theoretical development I will pursue in this book. For now, however, I shift focus to a related set of empirical patterns that must be explained but that, for the most part, have not been. In addition to sorting out the causal primacy of the many predictors of educational attainment, sociologists also need to develop explanations for change over time in these associations, especially since these are the crucial patterns on which policy decisions are based, and, perhaps more importantly, by which policy effectiveness is assessed.

Recall the college entry patterns presented in Figure 1.1. Researchers have been unable to identify specific and sufficient explanations for important trends such as these, using the theoretical machinery and data currently available. The decline in the entry rate of blacks in the early 1980s has proven exceedingly challenging. Presenting results very similar to those, Hauser (1993a, 1993b) labeled the trends "Findings in Search of Explanations." To investigate the decline, many candidate explanations were evaluated with regression-based methods: relative changes in social background, declines in achievement, increases in military service, changes in college plans, selection effects induced by changes in high school graduation rates, and changes in the composition of enrollment at two-year and four-year colleges. However, two incentive-based explanations attracted the most attention—rising costs of college tuition and decreases in the availability of financial aid. The second explanation received the most support from the research community, but even its most ardent proponents recognized the lack of any direct evidence for it. For example, even though he favored the financial aid explanation, Hauser (1993a:305–6) wrote:

> This evidence . . . is indirect and speculative. We have almost no direct information about the effects of college funding on college entry in any year and even less about its role in changing rates of college entry. We know a great deal about how much money has been given or loaned to college students, but almost nothing about who did not enter college for lack of funds, or who did

obtain grants or loans but would have attended college without them. Changing relationships between the costs of college and the availability of financial
resources may be the most likely explanation for recent trends in black college
entry, but they remain no more than a likely story.

Kane (1994:906) held the same view of the emergent consensus: "Though
this has been the primary hypothesis to explain the decline in college entry
by black youths in the early eighties, it has always been a residual hypothesis, invoked when alternative explanations failed." [11]

A number of more recent trends appear to warrant careful examination
as well. Why did the college entry rate of white females soar in the 1990s?
Was this simply a response to increases in labor market participation among
women (and perhaps, in particular, that women are increasingly entering a
part of the labor market that demands relatively more education)? Or, must
researchers instead explain why white men have not responded as strongly
to increases in labor market returns to college degrees? And, in line with this
latter possibility, why did the gap in the college entry rates of black and
white males narrow steadily throughout the 1990s? Could this narrowing
merely reflect changes in race-specific incarceration rates in the 1990s, or has
there been genuine progress in closing the racial gap? [12] Finding explanations
for these trends will be necessary to construct causal explanations for
changes in gender and racial inequality in the labor market in the next several decades.

The failure to identify solid explanations for these trends in college entry is, on its surface, directly attributable to a lack of appropriate data, as
Hauser (1993a, 1993b) argued for the decline in the college entry rate of
blacks in the early 1980s. Nonetheless, as I will argue in this book, the problem is more fundamentally a result of the lack of explicit theorizing. No adequate theoretical model exists that can be used to model how high school
graduates and their parents form beliefs in order to make decisions about
college enrollment. If such a model did exist, it would suggest exactly what
sort of data should be collected in order to evaluate incentive-based explanations such as shifts in tuition and financial aid.

INADEQUATE GUIDANCE FOR POLICYMAKERS

Trends in the college entry rates of high school graduates are an important
concern of policymakers. Total federal expenditures for Pell Grants, the main

federal program designed to help high school graduates from low-income families pay for the costs of college, exceed $6 billion per year. In the Taxpayer Relief Act of 1997, two new tax credits—the Hope Scholarship Credit and the Lifetime Learning Credit—were introduced to further subsidize enrollment in higher education. Together with the costs of supporting guaranteed student loans, the federal government spends more than $12 billion per year to subsidize enrollment in higher education (see Kane 1999a).[13]

Common sense suggests that all of these federal subsidies should be effective, and in the absence of evidence to the contrary, one can argue that all such programs should be funded. On the other hand, if through a careful analysis a social scientist were to conclusively determine that prospective college students are twice as responsive to increases in Pell Grants than they are to increases in Hope Scholarship Credits, then it would be wise to redistribute funds toward the Pell Grant program.[14]

Social scientists have not offered effective guidance to policymakers on such issues because we have almost no knowledge about how prospective college students respond to subsidies such as Pell Grants. Pell Grants may not even be as effective as straight subsidies to public institutions of higher education that lower tuition levels, for it is quite possible that many students and parents are unaware that Pell Grants exist (see Orfield 1992).

As I will demonstrate in the following chapters, we lack the tools to fully evaluate incentive-based policy prescriptions. But the problem is more general. We cannot effectively evaluate non-incentive-based policies either, even those that sociologists can be credited with proposing. Along with educational psychologists and the Educational Testing Service (who appear to be responsible for initiating some of the first relevant research in the early 1950s), sociologists have been actively engaged in the study of educational expectations for more than forty years. As mentioned earlier for the results in Tables 1.2 and 1.3, educational expectations are the answers that adolescents give to survey questions such as "Do you plan to go to college?" and "How far in school do you expect to get?" Consider how this broad research program has infiltrated the policy arena.[15]

As part of the 1998 amendments to the Higher Education Act of 1965, the secretary of education was authorized to form a new program—later named Gaining Early Awareness and Readiness for Undergraduate Programs (Gear Up)—and appropriated $120 million a year to fund it. The 1998 legis-

lation (P.L. 105-244, Section 404a; see http://www.ed.gov/policy/highered/
leg/hea98/sec403.html) authorized a program that:

> supports eligible entities in providing—(a) additional counseling, mentoring,
> academic support, outreach, and supportive services to elementary school,
> middle school, and secondary school students who are at risk of dropping out
> of school; and (b) information to students and their parents about the advan-
> tages of obtaining a postsecondary education and the college financing options
> for the students and their parents.

The specific wording of the legislation lays out a potentially important program, where eligible entities (such as partnerships of higher education institutions and secondary schools in low-income communities) apply for grants
to establish local programs to support and prepare low-income adolescents
for college.

But, consider how the program was subsequently announced. On the
Department of Education website, the program was introduced in 1999 with
the statement: "GEAR UP is a new national initiative to encourage more
young people to have high expectations, stay in school, study hard and take
the right courses to go to college." When President Clinton introduced the
first grants for Gear Up, he declared:

> "These programs can make all the difference in whether a young person goes
> to college," said President Clinton. "These innovative programs start early,
> reaching out to students no later than seventh grade, staying with them all the
> way—from providing students with mentors who encourage them to have
> high hopes and high expectations for themselves, to ensuring that schools
> teach the classes that prepare young people for college entrance exams, to
> helping families figure out how to pay for college." (Department of Education,
> August 7, 1999, press release)

Thus, shortly after the legislation was passed, one of the main objectives of
Gear Up became the encouragement of at-risk students "to have high hopes
and expectations for themselves."

How are funded Gear Up programs evaluated? The Department of
Education requires them to submit annual reports (see http://www.ed.gov/
programs/gearup/performance.html) demonstrating effectiveness in meeting
the goals of the legislation. Many of the indicators of success are straightforward, such as course-taking patterns of Gear Up participants and ensu-
ing rates of high school graduation. Others closely reflect the information-

propagation aspect of the legislation, as individual programs are required to assess the degree to which Gear Up students and their parents have been made aware of the true costs of a college education. And yet, in the midst of these straightforward indicators, Gear Up students' expectations of their own future chances of going to college are assessed, with (presumably) programs that raise students' expectations deemed successful.[16]

All would agree that it is important to assess whether low-income families are aware of the costs of a college education and the government support programs that are available to meet them. But, for this information to be maximally useful, we also need to know whether and how learning about the costs of education affects subsequent enrollments. We do not know much about these effects, as we have few reliable studies of them.

Regarding the increased hopes and expectations of Gear Up participants, is evidence that a local Gear Up program has convinced participating students that they will indeed go to college a good criterion for judging success? In order to answer this question, one needs to know whether making high school students think that they can and will attend college makes a difference for their future educational attainment, either by making them more likely to experiment with college or by increasing their academic effort while still in secondary school. Unfortunately, despite at least forty years of research on educational expectations, as I will demonstrate in Chapter 3, we still cannot conclusively state that increases in educational expectations have a measurable causal effect on educational attainment.

Accordingly, since social scientists cannot judge the impact of Gear Up effectively, we cannot advise policymakers about the relative prospects of Gear Up in comparison with other policy alternatives. The $120 million spent in the first year of the program, 1999, could have been used instead to increase the Pell Grant maximum by $50. As of fiscal year 2003, by which time the Gear Up budget had swelled to $293 million, the implicit opportunity cost to the Pell Grant program was at least a $100 increase in the Pell Grant maximum. If Gear Up substantially increases the number of low-income students who enroll in college and therefore take advantage of the Pell Grant program, then Gear Up will have been a good use of funds (although, not necessarily the optimal use of funds). If, on the other hand, net rates of college entry for students from participating communities do not measurably increase, then the money will not have been a good use of public funds (assuming, as seems reasonable, that other useful policy proposals are either underfunded or worthy of initial trial).[17]

The ultimate goal for the academic community's contribution to policy development and evaluation for higher education is clear. Researchers need a set of tools that will enable them to jointly evaluate incentive-based programs such as Pell Grants and information-propagation and preparation programs such as Gear Up. Sociologists will be most helpful to policymakers when we are able to write: "Out of the $Z billion that Congress is prepared to spend to increase the college enrollment of low-income students, Congress should allocate $W billion for direct grants, $X billion for guaranteed loans and tax credits, and $Y billion for programs designed to teach high school students and their parents about both the sources of government support available for college tuition and the preparation that will be needed to make an investment in a college education worthwhile." No omnibus policy evaluation framework currently exists that can be used to assign dollar values to W, X, and Y in this statement.

The inability to provide adequate guidance to policymakers for initiatives such as Pell Grants and Gear Up is just the beginning. For higher education, social scientists have been unable to inform policymakers in any convincing way of the consequences for enrollments of raising tuition at public universities. We simply do not know how responsive high school students are to the costs of higher education.[18] And for secondary education, we still have no solid basis for informing policymakers about the effects of statewide mandatory tests on high school graduation rates. This debate is particularly depressing, as researchers are generically polarized along party lines (see Orfield and Kornhaber 2001 for a set of essays). Relatively conservative scholars argue that tests will create incentives for students to learn and for teachers to teach. Their liberal combatants argue that the tests will decrease students' motivation to succeed because the tests will be seen as unfair and punitive. Worse yet, critics also claim that teachers will simply become unreflective test-taking coaches. Surely there is a truth to be discovered somewhere in the midst of these claims, but no one has yet found it.

The general problem that weakens our capacity to inform policymakers is that we do not have a good mechanistic model that enables us to model students' beliefs about their futures and how these beliefs affect effort in schooling in the present and enrollment decisions in the future. As I will now discuss, sociology is just as likely as any other discipline to produce the theoretical framework necessary to enable effective policy guidance.

SOCIOLOGY IS READY TO EMBRACE A NEW MODEL

The status socialization theory of educational attainment, as is discussed in depth in Chapter 2, dominated sociology through the mid-1970s. The theory was generally understood at the time as a model of achievement socialization; if adolescents' motivation could be compelled through the internalization of achievement aspirations, then educational attainment would result. Embodied in what is now known as the Wisconsin model (Sewell, Haller, and Portes 1969), status socialization theory has a strong legacy in current applied work in the sociology of education. But, the basic theory has received little development since the late 1970s when observed racial differences in the processes that it hypothesized overwhelmed it. Nothing in the theory as originally specified could explain why black high school students had more ambitious college plans than white high school students with similar characteristics and yet did not attain comparably higher levels of education. Critics, such as Alan Kerckhoff (1976), argued that structural constraints embedded in the opportunity structure of society need an explicit place in models of educational attainment.

One of the most celebrated assaults, worthy of a lengthy quotation because of its flair, was issued by Pierre Bourdieu (1973:83):

> The functionalist sociologists who announce the brave new world when, at the conclusion of a longitudinal study of academic and social careers, they discover that, as though by a pre-established harmony, individuals have hoped for nothing that they have not obtained and obtained nothing that they have not hoped for, are simply the least forgivable victims of the ideological effect which is produced by the school when it cuts off from their social conditions of production all predispositions regarding the school such as "expectations," "aspirations," "inclinations," or "desire," and thus tends to cover up the fact that objective conditions—and in the individual case, the laws of the academic market—determine aspirations by determining the extent to which they can be satisfied.

Has anything come of this dissatisfaction? Bourdieu (1973:83) argued that much of the educational attainment process should be modeled as "an anticipation, based upon the unconscious estimation of the objective probabilities of success." But in his later writing, he did not attempt to model this process explicitly. Rather, he continued to develop his theory of social reproduction, focusing on the connections between cultural capital endowments and the differential valuation of academic achievement.

Nonetheless, it may now be possible to rectify some of the weaknesses of status socialization theory by adopting a framework that can be used to explicitly model a student's anticipation and estimation of objective probabilities of success. But, this change will necessitate greater theoretical specificity, including some rational choice theory. Diego Gambetta's 1987 book, *Were They Pushed* or *Did They Jump? Individual Decision Mechanisms in Education*, is one of the first systematic attempts to build an explicitly sociological rational choice model of educational attainment.[19] Unfortunately, Gambetta rejects the basic decision tree framework on which all other rational choice researchers rely in other branches of decision theory (for example, in economics, Bayesian statistics, and artificial intelligence). As a result, he could not formulate an explicit model and had to rely on an assertion of unobserved class-differentiated preferences in order to provide an answer to the question that is the title of his book.

Prior to its publication, Anthony Giddens nonetheless recognized the merit of Gambetta's project. In a general discussion of how Gambetta's study is valuable for its attempt to address, at least implicitly, the classic duality in social theory between structure and agency, he praised Gambetta's general approach without mentioning its foundation in rational choice theory. Giddens (1984:310) wrote:

> Gambetta's study is concerned with the influence of structural constraint within the immediate situation of action which confronts school-leavers. Such a restricted focus is no doubt justified, given the inevitably confined nature of any individual piece of research. But obviously the influence of structural constraints over the course of action in question could potentially be examined in much more depth. Thus one could investigate how the actors' motives and processes of reasoning have been influenced or shaped by factors in their upbringing and prior experiences and how those factors have in turn been influenced by general institutional features of the wider society. However, such "social forces" could in principle themselves be studied in exactly the same way as the phenomena directly involved in Gambetta's research. Structural constraints, in other words, always operate via agents' motives and reasons, establishing (often in diffuse and convoluted ways) conditions and consequences affecting options open to others, and what they want from whatever options they have.

Like those of Bourdieu, these are wise words, and much of what I will offer in this book can be regarded as an attempt to build on Giddens' admonishment of Gambetta. After all, Giddens left this theoretical agenda to others, and Gambetta has written little on educational attainment since he published *Were They Pushed or Did They Jump?*[20]

The stage was set at least as early as the late 1980s for the full development within sociology of a model of educational attainment that provides mechanisms for the exogenous impact of shifts in costs and benefits (drawn in part from rational choice theory) along with mechanisms for belief formation (drawn in part from status socialization theory and criticism of it). These joint mechanisms can be used to incorporate structural dynamics into the process of educational attainment—structure that is imposed from the outside as the rigid constraints maintained by institutions along with complex individual responses to perceived structural constraints.

The model of educational attainment that I develop in this book represents a revival of status socialization theory, rendered relevant for the more precise rational choice models first developed by researchers in other disciplines but that now have a place in sociology as well. Less obviously, however, the model also represents an attempt to bring the related forms of structuralism advanced by Bourdieu and Giddens into usage, but only indirectly and (perhaps somewhat heretically) via mechanisms drawn from a bounded form of rational choice theory.

Bourdieu's conception of the habitus and Giddens' model of agency are in many respects appealing, but they are too general to serve my purposes. I wish to explicitly model the anticipation and (somewhat unconscious) estimated probabilities of success that Bourdieu consigns to the practical logic embodied in the habitus.[21] To do so in a sufficiently complete and explicit way, I will use some of the forward-looking apparatus of expected utility theory. Devotees of Bourdieu will surely bristle at this integrative effort, as in using ideas from rational choice theory it necessarily betrays most the processual and relational rhetoric of Bourdieu's writing. But, at least to me, it is unclear how the habitus can be deployed in particular applications without taking a stand on how it is generated and subsequently evolves as individuals progress through the institutions that allocate them to positions in the social structure. I see no practical way forward for models of educational attainment than to rely on the simplicity of decision trees and then model individuals' limited capacities to deliberate about them.

For Giddens' work, however, introducing some of the apparatus of expected utility theory represents less of a departure. Movement between his levels of discursive and practical consciousness is determined in part by the context of action but also by individuals' reflexive monitoring and rationalization of action. My concepts of prefigurative and preparatory commitment, which I will later define in Chapter 4, fit quite naturally into Giddens' framework, but they are more specifically tailored to the type of everyday action I will model.

Finally, from the opposite direction, it is important to note that practitioners of orthodox rational choice theory have been moving considerably closer to these positions as well.[22] Consider the following recent research in economics on the relative importance in accounting for differences in college entry of short-term resource constraints versus long-term family disadvantage. Cameron and Heckman (1999) offer a variety of explanations for why children from high-income families tend to obtain relatively more education than those from low-income families. After outlining the standard economic predictions—innate ability, capacity to buy higher quality high school education, resources to cover college tuition—Cameron and Heckman (1999: 84) wrote:

> Children's tastes for education and their expectations about their life chances are shaped by those of their parents. Educated parents are better able to develop the scholastic aptitude in their children by assisting and directing their studies. The influences of family factors that are present from birth through high school completion accumulate over many years to produce ability and college readiness.

While this explanation is only a modest departure from typical predictions in the economics of education, consider the blatantly sociological nature of this explanation of Cameron and Heckman (1999: 85):

> Children who grow up in inferior environments may expect less of themselves and may not fully develop their academic potential because they see little hope for ever being able to complete college or use their schooling in any effective way.

Following on these musings, Cameron and Heckman (1999: 85) note that in contrast to policy interventions that seek to relieve short-term credit constraints, "Policy that improves the environments that shape ability may be a more effective avenue for increasing college enrollment in the long run."

They conclude with the lament: "The issue could be settled empirically, although surprisingly little data have been brought to bear on it."

My contention, fully developed in subsequent chapters, is that we lack a specific model that can tell us what sort of data we need to collect in order to evaluate the possible importance of belief formation mechanisms. At least implicitly, sociologists have always maintained that such mechanisms are important, even though few explicit models have been proposed. Now that some economists are willing to concede that belief formation mechanisms are important as well, an even wider group of social scientists is ready and willing to accept a new and more complete model of educational attainment.

MODE OF THEORETICAL DEVELOPMENT AND PLAN OF THE BOOK

After coming to terms with the deficiencies of a prominent strand of sociological literature on educational attainment in Chapters 2 and 3—the first of which analyzes the structure and lineage of the status socialization theory of educational attainment and the second of which assesses the support for its central expectation formation mechanism—I will then construct in the remaining chapters of the book a foundation for a new sociological model of educational attainment. Three warnings about the mode of theoretical development I will pursue are in order.

First, I pursue an integrative agenda. At the present moment in modeling educational attainment, this strategy seems appropriate. Among candidate theories for educational attainment patterns, the family of rational choice models of educational attainment developed by economists is the strongest. Long central to policy design, these models now dominate demographic research and applied policy evaluation. Most sociologists of education have refused to recognize this dominance. Instead, as in other substantive areas of research, many have rejected rational choice models out of hand, braced by romanticized arguments against assumptions that students and parents are motivated to some extent by self-interest and/or by arguments that the choices of students and parents are so severely circumscribed by structural factors that little value is gained (and much ideological harm is done) by adopting a choice-theoretic framework.

I do not see such scholastic boundary maintenance as productive. As mentioned earlier, I will therefore use components of rational choice theory to build my model. But, I will not blindly adopt economic orthodoxy. I will avoid restrictions on which economists relied when building many of their models between 1960 and 1990—perfect information processing, redundant belief formation, and permissive revealed preference. Relaxing these restrictions will enable me to demonstrate within the rational choice framework the continuing relevance of the core mechanism of the sociological theory of status socialization. This is only one example of how I seek to be integrative, but it is also the one that it seems most appropriate to (again) forewarn.

Second, I will exercise mathematical restraint. Virtually every claim in this book could be developed in more mathematically elegant ways. I engage in formalism only when there is a substantial payoff for doing so. There is value in laying out some basic proof sketches for the core claims of the stochastic decision tree model I will develop in Chapter 4. But, thereafter, little would be gained by continuing to introduce proofs for what are relatively simple and straightforward implications of the basic framework. And therefore, in Chapters 5 and 6, which lay out the theoretical possibilities for jointly modeling both belief formation and social influence, the mathematical apparatus is considerably simplified. But, for purists, clarification of most of the mathematical simplifications can be found in the endnotes.

Third, I will not allow my efforts at theory construction to be needlessly constrained by available observational data. I will engage in an open-ended form of theory construction, and accordingly I will not offer along the way a systematic effort to empirically validate my theoretical proposals. In part, this is born of necessity, as I simply cannot offer up all of the supporting evidence I might wish for. But, it is also my position that this is the appropriate strategy for theory construction in the social sciences (especially for those who are willing, in other publication venues, to engage in their fair share of empirical analysis).

Nonetheless, to bolster this case for freedom from data, I will draw on some wise words of others. Aage Sørensen (1998) argued effectively that theoretical elaboration via regression modeling has proven to be a dead end, and I interpret his argument as more generally about the usefulness of survey data for theory construction. Sørensen (1998:241) wrote:

> With the advent of the high-speed computer . . . social scientists could now calculate almost everything with little manual labor and in very short periods of time. Unfortunately, the sociological workers involved in this revolution lost

control of their ability to see the relationship between theory and evidence. Sociologists became alienated from their sociological species being.

Accordingly, quantitative sociology, according to Sørensen, came to regard the selection of variables from available survey data as a legitimate and useful form of theory construction and elaboration. With a list of variables in hand, the data analyst simply apportioned variance in the outcome of interest across the selected variables and declared victory.

Sørensen's proposed remedy is for more careful conceptualization of the functional dependence—especially dependence through time—of the few most fundamental variables of interest. And hence, along with others in the same volume (Hedström and Swedberg 1998), he extolled the virtues of the language of mechanisms in order to transcend the vacuousness of using linear additive models estimated for their statistical and computational simplicity to classify "independent variables" as exogenous, control, or intervening.

My position is that Sørensen and others got it only partly right. Without a doubt, they correctly identified a major problem with quantitatively oriented sociology. But, they did not offer a sufficiently complete remedy. To some extent, their appeal for mechanisms is little more than a return to the strategy of empirical analysis that James S. Coleman advocated (but which, in the same piece, Sørensen argued he did not always follow). Coleman's mode of analysis was one in which a mathematical model was first worked out in theory, perhaps with reference to some available variables. Afterward, Coleman then advocated the use of data to calibrate and/or evaluate the model. Although far from his most elegant of written work, the following paragraph represents Coleman's basic strategy:

> This indicates the general strategy I will pursue: to use a model that generally conforms to the idea one has of the substantive process, but to constrain the processes in ways that make possible estimation of parameters, although the assumptions implied by the constraints may not be met in reality. With this as a starting point, it then becomes possible to relax certain of the constraints (or to test the assumptions they imply) when richer data or more powerful estimating methods become available. (1981:9)

In one sense, this is a practical and useful way for social scientists to proceed. One develops a model and then estimates a constrained version of it, hoping one day that the full model can be evaluated. This practical orientation, however, has not led to the necessary breakthroughs for models of educational attainment. The problem is that, as a discipline, we never seem to get back to the full model and instead seem to roll around in the empirical mud generating coefficient after coefficient (and, sometimes, remembering to appeal for more data in the future).

I am therefore reminded of a much more radical quotation from one of our best sociologists, Otis Dudley Duncan. At the end of his introductory book on structural equation models, written after he published groundbreaking models of educational and occupational attainment, Duncan (1975) wrote:

> A strong possibility in any area of research at a given time is that there are *no* structural relations among the variables currently recognized and measured in that area. Hence, whatever its mathematical properties, no model describing covariation of those variables will be a structural model. What is needed under the circumstances is a theory that invents the proper variables. (p.152; emphasis in the original)

It is unclear whether Duncan felt that the models of status attainment that he had developed should be seen as sufficiently "structural" (and references to his work on education, such as Duncan, Haller, and Portes [1968], are notably absent from the book). Regardless of his perception, I am prepared to say that they were not, and thus that subsequent efforts to invent new variables to explain patterns of educational attainment were and continue to be justified.[23]

From this tour of the wise words of the past, I am emboldened to engage in conceptual analysis, mechanism delineation, and (dare I say) variable creation.[24] Where possible, I will use available data and relate my theoretical proposals to some of our favorite existing variables. However, I will throw caution to the wind in many places in Chapters 4 through 6, creating concepts, mechanisms, and variables as I go, on the justification that caution is for journal articles, not books. Nonetheless, the dreary seriousness of science dictates that I must lay out an empirical agenda for model validation, and I therefore offer this in the concluding Chapter 7 of the book, leaving the task for my own future work and that of others.

NOTES

1. There remains considerable controversy over the determinants of these changes, and hence some debate about whether one should conceive of them as

changes in the wages of different educational groups, as opposed to exogenous growth in inequality across labor market positions into which differentially educated individuals are allocated. Even so, few scholars would be willing to argue against the growing relevance of the parental advice that staying in school does indeed pay off.

2. See Ellwood and Kane (2000) for elaboration of this credit constraint hypothesis and Carneiro and Heckman (2002) for a more skeptical view.

3. These percentages exclude individuals who did not receive a high school degree of some form, as is the traditional mode of analysis for college entry rates. According to census figures, the proportion of each age cohort that dropped out of high school declined between 1982 and 1992 from 11.33 to 8.17 for whites, 18.27 to 12.63 for blacks, and 32.17 to 30.73 for Hispanics (see the years for 1981–83 and 1991–93 in Supplemental Table 19-1, U.S. Department of Education, National Center for Education Statistics 2002). My estimates from the *HS&B* and *NELS* are similar, with declines from 12.40 to 6.75 for whites, 18.10 to 10.91 for blacks, 25.17 to 16.10 for Hispanics, and 7.64 to 6.28 for Asians. As a result, the set of individuals at risk of entering college, as defined for Table 1.1, changed between cohorts. The class of 1992 included students who, if they had been in the class of 1982, would likely not have graduated from high school, and who, it is reasonable to assume, would also have been less likely to enter college. Thus, the claims in the main text about the increases between cohorts in the college entry and completion rates may underestimate the true trends (that is, the counterfactual trends that would have evolved if the rate of high school graduation had remained the same).

4. Moreover, students who delay college entry are much less likely to obtain a bachelor's degree, although to some extent this is an artifact of measurement. Individuals are only observed for eight years following high school graduation, so that those who enter college more than three years after graduating high school would likely not have obtained a bachelor's degree even if attending college full time. Nonetheless, I have analyzed *NLSY* data (where, because of its longer panel this right censoring problem is less severe) and found the same pattern.

5. For Figure 1.1, as for Table 1.1, no distinction is made between entry into two- and four-year colleges. And, the *Current Population Surveys* necessitate the use of a slightly less clear race/ethnicity breakdown. The category "black" includes those who self-identify as black, regardless of whether or not they also self-identify as Hispanic. The category "white" includes those who neither self-identify as black nor as Hispanic. The *NELS* and *HS&B* employ a mutually exhaustive classification, such that Hispanics cannot self-identify as white or black.

6. Using the *CPS* data, one can attempt to estimate college completion rates as well, by lining up entry and attainment rates for age cohorts. I tried this and generated estimates of the college completion rates for college entrants from 1976 to 1994 (limiting the college entrants to those who entered college within one year of graduating high school). The estimates were formed by generating synthetic cohorts. For example, for the completion rate for 1976 college entrants, I first esti-

mated the percentage of 23–26-year-olds who reported having obtained bachelor's degrees in 1981 and then divided this percentage by the number of 18–21-year-olds who entered college in 1976 having graduated from high school in the prior year. An obvious problem with this method is that individuals who entered college late but who completed their bachelor's degrees in an especially timely manner should be removed from the numerator of the rate calculation, but there appears to be no way around this problem with the *CPS* data. Nonetheless, the findings were interpretable, and two patterns stood out. The estimated completion rates of whites remained fairly steady even as entry rates increased over the same time period. But, the estimated completion rate in the early 1980s of blacks increased slightly, followed by a decline thereafter. This latter pattern was produced by relative stability of bachelor's degree attainment rates in spite of the changes in initial college entry rates, as shown in Figure 1.1.

7. In no way am I suggesting that these contrasts represent causal effects. Indeed, I see no justification even for asserting the ultimate appropriateness of a multinomial distribution for modeling the three-category outcome. I merely wish to show what the data imply about patterns of college entry and college completion if one applies generic logit modeling to the patterns in Table 1.1.

8. Occupational prestige is measured with SEI scores, drawn from the analysis of Nakao and Treas (1992) using the 1989 General Social Survey.

9. This multinomial logit is actually specified with the natural logarithm of family income as the predictor variable. This also means that the "observed mean" referenced in the main text is actually the mean of logged family income. To calculate the levels for the discrete change in family income reported in the first two columns of Table 1.2, I exponentiated the mean of log income, added and subtracted $2,075 and $3,000 (respectively 1982 and 1992), took the logs of these resulting values, and then figured the discrete change in estimated probabilities using the corresponding logged values.

10. I used the personal consumption expenditures deflator to determine that $6,000 in 1992 would have been equal to approximately $4,150 in 1982.

11. To his credit, Kane (1994) attempts to capitalize on variation in state differences in college costs and available financial aid to more directly assess the hypothesis. Nonetheless, his analysis only penetrates so far, for with his limited data he is unable to offer direct evidence that differences in the net costs of college were accurately perceived by prospective college students and their parents. And it appears that the majority of his additional variance explained is a function of stable cross-sectional state differences, rather than more directly relevant differential trends within states.

12. And what about the slight increase in the college completion rate of blacks in the early 1980s, mentioned in note 6? It could be explained by at least one of four non-mutually exclusive narratives: (1) the decline in college entry was most pronounced for individuals who were least likely to complete college; (2) if the decline in the college entry rate was a response to changes in financial aid, these

changes did not have a measurable impact on funding subsequent years of college among those who enrolled; (3) the decline in the college entry rate was merely a delay in entry, since the percentages of blacks who obtained BAs in subsequent years did not show a sympathetic decline; or (4) the decline in the college entry rate was an artifact of the small sample sizes of black high school graduates in the *CPS*, and the years between 1981 and 1983 represent a run of sampling errors on the same underside of the true underlying trend. I am inclined to accept this last explanation, as it also resolves the college entry puzzle, which I have ultimately come to believe (based mostly on the lack of a sympathetic decline in bachelor's degree attainment in the mid-1980s) is merely statistical noise.

13. These expenditures are far exceeded by state-level subsidies of public higher education institutions, and these subsidies are in large measure aimed at reducing tuition levels to enable low-income students to attend college. Of course, in the last few years, these state-level subsidies have declined.

14. Most sensible theoretical predictions imply that Pell Grants should be more effective than Hope Scholarship Credits, since the latter are tax credits and are therefore only incentives to students/families who otherwise have enough income to be taxed. See Kane (1999b) for more discussion.

15. William Sewell's presidential address to the American Sociological Association, published in the 1971 volume of the *American Sociological Review*, probably marks the beginning of this type of policy proposal. His entire address is devoted to an explication of the Wisconsin model, discussed in detail in Chapter 2. He concludes his address with a "Policy Implications" section where he argues in part that in order to reduce inequality of educational opportunity, programs should be developed for the "stimulation of educational and occupational aspirations" of low-SES children (Sewell 1971:803).

16. For example, on the sample student survey that the Department of Education suggests individual programs administer to high school students (see http://www.ed.gov/offices/OPE/gearup/gu-grantee-info.html), two questions figure prominently: "Do you think you will continue your education after high school?" and "How far in school do you think you will get after high school?"

17. It is unclear how Gear Up fits into the Bush administration's No Child Left Behind initiative. Funding of existing Gear Up programs continues (having increased from $120 million in 1999 to 200, 295, 285, and now $293 million from 2000 through 2003), but no competition for the funding of new local Gear Up programs was scheduled for the 2003 fiscal year. The Department of Education does, nonetheless, tout on its website that 1,236,606 students were served through Gear Up in fiscal year 2002.

18. The reported elasticities of college enrollment in the economics of education literature are little more than correlations derived from survey data and aggregate time series. As all first-year statistics students know, correlation is not causation. See Cameron and Heckman (1999) and Carneiro and Heckman (2002) for

enlightening critiques from within the economics of education of such reported elasticities.

19. Boudon (1974) is an even earlier possible example, but its rational choice foundation is both less explicit and less well developed.

20. See Gambetta (1998:111–13).

21. Indeed, the stochastic decision tree model that I propose later can be interpreted as an attempt to formally specify Bourdieu's claim that individuals act within a relational field of structural opportunities and constraints that "presents itself as a structure of probabilities—of rewards, gains, profits, or sanctions—but always implies a measure of indeterminacy" (translated and quoted in Bourdieu and Wacquant [1992:18] but written by Bourdieu two years earlier in 1990). To formalize the indeterminacy, I allow individuals to rely on simple decision trees that only approximate the complexity of their future choices, but then allow individuals to maintain stochastic parameters for their decision trees.

22. Indeed, an economist (who will remain nameless for now) has contacted me, asking for help in translating Bourdieu's ideas into an economic framework.

23. Explaining and supporting this claim would take me into a much longer discussion of structural and causal models than I have the space for. Some of this discussion will occur in Chapter 3, but some of it can also be found in Morgan (2004), which relates the Duncan quotation in the main text to the definition of causality developed by Judea Pearl (see Pearl 2000).

24. The appeal for mechanisms is a useful rallying cry, but the originality of a mechanism-based sociology has been oversold. Mechanisms are composed of functions, which relate inputs to outputs. Arguing that mechanisms are concatenations of nonlinear functions is not an argument against the use of variables, since the primitive elements of functions—defined as inputs and outputs—can be redefined as variables. That the word "variable" has become almost a forbidden word in some corners of sociology is therefore quite bizarre, since the problem is merely with how measured variables have been deployed in recent empirical research.

PART I

COMING TO TERMS WITH THE SOCIOLOGICAL LITERATURE ON EDUCATIONAL ATTAINMENT

Expectation Formation and the Status Socialization Theory of Educational Attainment

In Chapter 1, I claimed none of the theories of educational attainment that dominate social science offers an explicit model of educational attainment that can be used to explain in sufficient detail important empirical patterns. In this chapter, I further justify this claim, examining the status socialization theory of educational attainment while laying the groundwork for the related model I develop in subsequent chapters.

I first introduce the Wisconsin model of status attainment, which is the theory's principal embodiment. I then examine its origins in functionalist sociology, as well as classical social psychology. After then summarizing its legacy in everyday empirical research in current sociology, I argue that what I regard as the core idea of the framework—that one's current behavior is contingent on the factors that shape one's beliefs about the future—provides a sound basis for a model of educational attainment. In particular, it provides a solid grounding for modeling the everyday preparatory commitment decisions that prospective college students must confront. I conclude by laying out a simple rational choice model of educational attainment, in part to explain why rational choice researchers have not attempted to model the same basic expectation formation mechanism that is at the heart of status socialization theory. But, I then show that the recent movement within economics to model both beliefs and social influence processes is entirely consistent with a revival of the Wisconsin model framework within the rational choice tradition, which I then develop in the remaining chapters of the book.

THE WISCONSIN MODEL OF STATUS ATTAINMENT

Status socialization theory is most closely associated with the Wisconsin model of status attainment (see Sewell and Hauser 1980, 1992). I will therefore introduce status socialization theory by presenting the initial formulation of the Wisconsin model, carrying on thereafter to an analysis of its origins and subsequent revisions. The model originated in early analyses of the Wisconsin Longitudinal Survey—a random sample of all high school seniors in the state of Wisconsin in 1957 (see Sewell 1964).[1] And yet, the Wisconsin model is commonly seen as a social-psychological elaboration of the path-breaking status attainment model of Blau and Duncan (1967). The full model was first fully specified in two articles published in the *American Sociological Review* *(ASR)*—Sewell, Haller, and Portes (1969) and Sewell, Haller, and Ohlendorf (1970)—that reported results from both the original 1957 data and the second-wave 1964 data on the educational and early occupational careers of the young men. Although these articles aim to explain both the process of educational and occupational attainment, I will focus attention narrowly on the nested path-model of educational attainment.

According to the original 1969 Wisconsin model, presented in Figure 2.1, the joint effects of a student's family background and mental ability on his eventual educational attainment can be completely explained by the expectations that others hold of him. In particular, significant others—parents, teachers, and peers—define educational expectations for students that they then internalize as educational aspirations. Because the theory assumes that students are compelled to follow their own aspirations, the model is powerfully simple and implies that significant others can increase a student's educational attainment merely by increasing their own expectations of him. Of course, in framing their expectations of a student's future, significant others reflect on the social origins of a student, as well as his demonstrated academic performance. But, the contours of such reflection are merely an ignorable intervening mechanism that explain how family background and intelligence affect later educational attainment.

Although the theory underneath the Wisconsin model is bold, its creators were well aware of its many limitations (see Haller 1982; Sewell and Hauser 1980, 1992). Almost immediately on publication, they began to qualify its basic mechanisms, and in the process weakened its most parsimonious theoretical claims. The data analyzed for the 1969 article were based only

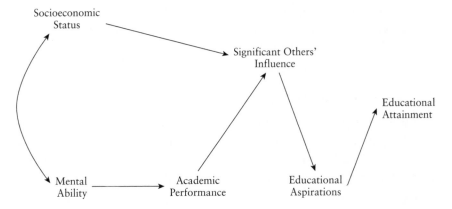

Figure 2.1.   Initial Formulation of the Wisconsin Model of Educational Attainment.

SOURCE: Sewell, Heller, and Portes, 1969

on the boys of farmers (the original model having been prepared for consumption by rural sociologists), and as a result the authors were understandably concerned that their model might not adequately represent the status attainment process for a fully representative sample of Wisconsin high school seniors. Partly to address this possibility, Sewell, Haller, and Ohlendorf (1970) reestimated their original model on the full sample of young men drawn from the entire state of Wisconsin. Direct effects of academic performance on educational aspirations and educational attainment were added to the model, along with the direct effect of mental ability on significant others' influence and the direct effect of significant others' influence on educational attainment, which were considered debatable at the time the 1969 model was estimated.

The addition of paths not predicted by the original socialization theory presented problems for the powerful claims of the 1969 article. The implication that significant others could raise a student's educational attainment by simply imposing higher educational expectations on him began to seem less credible. Instead, the revised 1970 path-model suggested that significant others and educational institutions may have some direct control over the educational attainment process and thus that structural constraints (and perceptions of them) must have an explicit role in models of educational attainment.[2]

In order to see how these additional mechanisms can be modeled, and to determine whether they are necessarily inconsistent with the Wisconsin model, one must first examine the foundational literature on which the core aspiration mechanism of the Wisconsin model is based. The crucial ideas are grounded in two separate traditions that took hold in the 1940s and 1950s —functionalist sociology and a particular form of social psychology.

Origins of the Aspiration Mechanism

The Wisconsin model has an impressive lineage, stretching back to the functionalist paradigm of sociological inquiry. In his famously meandering 1953 essay, "A Revised Analytical Approach to the Theory of Social Stratification," Talcott Parsons stressed the "fluidity of the shadings" between class and status groups and yet then declared:

> Probably the best single index of the line between "upper middle" class and the rest of the middle class is the *expectation* that children will have a college education, as a matter that is of status-right not of the exceptional ability of the individual. . . . It is important to be clear about the meaning of this expectation. It is, primarily, that the son of such a family will thereby be able to qualify for an acceptably high-level occupational role rather than that he should become a sufficiently educated man to have the manners and humanistic interests appropriate to the cultural status of the family. (p. 124; italics in the original)

Accordingly, upper middle class parents (and, surely, upper class parents as well) maintained future status expectations for their children into which adolescents were socialized and toward which they were then taught to strive.[3] In contrast, for members of the lower classes, Parsons (1953) saw

> a shift from predominance of the "success" goal to that of the "security" goal. More concretely it is a loss of interest in achievement, whether for its own sake and for opportunity to do more important things, or for advancement of family status through more income and enhanced reputation. Occupational role then becomes not the main "field" for achievement, but a means for securing the necessities of a tolerable standard of living, a necessary evil. The basic focus of interest is diverted from the occupational field into the family, avocations, friendship relations and the like. (p. 125)

This preference for security over success led lower class parents to deemphasize the importance of striving for achievement in school.

Parsons developed these ideas while leading the "Mobility Project," for which a group of scholars in the department of social relations at Harvard University studied the educational careers of boys from Boston area high schools. Among the research reports generated, the 1953 article entitled

"Educational and Occupational Aspirations of 'Common Man' Boys," written by Joseph A. Kahl, became one of the most widely read. In the essay, Kahl opens his analysis with support for Parsons' claims, which one can assume Kahl helped to shape. Accordingly, Kahl duly notes that the association between measured IQ and college plans can be separated from a complementary association between social class and college plans.

This pattern of findings, however, was merely the beginning of Kahl's analysis, after which he then asks the central question of his study: "What influences the aspirations of the boys in the lower middle levels of the status range whose environment gives them a wide choice?" (Kahl 1953:189). In order to show that "these boys must make a conscious and pointed decision at some stage of their careers," he then reported the results of in-depth interviews with twelve boys who expected to attend college and twelve boys who expected to forego college.[4] The key to the study was the matching, albeit coarsely, of the boys on social class and measured IQ; all were in the top 60 percent of the IQ scale and all had fathers who were petty white collar, skilled artisans, or unskilled workers. As these boys were neither at the bottom nor the top of the social class hierarchy, he labeled them members of the "common man class." His goal was then to "explore the decision making of such boys," whose beliefs about the future were not predetermined either by expectations grounded in their class origins or by their cognitive abilities.

Kahl's explanation for the generation of college plans is easily recognizable as the direct forerunner of the Wisconsin model, and yet it was also considerably different. The "common man" boys considered the costs of a college education and the consequences that their everyday behavioral choices would generate for their relations with valued peers. And yet, beyond these concerns, Kahl identified parental pressure as the most crucial determinant. Corresponding roughly to two types of students, he saw two types of parents, those who sought to raise "getting by" children and those who sought to raise "getting ahead" children. Many of the factors that determined whether parents adopted the getting ahead rearing strategy were idiosyncratic, and yet there were some systematic differences, relating primarily to parents' own experiences with the labor market. Kahl (1953:200) wrote:

> If a boy had a rational conviction about the importance of schoolwork for his future career, he would strive to keep up his performance. But that conviction never appeared unless the parents emphasized it.

and he continued with

> the boys learned to an extraordinary degree to view the occupational system
> from their parents' perspective. They took over their parents' view of the op-
> portunities available, the desirability and possibility of change of status, the
> techniques to be used if change was desired, and the appropriate goals for
> boys who performed as they did in school. (p. 202)

Kahl's common man boys made deliberative decisions in the course of their
adolescence, and these decisions were influenced by the beliefs and practices
of their peers and, especially, parents.[5] The extent to which parents saw college as having a genuine payoff for occupational attainment appeared crucial.

The Wisconsin model can be regarded as an elaborate updating of Kahl's
basic explanatory narrative. First, Sewell and his colleagues laid the groundwork, just as did Kahl, by claiming in Sewell, Haller, and Straus (1957) that
there are separable effects of intelligence and social origins on college plans.
Then, in the late 1960s, with a new round of data on Wisconsin high school
seniors, they laid out a mechanistic explanation, relying on significant others' influence, to explain how students formed their educational aspirations,
and then endeavored to realize them in early adulthood.

Retrospective accounts of the construction of the Wisconsin model best
explain how the generation of educational aspirations became the central
piece of the model (Haller, Otto, Meier, and Ohlendorf 1974; Haller 1982).[6]
The principal social psychological theorist, Archibald Haller, maintained
that, for the most part, students' aspirations are constructed and internalized
prior to entering high school. Regarding the specific processes, he wrote:

> aspirations are formed in at least three ways. The first is imitation—adopting
> the statuses illustrated by models. The second is self-reflection—adjusting as-
> pirations to correspond with performance in status-related arenas of behavior.
> The third is probably most important—adopting the status expectations that
> one's definers hold for one. The theory also holds that, once aspirations are
> formed as status-specific conceptions of oneself, they are extremely resistant to
> change. Embedded in a mass of approximately consistent and mutually rein-
> forcing cognitions, they come to have an inertia of their own and are ex-
> pressed in corresponding behavior. (Haller 1982:5–6)

A student's educational aspiration thus became an abstract motivational orientation, solidly grounded in his or her cognitive structure. The measured
Wisconsin model variable—college plans—was merely a realistic indicator

of one's latent educational aspirations. However, as I have pointed out elsewhere (Morgan 1998), Haller and his colleagues, in pushing their behaviorist theoretical orientation, de-emphasized the self-reflection mechanism for the construction of college plans, which had the effect of ignoring the subtleties of Kahl's earlier explanation. Students were not seen as spending time and effort actively weighing the consequences of their everyday courses of behavior, nor independently calculating the labor market payoff to higher education, but rather were simply compelled to live up to expectations that were largely determined by the beliefs of their significant others.

Although Haller identified behaviorism as the inspiration for the significant others' influence mechanism (and, in particular, George Herbert Mead's variant of it), he identified the general aspiration mechanism as an application of Kurt Lewin's field theory and attendant concept of "Level of Aspiration." Although it would have been reasonable to regard students' reported college plans as simply expectations for future behavior (in line with many articles in the sociology of education over that time period), Haller (and one must assume Sewell as well) preferred to interpret college plans as an indicator of internal motivation (see Spenner and Featherman 1978). This decision was, unfortunately, a misapplication of Lewin's own framework, as I discuss next.

What Was Lewin's Model?

Kurt Lewin, in the course of developing his influential field theory in psychology, joined with colleagues to develop models of goal-setting and goal-seeking behavior (see Lewin, Dembo, Festinger, and Sears 1944 for a classic review of the early research). The main outcome of this research program was the concept of Level of Aspiration (LOA). In a series of laboratory experiments, subjects were asked to set a goal, execute a simple task, set a new goal, repeat the task, and so on. A subject, for example, would be asked to throw darts at a bull's-eye after selecting a distance from which to throw at the dartboard. All of the experimental evidence showed that subjects consistently select goals that are more ambitious than their past performance but not unrealistically beyond the range of their abilities. Lewin and his colleagues referred to these goals as aspirations, claiming that the level of aspiration is generally beyond the "50–50 level of subjective probability" or "expectancy" level of even-chance success.

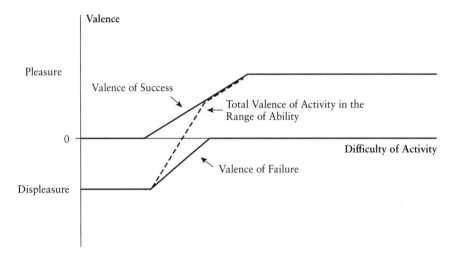

Figure 2.2.   Lewin's Valence of an Activity as a Function of Its Perceived Difficulty

In order to account for the relatively optimistic nature of aspirations, Lewin developed a valence theory of goal setting, asserting that individuals enjoy triumph over difficulty.[7] As shown in Figure 2.2, the valence of success (or positive sentiment) and the valence of failure (or negative sentiment) vary with the difficulty of an activity. Imagine an individual attempting to hit a bull's-eye on a dartboard from one foot away and from twenty feet away. Clearly, he would feel disappointed if he missed the bull's-eye in the first case and perhaps ecstatic if he hit it in the second case. Total valence, represented by the dashed line in Figure 2.2, is the simple sum of valence of success and valence of failure within discrete intervals of the difficulty continuum.[8]

For Lewin, an aspiration is then a success-probability scaled maximum expected valence. After partitioning the scale of difficulty D into discrete intervals d, the subject selects a level of aspiration such that:

$$\text{LOA}(D) = max_D\{v(d)\,\pi(d)\} \tag{2.1}$$

where $v(d)$ and $\pi(d)$ are the total valence and probability of success that are functions in d. As such, desire for triumph defines valence as a nonlinear function of perceived difficulty. The scaling of valence by the perceived difficulty of achieving success ensures that reported aspirations remain within a reasonable range of possible success.

As long as individuals can improve their performance, they should set higher and higher goals for themselves. To an outside observer, therefore, it may appear as if aspirations drive increases in performance, but Lewin never explicitly claimed that this was so. Rather, he simply proposed a mechanism that converts the desire for triumph and subjective probability evaluations of future success into aspirations. Individuals may relish triumph, but their performance cannot necessarily be improved by increasing their goals for action, as would be the case if aspirations themselves could cause behavior.[9]

Lewin recognized the fundamental indeterminacy of his theory, acknowledging that the same wishes and fears can partly determine valence and subjective probability of success so that "the subjective probability scale is not entirely independent of the valence scale" (Lewin et al. 1944:372). Even more broadly, he maintained that valence and subjective probability "depend on many aspects of the life space of the individual at that time, particularly on the way he sees his past experience and on the scales of reference which are characteristic for his culture and his personality" (p. 376). It would appear that comments such as these were influential in capturing the theoretical imagination of Haller and his colleagues, since aspirations could then quite easily be seen as functions of the social contexts defined by socioeconomic status and significant others' influence.

And yet, Lewin's theory concerns the repeated performance of simple tasks over which an individual has substantial control. Progress through the educational system is largely a one-shot performance that is only partly under the control of the individual. One could argue that, if an individual regards every level of education as a different performance, then an aspiration-based model of the completion of higher education is possible. That is, if the probability of success declines at higher levels of education, and if individuals seek triumph over challenges, then they will form aspirations that are higher than their expectations of actual attainment. Nonetheless, such a model could only be regarded as weakly related to Lewin's ideas.

According to Lewin, individuals maintain, as separate concepts, goals for future behavior on the one hand and beliefs about future behavior on the other. Accordingly, goals are aspirations while beliefs are expectations. There is simply no justification in Lewin's writings for regarding a self-expressed expectation for one's future behavior as an aspiration that compels future behavior. Largely for this reason, variables for college plans are now more typically labeled educational expectations than educational aspirations (as in Chapter 1; see Tables 1.2 and 1.3).

Status Socialization Theory in Current Research

In response to dozens of articles throughout the 1970s, paths were successively added to the Wisconsin model so that by 1980 it was conceded that all prior variables—SES, mental ability, academic performance, significant others' influence, and college plans—can be seen as determinants of educational attainment (see Figure 1 in Sewell and Hauser 1980). One intriguing contrarian article emerged in 1983. Hauser, Tsai, and Sewell (1983) corrected for measurement error and, in the process, reaffirmed the support in the original data for the "modified causal chain" of the 1969 path-model. By then, however, it would appear that the theory itself could not be saved from its detractors. After studies of race differences in the status attainment process (for example, Portes and Wilson 1976), scholars such as Kerckhoff (1976) argued convincingly that structural constraints should be explicitly modeled.

Nonetheless, the Wisconsin model has a strong legacy in current research. Figure 2.3 presents five-year moving averages from 1960 through 2002 of the number of articles published in the journal *Sociology of Education* that use a variable in empirical analysis that is labeled either educational aspirations or educational expectations. From 1960 to 1969, the moving average for the number of articles published per year increased slightly from about one to two (and this must partly be a response to early articles such as Haller and Butterworth 1960 and Sewell, Haller, and Straus 1957). Following the appearance of the Wisconsin model in the flagship journal of sociology, the moving average increased to approximately four articles per year, remaining at that level until 1982. In recent years, the variable educational expectations has become a standard covariate in the sociology of education for the analysis of many other outcomes, as shown by the lower trend line, which is the five-year moving average of the number of articles that use educational expectations as a predictor variable only.

Thus, as shown in Figure 2.3, status socialization theory is deeply entrenched in data analysis practices in the sociology of education, and to some extent within social stratification research in general. However, because it is often applied without attention to the details of the original theory, its fine-grained details are often lost in application, and it would seem few re-

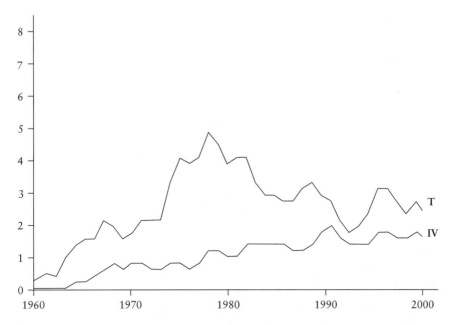

Figure 2.3.   Number of Articles in *Sociology of Education* That Use the Variable Educational Expectations or Aspirations (five-year moving average). T = total number of articles, IV = as independent variable only

searchers any longer appreciate the complexity and promise of some of the core tenets of status socialization theory. In the next section, I re-specify the core mechanism of the Wisconsin modeling, focusing attention on the ways in which future behavior is conditioned by forecasts of the future.

EMBRACING THE CORE CLAIM OF THE WISCONSIN MODEL

Stripping away the misapplication of Lewin's theory of aspirations, and restoring to students and parents the genuine deliberative powers recognized long ago by Kahl, one can then argue that the distinguishing feature of status socialization theory is the explicit modeling of future behavior as the outcome of one's own expectations and how they are conditioned by the expectations of others. In this second half of the chapter, I embrace this claim and demonstrate how it is consistent with a complementary movement within economics to model expectation formation mechanisms.

To represent the generality of the basic Wisconsin model mechanism, consider the following two equations for the generation of educational expectations and educational attainment:

$$EXPECT = f(SES, ABILITY, SOI) + e_1 \tag{2.2}$$

$$ATTAIN = g(EXPECT, SES, ABILITY, SOI) + e_2 \tag{2.3}$$

where *EXPECT* is years of expected educational attainment (an answer to a question: "As things stand now, how far in school do you expect to get?" as for the last variable in Table 1.2), *ATTAIN* is years of eventual educational attainment, *SES* is socioeconomic status (a composite of parents' educational attainments, occupational prestige, and family income, such as the first five variables in Table 1.2), *ABILITY* is inherited and accumulated cognitive skill, and *SOI* is significant others' influence (a composite of the educational expectations that parents, peers, and teachers have for a student, again as in Table 1.2). Other determinants of expectations and attainment are represented by mean-zero vectors e_1 and e_2.

According to status socialization theory, as specified above in the quotation by Haller (1982), educational expectations are generated by three mechanisms: self-reflection, imitation, and adoption. Equation 2.2 is a generalized representation of these three mechanisms, written as an unspecified function with inputs as arguments of $f(.)$. In applied work (especially when measurement error and the ambiguities of scaling are acknowledged), $f(.)$ is usually specified as a linear combination of *SES, ABILITY,* and *SOI*. However, there is nothing in status socialization theory that justifies such a restrictive functional form. Indeed, there are good reasons to believe that nonlinearities might be important (see Haller and Portes 1973; Jencks, Crouse, and Mueser 1983).

Equation 2.3 expresses educational attainment as a function of *SES, ABILITY, SOI,* and the educational expectations that are the outcome of Equation 2.2. As written, Equation 2.3 implies two, somewhat contradictory, claims about the process of educational attainment. First, educational expectations are self-fulfilling prophecies. Once they are formed in adolescence, they compel future behavior. Second, however, educational expectations are imperfect prophecies because they do not fully account for all of the future factors that lead *SES, ABILITY,* and *SOI* to generate educational attainment on their own.

Equation 2.3 could be simplified by applying exclusion restrictions to the arguments of $g(.)$, as did Sewell and his colleagues for their 1969 article. The direct effect of *SES* on educational attainment could be removed, by constraining to 0 all parameters that define its contribution to $g(.)$, in order to maintain that adolescents fully incorporate (with the help of their significant others) all social background effects on eventual attainment into the formation of their self-fulfilling educational expectations (as in Figure 2.1).

Most researchers are unwilling to make arguments like those of Sewell and Haller. What is not under debate among most of the researchers whose articles are plotted in Figure 2.3, however, is that educational expectations have an effect on educational attainment (or whatever outcome is modeled), and not just as a mediator for the indirect effects of prior variables on educational attainment.

Haller (1982) and Sewell and Hauser (1980) recognized that other important variables are likely embedded in the error term of Equation 2.2 (and thus embedded in educational expectations), and these additional variables have important effects on educational attainment. Other researchers (Hout and Morgan 1975; Kerckhoff 1976; Kerckhoff and Campbell 1977a, 1977b; Morgan 1996, 1998) have argued that these unmeasured variables include beliefs about the opportunity structure and beliefs about labor market rewards.

Indeed, if educational expectations have a causal effect on educational attainment "independent of its relationship to measured intelligence and socioeconomic status" (Sewell and Hauser 1980:70), then educational expectations may be a useful summary measure of at least some of the underlying beliefs that have effects on educational attainment. If this is the case, then the Wisconsin model may properly function as one piece of the foundation on which new and improved models of educational attainment should be constructed. And, if the constraints of the opportunity structure, along with the labor market benefits of educational training, must somehow find a place within an expanded Wisconsin model framework, the long tradition of rational choice scholarship in the economics of education must be considered for possible co-optation.

Should Rational Choice Theory Be Used to Construct a New Sociological Model?

A basic educational attainment model derived from rational choice theory can be represented by a few general equations (although see Chapter 4 for a

more complete presentation). First, assume that educational training generates returns on the investments of time and money of students, where

$$RETURNS = h(BENEFITS, COSTS) + e_3 \qquad (2.4)$$

Equation 2.4 expresses the future investment returns on educational training as a sum of an unspecified function $h(.)$ of labor market benefits and the
costs of educational training along with a vector, e_3, that summarizes purely
stochastic individual-level determinants of returns.

For Equation 2.4, the arguments of the function $h(.)$ are written in their
most general form as simply unspecified costs and benefits. In any particular application, the specific determinants of returns differ. Benefits, for example, may encompass expected earnings returns, nonmonetary job satis-
faction, and employment prospects. Costs may be relatively more weighted
toward direct costs than opportunity costs, depending on the extent and
commitment of parental resources. Moreover, benefits likely vary according
to level of cognitive skill, and opportunity costs may depend on exogenous
allocation to local labor market conditions. And, with an appropriately
strong and comprehensive theory, e_3 might even be justifiably removed from
Equation 2.4, such that all returns are determined by the characteristics of
the choices being made and the characteristics of individuals.

With an acceptable model of investment returns on education in hand,
educational attainment can then be modeled as a choice-based outcome of
expected returns:

$$ATTAIN = u(E[RETURNS], TASTE) + e_4 \qquad (2.5)$$

where *ATTAIN* is eventual educational attainment, $E[.]$ is the expectation operator from probability theory, *RETURNS* is the outcome of Equation 2.4,
TASTE is the appeal of education as consumption, and e_4 is a random mean-
zero vector of idiosyncratic determinants of educational attainment. In practice, attainment is usually analyzed as a single dichotomous choice (although
sometimes extended to a series of choices), and a threshold τ is specified (or
estimated) above which attainment results if exceeded by the right-hand side
of Equation 2.5.

Although a gross technical oversimplification of typical applications of
rational choice theory to educational attainment outcomes, the general modeling strategy characterized by Equations 2.4 and 2.5 still illustrates the es-
sentials of the approach (see Manski 1993a for a similarly simple character-

ization). The issue that confronts the rational choice scholarship, especially in the economics of education, is whether students can formulate Equation 2.4 on their own, and hence know the expected returns on which they are assumed to be making their enrollment decisions using a decision rule as in Equation 2.5.[10] Manski (1993a) argues that economists, by and large, do not know, writing:

> If youth form their expectations in anything like the manner that econometricians study the returns to schooling, then prevailing expectations assumptions cannot be correct. Without an understanding of expectations, it is not possible to interpret schooling behavior nor to measure the objective returns to schooling. As a consequence, the economics of education is at an impasse. (p. 55)

Manski's call to arms is for greater investment in research projects that attempt to model expectation formation processes, which necessarily entails the collection and subsequent analysis of data on prospective students' beliefs about the costs and benefits of alternative trajectories through the educational system.

In response, some research has been completed, and researchers now know more about the formation of expectations for the returns to education than when Manski wrote in 1993. And, ironically, two of the most informative studies are based on subjects from Wisconsin and Boston. Dominitz and Manski (1996) studied high school students from the state of Wisconsin, developing a new technique for measuring students' earnings expectations. Although far fewer in number, their subjects are similar to the Wisconsin high school seniors who were studied by Sewell and his colleagues in the 1960s and 1970s when the Wisconsin model was developed. Likewise, Kane (2001) studied the earnings expectations of students from Boston—one group from the central city school district and one group from surrounding and relatively affluent suburbs. His sample was drawn from the Boston area in much the same way as was the sample of students for the social mobility project of Talcott Parsons in the 1950s, from which Kahl (1953) selected respondents for his study of common man boys.

For the study by Dominitz and Manski (1996), seventy-one high school students from Madison, Wisconsin were asked to predict their own earnings, unconditional and conditional on completing different amounts of schooling. Although the sample was quite small, the high school students provided reasonably informative probability distributions for their future earnings.

They recognized a substantial labor market payoff for the acquisition of a college degree, and yet they also recognized substantial uncertainty in their prospects.

In his larger and more recent study, Kane (2001) collected data on 277 students from suburban schools and 286 students from central city schools. Eighty-two percent of the suburban students were white, non-Hispanic, and 97 percent had a parent with a bachelor's degree. In contrast, only 10 percent of the city school students were white, non-Hispanic, and only 22 percent had a parent with a bachelor's degree. Despite these differences, both groups of students in Kane's study had somewhat similar beliefs about the tuition costs and labor market benefits of a college degree. Both groups of students overestimated the tuition rate at the University of Massachusetts-Boston, with the suburban students expecting, on average, that tuition was $11,191 and with the city students expecting, on average, that tuition was $12,730. The true tuition rate was only $4,222.

Nonetheless, both sets of students saw a strong relationship between their potential future earnings and alternative levels of educational attainment. The median responses for earnings levels at age 25 having completed college were $50,000 for both sets of students, whereas the median responses for earnings levels at age 25 having only completed high school were $30,000 for suburban students and $28,900 for city students. The difference in the beliefs of these two groups of students was found in the lower tails of the distributions of expected earnings, with a higher proportion of city students expecting relatively low earnings no matter what their educational attainments. As will become obvious in Chapter 4 (which is built on Morgan 2002), I do not regard this last difference as trivial, but rather see it as a potential reason that Kane also observed a lower rate of preparation for college among city students, and a correspondingly lower rate of city students who expected to obtain bachelor's degrees.

Although these two studies are presented by the authors as if they are mere exploratory exercises, this is, it would seem, misplaced modesty. Their findings demonstrate what sociologists need to take to heart. High school students do have expectations about the costs and benefits of postsecondary education, and their expectations are not complete fantasy.[11] What remains to be determined by sociologists is how these expectations about returns are translated into plans for action and into the formation of one's educational expectations, or, as I will argue later, into prefigurative commitments that compel everyday behavior.

But, returning to the rational choice literature, one question still has to be addressed. Can the economics of education break the impasse that Manski (1993a) identifies without formulating a model for students' beliefs about their own future behavior? In other words, can the impasse be broken merely by constructing lower-order models of beliefs about the determinants of the returns to schooling? Or is there justification for also modeling expectations of one's own future behavior?

In one sense, nothing in rational choice models of educational attainment suggests that students' beliefs about their own future behavior should be ignored. Such a restriction could be developed, however. One could assume, accordingly, that educational expectations are uninformative when all expectations about component costs and benefits are specified. Under this assumption, knowing expectations does not help to account for attainment because:

$$EXPECT = u(E[RETURNS], TASTE) + e_5 \qquad (2.6)$$

where e_4 and e_5 are uncorrelated, although not necessarily of equal variance. Educational expectations are then regarded as rational expectations. On average, educational expectations would exhibit no patterned forecast error, except as would be produced by aggregate shocks affecting entire cohorts of students.[12]

Although I have seen no explicit claims that educational expectations are rational expectations, it is not unreasonable to surmise that at least some economists would be willing to assume that if enough incentives could be generated for students to spend as much effort forming educational expectations in response to a survey question as they must exert making actual decisions, the near equivalence of Equations 2.5 and 2.6 could be demonstrated. Any such economists would then likely argue that because no set of such incentives has ever been created, the existing survey data on educational expectations are probably too contaminated by response error to be considered worthy of study. I suspect, however, that most economists of education are either unaware that data on educational expectations exist or instead that trying to untangle their causes and consequences is a task best left for sociologists to ponder (since, in any case, they might argue, little additional information is contained in educational expectations that one would not wish to measure more directly as beliefs about the costs and benefits underlying the actual decisions).

Nonetheless, without explicit theorizing to the contrary, within the rational choice paradigm one is almost forced to assume that expectations of one's own future behavior must be updated continuously as new information becomes available. The re-creation of one's own expectations is not dampened by momentum, and the influences of others cannot induce the creation of self-fulfilling prophecies. Instead, the influences of others can only exist as the imposition or alleviation of the costs that determine returns. When cost mechanisms seem implausible, influence must then be packaged as unknowable taste (which, commonly, is then either entirely ignored in empirical analysis, or assumed stochastically exogenous).

The model I will propose later can be seen as a sociologically informed refinement of the basic rational choice model of educational attainment, which, built on a Bayesian learning foundation, allows educational expectations to become self-fulfilling prophecies by regulating everyday preparatory commitment decisions. In this framework, educational expectations summarize beliefs about future decisions on which students must condition their current behavior, and yet educational expectations are open to other mechanisms, some of which may have only a loose connection to the sorts of costs and benefits that one would customarily specify in a rational choice model of educational attainment. The model I will develop can be seen as an attempt to use the explicitness of rational choice theory to realize the core mechanism of the Wisconsin model, and, in the process, open that mechanism up to additional important causes of educational attainment.

CONCLUSIONS

Status socialization theory is a deeply entrenched set of practices but, as presently deployed, a collectively weak body of ideas. The expectation formation mechanism of status socialization theory is a compacted set of belief formation mechanisms that needs to be decomposed and explicitly modeled. In Chapter 3, I begin this process by thoroughly analyzing the central association of the Wisconsin model, the relationship between educational expectations and attainment.

NOTES

1. And, there exists even earlier relevant research reports based on 1947–48 data on Wisconsin high school seniors (see Sewell, Haller, and Straus 1957).

2. Even this round of revisions was incomplete. According to the guidelines set down in the original articles, there was a direct effect of socioeconomic status on college plans in the 1970 Wisconsin model. This initially overlooked effect has implications for both the conceptualization of college plans and the power of the socialization theory on which the model is grounded, and hence deserves some explication.

In the early days of path analysis in sociology, model estimation proceeded in the following steps. After first deriving a causal ordering of variables from a theory, every possible path in the chain of causality was first estimated. After the researcher established threshold criteria for the retention of theoretically and substantively important paths, the path-model was reestimated with the subset of paths whose first stage estimates met these criteria. The path-models presented in the 1969 and 1970 articles show only the final outcome of this process for the construction of the Wisconsin model.

For the 1969 Wisconsin model, the initial estimate of the standardized partial regression coefficient for the direct path from SES to educational aspirations was .07. Because this path was not predicted by the underlying socialization theory of the model, and because its initial estimate was so small, it was not included in the final model presented in *ASR*. However, because all of the respondents used in the 1969 sample were sons of farmers, variation in socioeconomic status was extremely narrow. Accordingly, it is unlikely that .07 was an informative estimate for respondents from the full range of social backgrounds.

When the entire sample was used for the more comprehensive 1970 model, the initial estimate of the direct effect of SES on educational aspirations was much larger. And if the numbers are examined closely, only one conclusion is possible: Sewell and his colleagues mistakenly omitted a nontrivial direct effect of SES on college plans. For the 1970 model, it was decided that statistical significance would not be the criterion for retention of paths "because the large size of the samples representing the various community size categories produces statistically significant beta values which have no interpretable importance" (Sewell et al. 1970:1020). They selected "a quite arbitrary" cutoff point of .15 for standardized regression coefficients. A path would only be retained in the model if the beta value was at least .15 in "the total sample and in three of the five community sizes" (p. 1020). The beta value for the path from SES to educational aspirations was .168 for the entire sample. While for boys raised on farms it was only .078, it was .120, .154, .174, and .169 for those raised respectively in villages, small cities, medium cities, and large cities. The path for the direct effect of SES on educational aspirations seems to have met all of their criteria and yet it was not retained. (By comparison, other paths with beta values for the entire sample as low as .150, .172, .177, and .176 were retained.)

Subsequent research within the community of Wisconsin modelers has not fully resolved the issue. Hauser (1972) reestimated a disaggregated version of the Wisconsin model and tentatively argued for the importance of a direct effect of SES on educational plans. However, Hauser, Tsai, and Sewell (1983) then recalculated Hauser's 1972 estimates, modeling measurement error with retrospective reports of significant others' influence and educational plans. They concluded that unmediated effects of SES on educational plans were not sufficiently supported by the data and thus reaffirmed the viability of the socialization theory—and its operationalization as a "modified causal chain"—underlying the original specification.

Nonetheless, when status socialization theory was developed in tandem with the estimation of the original specification of the model, a direct effect of SES on college plans was evident in the numbers. Had it been noted, college plans might have been recognized, even net of the influence of significant others, as responsive to resource constraints proxied by parental SES. College plans might then have been considered reasonable forecasts of future behavior, not mere internalized expressions of the status-defined expectations of significant others.

3. Although these class differences in expectations were based, presumably, in the everyday experiences of individuals, they were also shaped within educational institutions as well. For example, in his later essay "The School Class as a Social System," Parsons (1964[1959]) provided a comprehensive framework for understanding the central function that educational institutions play in inculcating the universal norms of the modern age while at the same time differentiating individuals by talent and then allocating them to appropriate stations in life. In laying out the details of the framework, Parsons stops and soberly contends that: "It is therefore not stretching the evidence too far to say broadly that the primary selective process occurs through differential school performance in elementary school, and that the 'seal' is put on it in junior high school" (p. 131). Nonetheless, the continuum of achievement along which students are ranked is, however, complex because "a *good* pupil is defined in terms of a fusion of the cognitive and the moral components, in which varying weight is given to one or the other." And, as a result, achievement can be thought of as: "relative excellence in living up to the expectations imposed by the teacher as an agent of the adult society" (p. 137–38).

4. It is unclear why, in many passages of the article and in its title, Kahl chose the label aspirations for what was a straightforward expressed intention for whether or not the boy planned to enter college (and hence was enrolled in a college preparatory program).

5. The fine points of this explanation, however, seem to have been lost in the secondary literature, for Kahl's article is often regarded as a statement about intergenerational value transmission, much like Hyman's 1953 article "The Value Systems of Different Classes." Scholars such as Boudon (1974) and Goldthorpe (1996) regard the Hyman article as an early example of explanation via class-specific cul-

ture and values. One can, however, also regard Hyman's explanation as one about quite rational beliefs. Much like Kahl, Hyman stresses the possible reasonableness of beliefs about the opportunity structure. For example, although Hyman (1953: 427) wrote, in an oft-cited phrase (e.g., see Keller and Zavalloni 1964:58), that lower class youth are characterized by a "value system" with components that "involve less emphasis upon the traditional high success goals, increased awareness of the lack of opportunity to achieve success, and less emphasis upon the achievement of goals which in turn would be instrumental for success," he then wrote that "Presumably this value system arises out of a realistic appraisal of reality and in turn softens for the individual the impact of low status. Unfortunately, we have at the moment little information on its genesis." Boudon (1974:22–23), nonetheless, labels Hyman's explanation as a "value theory." Unlike Boudon, Breen (1999:466) correctly identifies the belief-based foundations of Hyman's values, and begins to lay out a model for the "genesis" of these beliefs that Hyman considered, at the time, unknown.

6. In fairness to early critics of the Wisconsin model, it is possible that these later articles are best regarded as rearguard maneuvers, which develop a misleading case that the original article was substantially more theoretically developed in 1969 and 1970 than it truly was. However, I err on the side of crediting the Wisconsin modelers with substantial clarity of thought, for their model was uncharacteristically bold in the context of other work in the sociology of education at the time.

7. Valence is a somewhat awkward term, but in the construction of his field theory Lewin was obsessed with physics. The reader should not attempt to read much meaning into the etymology of the term. As for the notion of "triumph over difficulty," I introduce it into the presentation to qualitatively describe what I see as the implicit mechanism that governs the setting of valences for Lewin. Lewin never used the phrase in his writing, as far as I am aware.

8. Lewin's model of sentiment derived from success differs substantially from the one assumed by standard rational choice models, primarily because the assumed context of action differs across the two theories. Rational choice theories typically assume a background world of constraints where more rewards exist than can be captured in any period of time. As a result, individuals choose to perform tasks that yield the highest rewards for the least amount of effort. In contrast, Lewin's subjects performed their tasks in a completely different context. They repeated the performance of a single task in a highly controlled laboratory environment, a salient characteristic of which was the absence of any competing tasks with alternative rewards. This difference in the two theories could be shown in Figure 2.2 by adding a flat line for the utility of successful performance, which, according to the usual tenets of rational choice theory, would remain constant when plotted against the perceived difficulty of the task.

9. Lewin, however, does have a related set of ideas that might support such a mechanism. An "intention" for Lewin is a mental state that creates a quasi-need. The resulting quasi-need engenders tension that can only be relieved by an appro-

priate consummatory action (Lewin 1999[1926]). Thus, for Lewin the creation of an intention can compel action. Unfortunately, as far as I am aware, he appears never to have clearly specified the conceptual connection between aspirations and intentions.

10. This is not the only challenge, only the one that seems most troubling to rational choice scholars themselves. The other obvious challenge for the two-equation system is the input to Equation 2.5, labeled *TASTE*. Although often presented as crucial, taste is rarely specified and never measured. As a result, $u(.)$ is rarely given any specific form that incorporates tastes. Instead, rational choice researchers focus attention on the development and estimation of $h(.)$ from Equation 2.4, attempting to measure the associations between the determinants of returns and actual educational attainment through Equation 2.5. Claims that these observed associations support causal propositions rest on assumptions about $h(.)$ and the joint distributions of tastes, e_3, and e_4.

11. If anything, they are the sort of rational fantasy that I speculated about in Morgan (1998). Students seem to overestimate the returns to schooling and may then report to expect to attend college because they wish to bring their expressed intentions in line with their beliefs about what they should do.

12. More specifically, if $\varepsilon_i = ATTAIN_i - EXPECT_i$ for all individuals i and there are no aggregate shocks to individuals' behavior, then (1) $E[\varepsilon]$ must be 0 and (2) individuals must know and base their expectations on the true functional relationship between observable information and actual educational attainment so that ε is uncorrelated with all of the potentially observable information that will determine attainment. These two necessary conditions are satisfied by the assumptions that e_4 and e_5 are uncorrelated and that the nonrandom portions of Equations 2.5 and 2.6 are equivalent, as can be shown if the right-hand side of Equation 2.6 is subtracted from the right-hand side of Equation 2.5. Sheffrin (1996) gives an introduction to rational expectations assumptions in economic modeling, especially in macroeconomics where the concept has been most frequently deployed.

CHAPTER THREE

Do Beliefs Matter? A Reanalysis of the Relationship Between Educational Expectations and Attainment

Classic rational choice models of educational attainment generate predictions by assuming that individuals can be modeled as if they have engaged in perfect information processing and flawless expectation formation in advance of all relevant consequential decisions (see Willis and Rosen 1979). For example, students are thought to observe college and labor market entrance rates and then, on average, accurately estimate whether or not individuals with attributes such as their own are likely to receive adequate returns for enrolling in college (see Manski 1993a). When combined with axioms of consistent choice, perception-rationality assumptions ensure that observed behavior reveals preferences, and empirical analysis is simplified because discrete choice models then have simple behavioral interpretations. For this set of reasons, perception-rationality assumptions have proven useful for facilitating theoretical predictions and for motivating the analysis of the limited data that are available (see McFadden 1999).

Sociologists have rejected these assumptions as reasonable presuppositions for explanatory theories of educational attainment. Instead, sociologists have developed many competing explanations, most of which focus at least informally on the ways in which the behavioral orientations of students, parents, and teachers are shaped by beliefs about the educational system and which types of students are destined for success within it. The Wisconsin model, summarized in Chapter 2, is only one such model. For a celebrated alternative, consider the perspective of Bourdieu (1973), as quoted in Chapter 1 (see page 20). Or, consider the classic counterargument of Willis (1977), who wrote in *Learning to Labour* with Bourdieu in mind about why some adolescents commit to schooling whereas others rebel:

we must go to the cultural milieu . . . and we must accept a certain autonomy
of the processes at this level which . . . gives the social agents involved some
meaningful scope for viewing, inhabiting and constructing their own world in
a way which is recognisably human and not theoretically reductive. Settling
for manual work is not an experience of absolute incoherence walled from en-
lightenment by perverse cultural influences, nor is it that of atavistic innocence
deeply inscribed upon by pre-given ideologies. It has the profane nature of itself, neither without meaning nor with other's meaning. It is felt, subjectively,
as a profound process of learning: it is the organisation of the self in relation
to the future. (p. 172)

While one can applaud the passion of Willis' argument—which I interpret
as a plea for examining the individually contingent nature of belief formation processes as opposed to Bourdieu's stronger assumption of class homo-
geneity of beliefs—nothing in Willis' book specifies possible ways in which
students learn to organize "the self in relation to the future."

In the recent theoretical literature, a clear convergence in the theoretical
strategies of sociologists and economists is now evident, with sociologists
adopting more specific theoretical mechanisms and economists questioning
the usefulness of a priori assumptions of perception-rationality. I presented
some of this convergent literature in Chapter 2 and will return to it in Chapter 4, seeking to further develop it thereafter.

In this chapter, I draw together the sociology and economics literature
in jointly inspired empirical analysis of students' own beliefs about their future behavior. The five sets of results I will develop have a dual-headed pur-
pose: (1) to demonstrate that the data are consistent with the proposition
that students' beliefs do matter and should be explicitly modeled and also
(2) to demonstrate that the existing data and the underlying theoretical motivation for collecting them are sufficiently lacking such that the theoretical
work of the remainder of this book is worthwhile.

I organize analysis around the following questions: Can the association between educational expectations and educational attainment be given
a causal interpretation? If not, is it reasonable to instead treat educational
expectations as little more than alternative indicators of educational attainment that can be ignored when data on educational attainment are available? Finally, in order to provide analytical traction for these two questions,
while also addressing controversies from the 1970s and 1980s on the universal applicability of the Wisconsin model's explanatory narrative, I focus ex-

plicitly on black-white differences in the formation of educational expectations and their subsequent association with realized educational attainment.

WHY DOES THE MEASURED EFFECT OF EXPECTATIONS ON ATTAINMENT DIFFER FOR WHITES AND BLACKS?

Attention to students' beliefs about the educational attainment process has varied over the past three decades, and the vicissitudes of research on racial differences are partly responsible for the fluctuation of interest. In the 1960s, early research on students' college plans (for example, Educational Testing Service 1957; Kahl 1953) was superseded by the Wisconsin model and its claim of a universal status attainment process. When survey research then focused more narrowly on racial differences in the educational attainment process (for example, Kerckhoff and Campbell 1977a, 1977b; Portes and Wilson 1976), the Wisconsin model lost much of its initial appeal as a comprehensive explanation for the status attainment process, in large part because estimates of the correspondence between college plans and educational attainment differed for whites and blacks.

Following on the arguments of Kerckhoff (1976), the educational attainment literature in sociology then gradually shifted toward structural allocation models that focused primarily on institutions (for example, Arum 1998; Gamoran and Mare 1989; Raftery and Hout 1993), demographic effects (for example, Kuo and Hauser 1995; Mare and Tzeng 1989), and variation in resources other than stable family background characteristics (for example, Duncan, Brooks-Gunn, Yeung, and Smith 1998; Hofferth, Boisjoly, and Duncan 1998; Mayer 1997). Although these structural and demographic models generated important empirical results, for the most part they did not elucidate the micro-mechanisms with which prior status socialization models were appropriately concerned.

In this section, I engage a classic unresolved question in the status attainment literature (see Kerckhoff and Campbell 1977a, Table 1; Portes and Wilson 1976, Table 2): Why is the relationship between educational expectations and subsequent educational attainment weaker for blacks than for whites?

Figure 3.1 presents a graphical depiction of the traditional two-equation system that has been invoked to answer this question (see also Equations 2.2 and 2.3 from Chapter 2). The first two models presented below are con-

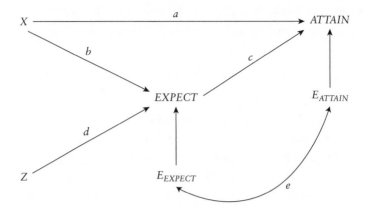

Figure 3.1.   A Structural Equation System for the Effect of Educational Expectations on Educational Attainment

strained specifications of this system—a path-model and an instrumental variable model. Both models are grounded on assumptions of temporal causal order (see Davis 1985): Variables in X cause both expectations and attainment, and expectations cause attainment.

The data were drawn for white and black respondents from the base year through fourth follow-up waves of the *HS&B*. For this survey, analyzed earlier in Chapter 1, all respondents were high school sophomores for the base year survey in 1980 and were subsequently resurveyed in 1982, 1984, 1986, and finally in 1992 by which time most respondents were 28 years old.[1]

A Traditional Path-Model for the Causal Effect of Expectations on Attainment

For a path-model specification of the structural equations system, an identifying assumption is asserted: None of the unobserved variables that determine attainment, E_{ATTAIN}, are correlated with those that determine expectations, E_{EXPECT}. Under this assumption, e is assumed equal to 0, and simple regression techniques can be used to estimate a set of coefficients for a, b, and c. With these coefficients, the causal effects of variables in X can be decomposed into direct effects on attainment and indirect effects that are mediated by expectations (see Alwin and Hauser 1975). Most importantly for the research question investigated here, the temporal causal order assumption allows the coefficient estimate of c to be interpreted as the direct causal effect of expectations on attainment.

Separately for white male, white female, black male, and black female *HS&B* respondents, the two panels of Table 3.1 present path-model estimates of the causal effect of sophomore year and senior year expectations on attainment by age 28. Expectations and attainment are scaled in years, and estimation is by ordinary least squares (OLS). For the estimates reported in the first column of each panel, socioeconomic status, family structure, and test scores are included as variables in X. For the estimates reported in the second column of each panel, the central variable of the Wisconsin model, significant others' influence, is added to the variables in X.

The point estimate of the direct causal effect of expectations on attainment is larger for whites than for blacks, for each sex in all four sets of models. For example, each additional year of education expected in the sophomore year is associated with .182 and .080 years of attained education respectively for white males and black males. When significant others' inuence is added to X, these estimates fall to .133 and .068 respectively, just as in the Wisconsin model. Nonetheless, the same pattern of race differences persists.

Four explanations for these race differences exist in the literature, the first three of which are closely related:

1. The *differential socialization* explanation is based on the assumption, developed for the Wisconsin model, that educational expectations are an operationalization of latent achievement ambition (see Spenner and Featherman 1978). Many status attainment articles of the 1970s demonstrated that status socialization models explain relatively less of the variance of black students' educational expectations (for example, Hout and Morgan 1975). Within the status attainment framework, this finding was interpreted as evidence that the socialization of black students differed from that of white students. In particular, because black students have access to a less powerful socialization process, their motivational orientations are less effectively targeted at the crucial levers of advancement in the educational system. As a result, the correspondence between their expectations and future attainments is lower because they are more likely to adopt expectations that they are less compelled to follow.

2. The *misperception of opportunity constraint* explanation is based on the assumption that educational expectations reflect perceptions of opportunity constraints in addition to latent achievement ambition. Because black

TABLE 3.1

Traditional Path-Model Estimates of the Effect of
Educational Expectations on Educational Attainment by Age 28

| | PATH-MODEL ESTIMATES OF C IN FIGURE 1 FOR SOPHOMORE YEAR EDUCATIONAL EXPECTATIONS (1980) | | PATH-MODEL ESTIMATES OF C IN FIGURE 1 FOR SENIOR YEAR EDUCATIONAL EXPECTATIONS (1982) | | |
	Family Background and Test Scores as X [a]	Family Background, Test Scores, and Significant Others' Influence as X [b]	Family Background and Test Scores as X [c]	Family Background, Test Scores, and Significant Others' Influence as X [d]	N
White males	.182 (.024)[e]	.133 (.026)	.303 (.024)	.221 (.026)	2,444
White females	.159 (.020)	.138 (.021)	.252 (.021)	.205 (.023)	2,860
Black males	.080 (.057)	.068 (.059)	.181 (.095)	.155 (.099)	350
Black females	.120 (.037)	.112 (.036)	.069 (.031)	.029 (.030)	539

NOTES: *High School & Beyond* sophomore cohort data (1980 through 1992 waves). Data are weighted by the fourth follow-up panel weight (panel5wt)

[a] Exogenous variables that are specified as having direct effects on both expectations and attainment are socioeconomic status, family structure, 1980 test scores, and the predictive probability of being included in the analysis sample of those who do not have missing data on either expectations, attainment, or the instrument.

[b] Additional exogenous variables for these models include 1980 significant others' influence.

[c] Exogenous variables that are specified as having direct effects on both expectations and attainment are socioeconomic status, family structure, 1980 test scores, 1982 test scores, and the predictive probability of being included in the analysis sample of those who do not have missing data on either expectations, attainment, or the instrument.

[d] Additional exogenous variables for these models include 1980 significant others' influence and 1982 significant others' influence.

[e] The standard errors in parentheses are robust heteroskedastic-consistent standard errors, further adjusted for clustering of students within schools.

students are more often subject to opportunity constraints that they do not recognize at the time they form expectations, black students find it relatively more difficult to realize the achievement motivation into which they have been socialized.[2] Foreshadowed within the early status attainment literature (for example, Duncan 1969; Kerckhoff 1976), this explanation is perhaps the most popular theme of subsequent literature on the expectations and attainment relationship that emphasizes "lost talent" (see Hanson 1994).

3. The *underachievement* explanation focuses on the self-regulation of academic performance in high school. For this explanation, it is assumed that the expectations of whites and blacks alike are shaped by a powerful and universal abstract attitude that educational attainment is of paramount importance for socioeconomic advancement. But because black college graduates earn considerably less than white college graduates, black high school students on average develop a less positive concrete attitude toward performance in schooling (see Mickelson 1990).[3] This explanation assumes that although concrete attitudes are inconsequential for educational expectations, they nonetheless lead blacks to underachieve in everyday school performance. This daily underachievement, by way of reduced college preparation, lowers resulting levels of educational attainment.

4. The *measurement error* explanation attributes the racial difference to a statistical artifact. If there is relatively more random measurement error in the expectations of black students and all else is equal, the estimated effect for blacks will be attenuated relative to the estimated effect for whites (see Fuller 1987 for the general argument). There is some evidence of relatively greater measurement error in reports of family background for blacks (for example, Bielby, Hauser, and Featherman 1977), but from these studies one cannot easily infer patterns of measurement error for expectations.[4]

Which of these four explanations is correct? Each of the three substantive explanations is theoretically interesting, consistent with the empirical results, and permits the incorporation of supporting qualitative, contextual, and historical evidence into their proposed narratives. And yet, all three explanations appeal to unmeasured variables, and none of the explanations necessarily implies that the true causal effect of expectations on attainment varies by race. Instead, as best I can determine, their implicit assumption is precisely the opposite: If the hypothesized omitted variables—differential socialization processes, misperceived opportunity constraints, and unmeasured concrete attitudes—had been observed and specified in the models, the path-model estimates of the effect of expectations on attainment would not vary by race. But that is only one possibility, since it could also be the case that if these omitted variables were specified, the net effect of expectations would actually be larger for blacks than for whites. Thus, it may be that a more narrowly defined relationship between expectations and attainment is greater for blacks than for whites, implying in contrast to the three traditional explanations that changes in core educational expectations are more consequential for final levels of educational attainment for blacks than for whites.[5]

Even more deeply, these explanations undermine the claim that expectations cause attainment for any group of students. When it is assumed that omitted variables are potentially of great importance, the claim that expectations cause attainment and hence that students' beliefs matter rests almost entirely on the temporal order assumption that expectations necessarily proceed, and thus cause, educational attainment. But, as will be discussed later, there is a plausible theoretical basis for questioning the temporal causal order assumption, on the alternative assumption that expectations are non-causal, best-possible forecasts.

An Instrumental Variable Model for the Average Causal Effect

Suppose that researchers could brainwash students, either erasing or creating their educational expectations at will. If researchers could then show that changes in expectations induced by this manipulation are associated with later educational attainment, they would be able to claim that educational expectations should be regarded as a cause of educational attainment. This would be powerful evidence that students' beliefs do matter. And if, in performing this experimental manipulation, they also uncovered race differences in the causal effect of expectations on attainment in the same direction as suggested by the path-model estimates above, they would then appropriately conclude that beliefs are probably more important for whites than for blacks.

Although effective experimental manipulation of expectations is infeasible, sociologists can attempt to take account of naturally occurring random variation. This is the goal of instrumental variables analysis, which in its classic form is an alternative to path-model identification of a structural equations system (Duncan 1975; see also Bollen 1989:415). For Figure 3.1, if a variable denoted by Z is available that predicts expectations but has no direct effect on attainment, then even in the presence of a correlation, e, between omitted variables that determine expectations and attainment, the causal effect of expectations on attainment, c, can be consistently estimated.

Are there any available instruments for expectations? Sociology has a long tradition of interpreting the positive correlation between the educational expectations of students and their best friends as evidence of a causal social influence process (for example, Cohen 1983; Davies and Kandel 1981; Duncan, Haller, and Portes 1968).[6] If it is assumed that friendship formation is in part a random process, net of the usual homophily predictors such as race and family background (see Hallinan and Williams 1990), then there is scope to regard some portion of the endogenous correlation as a source of quasi-experimental variation. Based on the assumption that when conditioning on family background, test scores, and significant others' influence, best friends' expectations have no direct effect on a student's own educational attainment and only an indirect effect by way of a student's expectations (as with Z in Figure 3.1), the quasi-experimental component of expectations can then be used to identify the causal effect of expectations on attainment by estimating a two-stage least squares (2SLS) model (see Greene 2000).

Table 3.2 presents 2SLS estimates of the effect of senior year educational expectations on educational attainment, using best friends' expectations as an instrument for students' expectations. The 2SLS estimates are positive and considerably larger than the corresponding OLS estimates reported in the fourth column of Table 3.1. Moreover, the 2SLS estimates provide no evidence of substantial race differences in the expectations and attainment relationship. In comparison to the path-model estimates, the 2SLS point estimates are similar for whites and blacks, and if anything are larger for blacks.

Two interpretations of these results based on the classical instrumental variables literature can be offered:

1. The true causal effect of expectations on attainment is positive but does not vary by race. Race differences in the path-model estimates are observed because the path-model identifying assumption that e is equal to 0 is unreasonable. Accordingly, the path-model evidence that the causal effect of expectations on attainment is stronger for whites than for blacks indicates that the correlation between omitted factors, e, is larger for whites than for blacks. For example, if the size of the effect of unmeasured opportunity constraints on attainment is the same for whites and for blacks, the path-model estimate of the effect of expectations on attainment will be larger for whites than for blacks if, as is suggested by the misperceived opportunity constraint explanation, the correlation between unmeasured opportunity constraints and educational expectations is stronger for whites than for blacks. Thus, these results are consis-

TABLE 3.2

2SLS Regression Estimates of the Effect of Senior
Year Educational Expectations on Educational
Attainment for Four Race and Sex Groups with
Best Friends' Expectations as an Instrument
for Respondent's Educational Expectations

	2SLS Estimates of c in Figure 1[a]	N
White males	.342 (.170)[b]	2,444
White females	.459 (.179)	2,860
Black males	.392 (.488)	350
Black females	.462 (.670)	539

NOTES: *High School & Beyond* sophomore cohort data (1980 through 1992 waves). Data are weighted by the fourth follow-up panel weight (panel5wt)

[a]Exogenous variables that are specified as having direct effects on both expectations and attainment are socioeconomic status, family structure, 1980 test scores, 1982 test scores, 1980 significant others' influence, 1982 significant others' influence, and the predictive probability of being included in the analysis sample of those who do not have missing data on either expectations, attainment, or the instrument.

[b]The standard errors in parentheses are robust heteroskedastic-consistent standard errors, further adjusted for clustering of students within schools.

tent with all three traditional explanations for the observed race difference in the path-model estimates, and with their common hidden conjecture that if relevant omitted variables were explicitly modeled in a path-model framework race differences in estimates of the causal effect might disappear.

2. Instrumental variable estimators are not susceptible to attenuation bias, primarily because they are ratios of covariances that can be consistently estimated even in the presence of random measurement error. Thus, the 2SLS estimates suggest that race differences in the path-model estimates can be attributed to larger amounts of random measurement error in the expectations of blacks. In order to sustain this interpretation, it must be assumed that there are distinct race differences in orientations to the survey questions (as will be discussed later) and that any greater variability in the responses of blacks is not on its own substantively meaningful.

There is a serious limitation to these traditional interpretations. Classical instrumental variable models assume that the causal effect of interest is absolutely constant across all individuals. For example, under the classical interpretation, the estimates of Table 3.2 suggest that for every white male the causal effect of expectations on attainment is equal to .342 years of attainment for every year of education expected for every white male in the sample. Fortunately, a new instrumental variables literature has arisen that relaxes the overly restrictive constant coefficient assumption by introducing a monotonicity condition on individuals' induced responses to the instrument (see Angrist, Imbens, and Rubin 1996). For this application, one would instead assert that the effect of best friends' expectations on students' own expectations is greater than or equal to 0 for all students. In other words, if students change their expectations in response to their best friends' expectations, they only change their expectations to make them more similar to their best friends' expectations. Under this monotonicity assumption, the 2SLS estimator identifies the average causal effect for the subset of students who would change their expectations in response to their best friends' expectations (Angrist and Imbens 1995). Thus, the new literature on instrumental variables offers a third interpretation:

> 3. Among those students who would change their expectations in response to a change in the expectations of their best friends, the average causal effect of expectations on attainment is positive and does not vary by race.

The claim that the true causal effect of expectations on attainment is positive is based on the instrumental variable identifying assumption that, net of family background, test scores, and significant others' influence, peers affect each others' attainment only by shaping each others' expectations. If there is a residual direct effect of best friends' expectations on attainment, net of students' own expectations and significant others' influence, then the 2SLS estimates are inconsistent and (asymptotically) biased upward. For this reason, causal claims based on instrumental variables invariably remain controversial, even though in this case such claims are no more controversial than the path-model-based claims of causality of the last section.

Given the possibility that these models may overstate the size of any causal effect of expectations on attainment, is there any reason to believe that possible violations of the identifying assumption have suppressed a true race difference analogous to the one suggested by the path-model estimates?

In order for this to be the case, the residual direct effect of best friends' expectations on students' own attainment would have to be considerably more serious for blacks than for whites. Although possibly consistent with the underachievement explanation of Mickelson (1990), such a difference in residual peer effects on attainment contradicts the ethnographic literature (for example, Fordham and Ogbu 1986) that stresses the self-conscious rejection of school performance by black adolescents.

In light of the new instrumental variable literature and the third interpretation of the 2SLS estimates offered above, there is a more subtle and yet also more serious threat to the conclusion that the true effect of expectations on attainment does not vary by race. Consider the best-case scenario: If researchers had many available instrumental variables, all of which satisfied analogous monotonicity conditions and also yielded the same pattern of coefficients—a positive effect that does not vary by race—then they would have confidence that no race difference in the expectations and attainment relationship needs to be explained.

What might such a set of instruments be? Educational expectations are a summary measure of underlying beliefs about the costs and benefits of educational attainment and about the availability of resources to meet the costs of postsecondary education. If some of these underlying beliefs are incorrect, then students' forecasts differ from the forecasts that they would have instead formed if all of their underlying beliefs had been correct. And if students' college preparatory commitment decisions while still in high school are regulated by their forecasts of their own future behavior, then educational expectations can be treated as if they are a cause of educational attainment. Variation in a set of component underlying beliefs could be treated as a set of instrumental variables for educational expectations.

Sociologists do not have a set of such instruments. As a result, the single set of 2SLS estimates presented in Table 3.2 does not reveal enough information about how much expectations would respond to shifts in underlying beliefs, and the average causal effect interpretation of the 2SLS estimates is thus quite limited. In particular, it does not rule out the possibility that other instruments might show that indeed a case can be made that there are important race differences in the expectations and attainment relationship.

Nonetheless, the average causal effect interpretation points the way toward future profitable research objectives, notably the explicit modeling of component belief formation processes on which expectations are based.

This objective is entirely consistent with the research objectives entailed by further attempts to directly model the differential socialization practices, misperceived opportunity constraints, and concrete attitudes stressed in the existing literature. But, unlike the path-model estimates, these estimates also compel sociologists to directly model the potential individual-level heterogeneity of causal effects and to explicitly model the potential impact of omitted variables.

Thus, the data simply cannot provide a clear-cut answer to the question that is posed at the beginning of this section. If I had to choose one, however, it would be the following. Educational expectations cause educational attainment, but there is no evidence that the effect of expectations on attainment varies by race. This conclusion implies that beliefs do not matter more for whites than for blacks. Rather, the path-model estimates simply suggest that additional belief-based effects for blacks operate outside of traditional status socialization models. This is justification for the model developed in later chapters.

IS THERE ANY EVIDENCE THAT THE MEASURED EFFECT OF EXPECTATIONS ON ATTAINMENT IS CAUSAL?

How strong is the evidence that beliefs matter? Unfortunately, not very strong. On balance, as I show in this section, there is only a modest amount of evidence. But, it is this ambiguity in the evidence that I regard as one of the best justifications for the more explicit theorizing I develop in subsequent chapters.

The starting point for a rigorous analysis of a claim of causality, and hence of an analysis of group differences in any such causal effect, is the careful definition of the causal effect of interest. For the effect of expectations on attainment, causal effects are most clearly defined using counterfactual-conditional statements of the form: "If a student who expected not to graduate from college and subsequently did not graduate from college had instead expected to graduate from college (and all else remained the same), then he or she would have graduated from college." [7]

Before introducing the specifics of the counterfactual framework that formalizes statements such as this one, I first provide a more basic representation of the relationship between expectations and attainment, one which is liberated from the interval-scaling assumptions of the models of the last section and one which more easily facilitates a discussion of the actions of individuals rather than the partial associations of measured variables. Accordingly, I dichotomize the yearly educational attainment variable into a dummy variable A that equals 1 if a respondent attains a college degree. Likewise, I dichotomize the yearly expectations variables into dummy variables E that equal 1 if a respondent expects to complete college.[8]

Column one of Table 3.3 presents the mean values of E for distinct strata of *HS&B* respondents delineated by race, sex, and a dichotomous variable for whether each student has at least one parent who completed college. Columns two and three present mean values of A conditional on alternative values of E. For example, the value .666 in the first row of column two indicates that 66.6 percent of white males who have a college-educated parent and who expected to graduate from college in their sophomore year actually did graduate from college by age 28.

The Counterfactual Model of Causality

Whereas the structural equations model presented in the last section relies primarily on a logic of temporal order for measured variables (see Davis 1985), the counterfactual framework asserts the theoretical existence of abstract and timeless potential outcomes that have distributions over all individuals in the population of interest.[9] For this application, potential outcomes are defined as: A^{ea}, a dichotomous attainment outcome for the action "complete college" under the theoretical state "expect to attain a college degree," and A^{ef}, a dichotomous attainment outcome under the alternative state "expect to fail to attain a college degree." The individual-level causal effect of expectations on attainment is then defined as the difference for each individual between the two potential outcomes:

$$\delta_i = A_i^{ea} - A_i^{ef} \tag{3.1}$$

where i indexes all individuals in the population. Individuals for whom δ_i equals 1 would be induced to complete college by an increase in their expectation from expect to fail to expect to attain. Individuals for whom δ_i equals 0 or -1 would not be induced to complete college by the same change in their expectations. Unfortunately, because individuals cannot be observed simultaneously in both theoretical states, δ_i cannot be calculated for any individual, and this observational reality is often referred to as the fundamental problem of causal inference (see Holland 1986).

TABLE 3.3
Mean Educational Expectations and Educational Attainment
for Four Race and Sex Groups and Level of Parents' Education

	Proportion of Students who Expected to Complete College	PROPORTION OF STUDENTS WHO COMPLETED COLLEGE		N
		Expected to Complete College	Did Not Expect to Complete College	
Sophomore Year Expectations:				
White males				
Parent with college degree	.632	.666	.193	744
No parent with college degree	.211	.399	.075	1,700
White females				
Parent with college degree	.595	.644	.239	827
No parent with college degree	.208	.314	.065	2,033
Black males				
Parent with college degree	.673	.234	.101	84
No parent with college degree	.275	.281	.099	266
Black females				
Parent with college degree	.506	.344	.033	93
No parent with college degree	.339	.183	.023	446
Senior Year Expectations:				
White males				
Parent with college degree	.642	.685	.147	744
No parent with college degree	.217	.495	.046	1,700
White females				
Parent with college degree	.613	.668	.182	827
No parent with college degree	.206	.409	.041	2,033
Black males				
Parent with college degree	.480	.381	.015	84
No parent with college degree	.243	.274	.109	266
Black females				
Parent with college degree	.600	.260	.085	93
No parent with college degree	.341	.150	.040	446

NOTES: *High School & Beyond* sophomore cohort data (1980 through 1992 waves). Data are weighted by the fourth follow-up panel weight (panel5wt) multiplied by the probability of having missing data on the expectations and attainment variables (estimated from separate race- and sex-specific logit models).

Progress is possible when individual-level potential outcomes are aggregated to the population level in order to form the population-level analog to Equation 3.1:

$$\delta = \overline{A}^{\text{ea}} - \overline{A}^{\text{ef}} \tag{3.2}$$

where the bar above each term denotes the population-level mean.[10] By aggregating to the population level, the fundamental problem of causal inference can be reduced to the more tractable challenge of estimating two population-level means.

To understand how difficult estimation can be, let E be a theoretical subset of the population that includes all individuals who, if observed, would report that they expect to attain a college degree. Accordingly, all individuals in the population are either members of E (denoted $i \in E$) or are not members of E (denoted $i \notin E$). Now, let π equal the true proportion of individuals in the population who are in E and decompose the population-level means of the potential outcomes in Equation 3.2 across inclusion in the subset E:

$$\delta = \left[\pi \overline{A}^{\text{ea}}_{i \in E} + (1 - \pi) \overline{A}^{\text{ea}}_{i \notin E} \right] - \left[\pi \overline{A}^{\text{ef}}_{i \in E} + (1 - \pi) \overline{A}^{\text{ef}}_{i \notin E} \right] \tag{3.3}$$

Which terms on the right hand side of Equation 3.3 can be effectively estimated with survey data on expectations and attainment? The proportion π of individuals who are in E is consistently estimated by the sample mean of the dichotomous educational expectations variable, E. Likewise, $\overline{A}^{\text{ea}}_{i \in E}$ and $\overline{A}^{\text{ef}}_{i \in E}$ are consistently estimated by the sample means of the observable attainment variable A, respectively for those who are observed expecting to attain a college degree and for those who are observed expecting to fail to attain a college degree (that is, those for whom $E = 1$ and $E = 0$, respectively). Unfortunately, no consistent estimator of $\overline{A}^{\text{ea}}_{i \notin E}$ and $\overline{A}^{\text{ef}}_{i \in E}$ is available for observational survey data because these counterfactual means are population-level means of individual-level potential outcomes that exist in theory but that are not observable.

Within this framework, in the remainder of this section I first offer naive estimates of the average causal effect defined by Equation 3.2 for different race and sex groups. I then assess the permissible range of the true average causal effect under three sets of theoretically grounded but inherently untestable alternative assumptions about the unobservable population-level means $\overline{A}^{\text{ea}}_{i \notin E}$ and $\overline{A}^{\text{ef}}_{i \in E}$.

Naive estimates of the average causal effect. Assume for the rest of this section that the population of interest is any one of the subpopulation strata defined for Table 3.3 based on race, sex, and parents' level of education. The naive estimator of the average causal effect $\bar{\delta}$ is:

$$\hat{\delta} = \hat{\bar{A}}^{ea}_{i \in E} - \hat{\bar{A}}^{ef}_{i \notin E} \tag{3.4}$$

Separately for distinct strata, estimates corresponding to Equation 3.4 are presented for *HS&B* respondents in column one of Table 3.4. Operationally, these estimates are formed by subtracting the conditional means in column three from those in column two of Table 3.3. For example, the naive estimate of the effect of sophomore year expectations for white males with a college graduate parent is .473, implying that if the expectations of a sample of such respondents were shifted from not expecting to attain a college degree to instead expecting to attain a college degree, an additional 47.3 percent of students would complete college. Note, however, that the corresponding conditional mean in column three of Table 3.3 suggests that 19.3 percent of these respondents would complete college anyway, regardless of their educational expectations.

Although very simple, and hence "naive," these estimates convey the same story as the path-model results.[11] The estimates of the average causal effect are larger for whites than for blacks for all similarly defined strata of students. Nonetheless, asserting that these differences are evidence of variation in a true causal effect requires additional assumptions, introduced below, about the unobservable population-level means $\bar{A}^{ea}_{i \notin E}$ and $\bar{A}^{ef}_{i \in E}$.

No-assumptions bounds on the average causal effect. Although with observational data, no consistent estimator of the counterfactual population means $\bar{A}^{ea}_{i \notin E}$ and $\bar{A}^{ef}_{i \in E}$ is available, each of these population means is no less than 0 and no greater than 1 because the individual-level potential outcomes are themselves no less than 0 and no greater than 1. If, for example, all individuals in the population who did not expect to complete college would have completed college if they had instead expected to complete college, $\bar{A}^{ea}_{i \notin E}$ would equal 1. And if none of these same individuals would have completed college given an increase in their expectation, then $\bar{A}^{ea}_{i \notin E}$ would equal 0. Thus, because the potential outcomes are bounded by 0 and 1, the permissible range for the true value of $\bar{\delta}$ can be expressed by substituting into Equation 3.3 the values for $\bar{A}^{ea}_{i \notin E}$ and $\bar{A}^{ef}_{i \in E}$ that would make $\bar{\delta}$ alternatively

TABLE 3.4

Estimates and Bounds for the Average Causal Effect of Expectations on Attainment for Four Race and Sex Groups and Level of Parents' Education

	Naive Estimate of the Average Causal Effect	NO-ASSUMPTIONS BOUND FOR THE AVERAGE CAUSAL EFFECT		BOUND FOR THE AVERAGE CAUSAL EFFECT, ASSUMING MONOTONE CAUSAL RESPONSE		BOUND FOR THE AVERAGE CAUSAL EFFECT, ASSUMING MONOTONE CAUSAL RESPONSE AND MONOTONE CAUSAL SELECTION		N
		Ignoring Sampling Error[a]	Conservative Bootstrapped Bounds[b]	Ignoring Sampling Error[a]	Conservative Bootstrapped Bounds[b]	Ignoring Sampling Error[a]	Conservative Bootstrapped Bounds[b]	
Sophomore Year Expectations								
White males								
Parent with college degree	.473	[−.282, .718]	(−.331, .767)	[0, .718]	(0, .767)	[0, .473]	(0, .570)	744
No parent with college degree	.324	[−.186, .814]	(−.211, .839)	[0, .814]	(0, .838)	[0, .324]	(0, .382)	1,700
White females								
Parent with college degree	.405	[−.308, .692]	(−.355, .739)	[0, .692]	(0, .737)	[0, .405]	(0, .494)	827
No parent with college degree	.249	[−.194, .806]	(−.216, .828)	[0, .806]	(0, .828)	[0, .249]	(0, .297)	2,033
Black males								
Parent with college degree	.132	[−.549, .451]	(−.778, .680)	[0, .451]	(0, .681)	[0, .132]	(0, .472)	84
No parent with college degree	.181	[−.270, .730]	(−.347, .807)	[0, .730]	(0, .808)	[0, .181]	(0, .324)	266
Black females								
Parent with college degree	.311	[−.348, .652]	(−.547, .850)	[0, .652]	(0, .846)	[0, .311]	(0, .512)	93
No parent with college degree	.159	[−.293, .707]	(−.354, .769)	[0, .707]	(0, .766)	[0, .159]	(0, .240)	446

Senior Year Expectations

White males							
Parent with college degree	.538	[−.255, .745]	(−.302, .793)	[0, .745]	(0, .793)	[0, .538]	(0, .628)	744
No parent with college degree	.449	[−.146, .854]	(−.167, .875)	[0, .854]	(0, .877)	[0, .449]	(0, .509)	1,700
White females							
Parent with college degree	.486	[−.274, .726]	(−.319, .772)	[0, .726]	(0, .771)	[0, .486]	(0, .571)	827
No parent with college degree	.368	[−.154, .846]	(−.174, .866)	[0, .846]	(0, .867)	[0, .368]	(0, .420)	2,033
Black males							
Parent with college degree	.365	[−.305, .695]	(−.493, .882)	[0, .695]	(0, .896)	[0, .365]	(0, .584)	84
No parent with college degree	.165	[−.259, .741]	(−.340, .821)	[0, .741]	(0, .822)	[0, .165]	(0, .323)	266
Black females							
Parent with college degree	.174	[−.478, .522]	(−.696, .739)	[0, .522]	(0, .738)	[0, .174]	(0, .433)	93
No parent with college degree	.110	[−.316, .684]	(−.385, .753)	[0, .684]	(0, .748)	[0, .110]	(0, .185)	446

NOTES: *High School & Beyond* sophomore cohort data (1980 through 1992 waves). Data are weighted by the fourth follow-up panel weight (panel5wt) multiplied by the probability of having missing data on the expectations and attainment variables (estimated from separate race- and sex-specific logit models).

[a] Bounds in brackets ignore sampling error.

[b] Bounds in parentheses are conservative bootstrapped bounds that take into account possible sampling error (1,000 replicated samples of size N with lower/higher end of the 95 percent confidence interval of the bootstrap distribution given for the lower/upper bound).

as small and as large as it could possibly be (see the derivation in the appendix to this chapter).

Column two of Table 3.4 presents no-assumptions bounds for the average causal effect that ignore sampling error in the estimates of $\overline{A}^{ea}_{i\in E}$, $\overline{A}^{ef}_{i\notin E}$, and π. Conservative bootstrapped bounds that take account of possible bias due to sampling error are presented in column three.[12] Without making any assumptions about the counterfactual population means $\overline{A}^{ea}_{i\notin E}$ and $\overline{A}^{ef}_{i\in E}$, these bounds imply, for example, that $\overline{\delta}$ is no smaller than $-.282$ and no larger than $.718$ (or if we allow for sampling error, no smaller than $-.331$ and no larger than $.767$ for white males with a college-educated parent.

Although indisputably true, the no-assumptions bounds are relatively uninformative, as by definition they always include 0. And, as shown in comparisons across levels of parental education, introducing additional variables into the analysis and forming yet more carefully defined strata would only shift the bounds up and down throughout the $(-1, 1)$ interval. Nonetheless, the no-assumptions bounds are a starting point, the estimation of which Manski (1995) effectively argues should precede the application of additional assumptions that generate stronger conclusions.

Bounds under a monotone causal response assumption. The no-assumptions bounds can be narrowed only by asserting additional assumptions. One such assumption is monotone causal response (Manski 1997). In this context, the assumption is operationalized by asserting the claim that having high educational expectations can do no harm. More specifically, shifting a student's educational expectation from "expect to fail" to "expect to attain" cannot make him or her less likely to attain a college degree. This monotone response assumption is useful because it narrows the lower bound of the no-assumptions bound for the average causal effect, thereby eliminating all negative values as permissible values for the average causal effect (see the derivation in the appendix).[13]

Bounds for the average causal effect under an assumption of monotone response are presented in column four of Table 3.4, alongside corresponding bootstrapped bounds in column five. For white males with a college-educated parent, the bound for the average effect is narrowed from the no-assumptions bound of $[-.282, .718]$ to $[0, .718]$ (ignoring sampling error). As can be seen across all of the strata, an assumption of monotone causal response does not eliminate 0 as a plausible value for the average causal effect.

Bounds under monotone causal response and monotone causal selection assumptions. In addition to monotone causal response, one can also assert (with perhaps a bit more hesitation) a monotone causal selection assumption. For this application, monotone causal selection stipulates that the college completion rate of those who do not expect to complete college, if they had instead expected to complete college, would still be no higher than the college completion rate of those who do expect to complete college. Or, in the opposite direction, individuals who expect to complete college, if they had instead not expected to complete college, would nonetheless complete college at a rate at least as high as those who do not expect to complete college. In constructing a bound for the average causal effect, monotone causal selection tightens the upper bound of the no-assumptions bound (see derivation in the appendix).

Joint bounds for the average causal effect under assumptions of both monotone response and monotone selection are presented in column six of Table 3.4, alongside corresponding bootstrapped bounds in column seven. For white males with a college-educated parent, the permissible range of the average effect is narrowed from the no-assumptions bound of $[-.282, .718]$ to $[0, .473]$ (ignoring sampling error). Again, as can be seen across all of the strata, these assumptions do not eliminate 0 as a plausible value for the average causal effect. Furthermore, the upper bound is what I labeled above the naive estimator of the average causal effect, as can be seen from a comparison of columns one and six.

The leap of faith: strong ignorability. What additional assumptions could tighten these bounds in order to establish the naive estimator in Equation 3.4 as a consistent estimator of the average causal effect in Equation 3.2? Often labeled a strong ignorability assumption (Rosenbaum and Rubin 1983), the assumption that $\overline{A}_{i\in E}^{ea} = \overline{A}_{i\notin E}^{ea}$ and $\overline{A}_{i\notin E}^{ef} = \overline{A}_{i\in E}^{ef}$ would suffice. Unfortunately, the only research design for which such assumed equalities can be easily justified is random assignment of students to the two states "expect to attain" and "expect to fail." Because such a design is infeasible for this application, the only available justification for asserting such equalities is "faith" (Clogg and Haritou 1997:105; also see Lieberson 1985).

For the bounds estimated in this section, the strong assumptions inherent in structural equations models have been replaced by weaker, more narrowly defined assumptions about educational expectations and their relationship with attainment. Two important interpretations of the results should be underlined:

1. None of the permissible weak assumptions about expectations and attainment can eliminate 0 from among the credible values for the average causal effect, and such elimination is what would be necessary to establish a firm claim of causality on the justification that for at least some students the counterfactual-conditional statement at the beginning of this section is true.

2. Because bounds for the average causal effect of expectations on attainment cannot eliminate a wide range of plausible estimates for both whites and blacks, no strong claims can be sustained about what race differences might remain in path-model estimates of the causal effect of expectations on attainment if all relevant omitted variables were measured and properly specified. Indeed, it may be the case that if differential socialization practices, misperceived opportunity constraints, and concrete attitudes were all observed and explicitly specified, the residual direct effect of expectations on attainment would be stronger for blacks than for whites.

In contrast to the structural equations models, the estimated bounds presented in this section are maximally defendable, and yet this epistemic security is purchased at a high price (perhaps too high, since no strong conclusions can then be advanced). One could, for example, adhere strictly to the counterfactual framework and claim that there is no irrefutable evidence that there is a causal effect of expectations on attainment. And if there is no evidence that there is a causal effect of expectations on attainment for any student, then there is no race difference to be explained.

Although this model conveys a stark message by revealing the limitations of observational survey data, and symmetrically the dependence of all conclusions based on traditional structural equations models on strong assumptions, all hope should not be abandoned.[14] In the next section, I use a similar analytic strategy to demonstrate that there is even weaker support for the only theoretical justification for treating expectations as universally noncausal, and hence of dismissing the well-studied race difference on the grounds that the survey data are simply uninformative.

A Model of Educational Expectations as Best-Possible Forecasts

Counterposed against the Wisconsin model, an influential contrarian strand of sociological literature argues educational expectations are survey-induced utterances that have no true salience to adolescents in their everyday lives. In this vein, Bourdieu (1973:83) criticizes "functionalist sociologists" who maintain that educational expectations cause educational attainment when it is shown with survey data that "individuals have hoped for nothing that they have not obtained and obtained nothing that they have not hoped for." Relatedly, Alexander and Cook (1979:202) raise the possibility that students' educational expectations are analogous to a "meteorologist's anticipation of fair or foul weather." The crux of these characterizations is the implicit claim that expectations and educational attainment are for all practical purposes two indicators of the same thing. As a result, the temporal causal order assumption depicted in Figure 3.1 is entirely inappropriate.

Alexander and Cook (1979) make some progress in evaluating this position, but no explicit framework has been adopted to formally test its plausibility. Since the limiting case of the contrarian position is that educational expectations are best-possible forecasts, rational expectations models of forecasting can provide such a framework. When educational expectations are best-possible forecasts, the association between expectations and attainment cannot be given a causal interpretation. Likewise, race differences in path-model estimates of the effect of expectations on attainment would reflect little more than the systematic predictability of the educational attainment trajectories typically traversed by whites and blacks. In this section, I test for whether expectations and resulting attainment conform to the analytic bounds implied by a best-possible-forecast conjecture, after first introducing a crucial threshold response framework.

Latent expectations and threshold response. The rational expectations forecasting framework must first be grounded on an assumption that individuals have latent probabilistic expectations. In response to a survey question—such as the *HS&B* question "As things stand now, how far in school do you think you will get?"—the assumption is that a student will select the level "Finish College" or a higher level only if his or her *ex ante* probability judgment of completing college, denoted $\hat{\Pr}(A = 1)_i$, exceeds a threshold value τ_i. Forecasting frameworks assume that a threshold is a function of an individual's latent loss function (see Chernoff and Moses 1959). In this application, the response threshold is based on a student's subjective evaluation of the consequences of his or her prediction error for false-positive and false-negative forecasts:

$$\tau_i = \frac{Loss(E = 1 \mid A = 0)_i}{Loss(E = 1 \mid A = 0)_i + Loss(E = 0 \mid A = 1)_i} \qquad (3.5)$$

If the expected subjective consequences of false-positive forecasts and false-negative forecasts are equal, students will set their response threshold equal to .5. I proceed to empirical analysis under the assumption that this is the case and thus that for all individuals τ_i is equal to .5. I will nonetheless interpret the results with recognition that this assumption may be violated (and, continuing with the focus on race differences, that it may be violated in race-specific ways).

However, before proceeding to the empirical analysis, consider a basic group-level implication of the threshold response framework. Suppose that a group of students has a common response threshold equal to .5 and that all students expect that their probability of graduating college is .51. In this case, all students will set E equal to 1. Nonetheless, if their probabilistic expectations are exactly correct, then only 51 percent of students will graduate from college, thereby rendering 49 percent of dichotomized forced-choice forecasts false-positive predictions. In general, even if students formulate their best-possible forecasts, the observed correlation between variables such as E and A may be moderate to small because of the coarse nature of forced-choice response categories posed in survey instruments.[15]

Bounds under a rational expectations conjecture. Formal forecasting models in the rational expectations literature are based on the delineation of overlapping sets of information on which to base a forecast of the future. The main issue in all such forecasting models is whether individuals use all available information when forming their forecasts and whether they accurately judge the relative likelihood of the occurrence of information-generating events that are at risk of occurring between the time when expectations are formed and modeled behavior is enacted.

Invoking a rational expectations framework, Manski (1990) derives permissible bounds on the range that subsequent aggregate behavior must be observed to obey if respondent-reported expectations are best-possible forecasts. The appendix to this chapter provides a derivation in this context of the implications of a rational expectations assumption (using implied restrictions on the attainment process, knowledge of available information I, and knowledge of the true probability distribution of unknown information U that determines attainment but that is unknowable at the time expectations are formed). The framework implies the following implication for each individual i,

$$E_i = 0 \Rightarrow \Pr(A = 1)_i \leq .5$$
$$E_i = 1 \Rightarrow \Pr(A = 1)_i \geq .5 \tag{3.6}$$

where .5 is the assumed common response threshold. If all individuals have rational expectations, then in the notation introduced for the counterfactual model:

$$\overline{A}_{i \notin E}^{\text{ef}} \leq .5 \leq \overline{A}_{i \in E}^{\text{ea}} \tag{3.7}$$

Equation 3.7 holds true for subsets of students defined by any set of characteristics X, such as the strata analyzed for Tables 3.3 and 3.4.

The modeling strategy for this section is thus the mirror image of the bounds analysis of the last section. The rational expectations assumption fixes a middle point that conditional means cannot cross if the assumption is valid. Accordingly, the assumption can be evaluated by determining whether or not, for every group of students with identical characteristics X, at least 50 percent of students who expect to graduate from college do graduate from college and no more than 50 percent of students who expect not to graduate from college do graduate from college.

As shown in columns two and three of Table 3.3, the educational expectations maintained by many groups of students violate the bound in Equation 3.7. While the percent of students from all eight strata who complete college having expected not to do so conforms to the bound, ranging from a low of .015 to a high of .239, rates of college completion for those who expect to graduate from college do not uniformly conform to the bound. Only for white students with a college-educated parent is the proportion of students who graduated from college having expected to do so greater than 50 percent. Likewise, for no group of black students who expected to graduate from college is the college completion rate greater than 50 percent, ranging from a low of .150 to a high of .381.[16]

Violations of the bounds based on the rational expectations conjecture suggest the following interpretation of the expectations and attainment relationship:

1. It is not permissible to treat the educational expectations of all students as noncausal, best-possible forecasts that can be ignored when data on educational attainment are available.

And since expectations predict attainment, at least one of two qualifications must be accepted:

2A. For at least some students, expectations are causes of attainment.

2B. For at least some (but not all) students, expectations are noncausal, best-possible forecasts.

If qualification 2a could be favored over qualification 2b, this model would be powerful evidence that students' own beliefs do matter. Unfortunately, qualification 2a cannot be so favored, and hence there is no ironclad proof that for at least some students' educational expectations are causes of educational attainment.

Because no information shows how students weigh the subjective consequences of false-positive and false-negative forecasts, assuming the existence of a common response threshold equal to .5 may be unreasonable. If so, one cannot infer from these results that expectations are not best-possible forecasts, since if it were the case that τ is equal to .25, then mean levels of educational attainment for *HS&B* respondents would in almost all cases conform to the bound in Equation 3.7.

When might τ equal a value such as .25? As shown in Equation 3.5, students will set τ equal to .25 if they associate three times as much subjective loss with reporting a false-negative prediction. Students would maintain such a loss function if they believe that they will be judged negatively by survey researchers or others who might have access to their answers if they underestimate their own future level of educational attainment.[17]

When focusing on interpretations of the group differences revealed in Table 3.3, it must be recognized that subjective loss functions and corresponding response thresholds may vary by race. Black students may associate more costs than white students with mistakenly underestimating their own future educational attainment, for it is possible that black students fear that their answers will confirm a stereotype that black students are less committed to schooling. Steele's theory of stereotype threat would, in some survey administration contexts, suggest that such a hypothesis is worth investigation (see Steele and Aronson 1995; Steele 1997).

Nonetheless, there is still no strong evidence that the relationship between expectations and attainment can be completely ignored, and hence that race differences in this relationship should not be subjected to explanatory effort. And although these results do not provide any evidence to adjudicate between the alternative explanations for race differences in the expectations and attainment relationship outlined earlier, the explicit attention to response thresholds formalizes the contention of Alexander and Cook (1979) that whites and blacks may respond in fundamentally different ways to the same survey question. Thus, to the explanations offered in prior sections, an additional explanation should be delineated: the *differential response threshold* explanation implied above.

If across both whites and blacks educational expectations are too optimistic in the aggregate to be best-possible forecasts in general, is there any evidence that the expectations of some students are persistent and salient enough that they become self-fulfilling prophecies? In other words, is there any evidence that expectations are based on relatively stable incorrect component beliefs that would cause students to shift their college preparatory commitment decisions while still in high school? Although submerged within relatively vague socialization mechanisms, I regard this as the central claim of the Wisconsin model. The final model presented in the next section addresses this possibility.

A PANEL DATA MODEL OF UPDATED EDUCATIONAL EXPECTATIONS

Because educational expectations are reported by *HS&B* respondents as high school sophomores in 1980 and then subsequently in surveys in 1982, 1984, and 1986, a panel data model of updated educational expectations is feasible. The goal of this final piece of analysis is to determine whether, after observable information is specified, net educational expectations are serially correlated across time as individuals progress along attainment trajectories. Autoregressive patterns of serial correlation are the signature of an underlying dynamic process, one that is inconsistent with a socialization-based claim that expectations are a stable indicator of latent achievement motivation. If expectations are serially correlated in this way, then these correlations are at least some evidence that educational expectations may be dynamically linked across time in an underlying causal process that generates forward-looking commitment decisions that are consequential for final levels of educational attainment.

Each individual's time-specific educational expectation, E_{it}, can be defined as a departure from a time-invariant projection onto variables specified as X. As detailed in the notes to Table 3.5, for the analysis reported below these variables will be the same Wisconsin model variables used for the path-models estimated earlier. The difference here is that the coefficients on the variables in X, analogous to those labeled b in Figure 3.1, will be weighted averages of four different time-specific variables for expectations projected onto a single set of stable characteristics in X. As a result, departures from the stable predicted values based on the variables in X and their estimated coefficients, collectively denoted by time-specific error terms e_{it}, represent that portion of individuals' time-specific expectations that cannot be accounted for by the variables specified in X.

Most importantly, because these residualized expectations exist for all four time periods, one can estimate the correlation between error terms across time, $\rho(e_{it}, e_{it+1})$. These estimated correlations then allow for examination of the effects of omitted variables (such as the differential socialization practices, misperceived opportunity constraints, and concrete attitudes invoked for the explanations of race differences earlier) collectively persist from one time period to the next and, if so, if in any particular pattern.

Using the panel data models of Liang and Zeger (1986), the expectations variables can be either dichotomous or interval-scaled. For consistency with the models presented in the last two sections, I will offer models for dichotomous expectations variables, again equal to 1 if an individual expects to obtain a bachelor's degree. Models with years of education expected as the dependent variable yield substantively similar findings (and even more consistency across race than I will claim below).

For separate race and sex groups, Table 3.5 presents estimated correlation coefficients between error terms from panel data models of college-completion expectations in 1980, 1982, 1984, and 1986 regressed on observed information in X available to sophomores in 1980.[18] Although the pattern for black males may differ (to be discussed later), the correlations follow the same pattern for whites and for black females. They are positive and strongest between adjacent survey years, declining regularly with distance between years as in an autoregressive time series model. Net of the ef-

TABLE 3.5

Estimated Correlations Between Error Terms from Panel Data Models
of Educational Expectations in 1980, 1982, 1984, and 1986

	MALES				FEMALES			
	e_{1980}	e_{1982}	e_{1984}	e_{1986}	e_{1980}	e_{1982}	e_{1984}	e_{1986}
Whites	—				—			
	.277 (.029)	—			.240 (.047)	—		
	.281 (.037)	.389 (.032)	—		.146 (.022)	.359 (.037)	—	
	.225 (.032)	.382 (.033)	.579 (.038)	—	.118 (.022)	.340 (.038)	.585 (.048)	—
Blacks	—				—			
	.024 (.057)	—			.306 (.062)	—		
	.102 (.070)	.207 (.075)	—		.243 (.055)	.342 (.066)	—	
	.074 (.073)	.057 (.079)	.452 (.097)	—	.256 (.064)	.325 (.079)	.490 (.065)	—

NOTES: *High School & Beyond* sophomore cohort data (1980 through 1992 waves). Data are weighted by the fourth follow-up panel weight (panel5wt). Numbers of respondents are 2,444 for white males, 2,860 for white females, 350 for black males, and 539 for black females. Information considered available in 1980 and specified as X for all models: socioeconomic status, family structure, sophomore year test scores, and significant others' influence. The predictive probability of being in the analysis sample is included as an independent variable in all models. Bootstrapped standard errors in parentheses.

fects of stable characteristics in X, a high expectation in one time period is more likely to be followed by a high expectation in the next period and then by a slightly less high expectation in the following period.

The common estimated pattern of correlations between residualized expectations suggests two related interpretations:

1. The positive correlations between net expectations at all years suggests that important component beliefs generate educational expectations that are not contained within the variables in X suggested by status socialization theory.

2. The autoregressive structure of the correlations is consistent with the existence of an underlying dynamic causal process relating expectations to each other across time.

A speculative interpretation of this pattern suggests the following line of reasoning. Initially incorrect component beliefs unaccounted for by X persist from time period to time period before being corrected by the arrival of a sufficient amount of correct information. These new corrected beliefs grow in relative importance to beliefs predicted by X, such that the correlations between net expectations increase in time. Under an additional assumption that incorrect component beliefs have effects on concurrent preparatory commitment decisions relevant to different courses of educational attainment, this dynamic relation of time-specific expectations to each other could then be considered evidence that dynamic expectation formation is a causal process that partly determines final levels of educational attainment.

Is this interpretation equally applicable to the expectations of black males? As shown in the lower left panel of Table 3.5, there may be some evidence of a different pattern. The point estimates of the correlation coefficients are in general smaller, and the estimate of the net correlation between expectations in 1980 and 1982 is too small to conform to an overall claim of an autoregressive structure. But these estimates are quite imprecise, as indicated by the bootstrapped standard errors in parentheses. It may simply be too much to ask only 350 cases, in contrast to 539 cases for black females, to clearly reveal the error structure of net educational expectations. Nonetheless, if a larger sample size revealed the same sort of pattern, it would be necessary to amend the interpretation above for black males, indicating that the omitted variables that account for the variation in the expectations of blacks are less correlated across time and implying less scope for expectations being interpreted as dynamically causal and more scope for expectations being regarded as either best-possible forecasts or unpredictable fantasies.

The panel data models of this section are useful because they provide a way to examine whether omitted variables may be important, by modeling gross correlations between them across time. The main threat to the substantive claim that they reveal an important dynamic causal process is that the omitted variables correlated across time are merely features of measurement or model misspecification. Although a genuine threat, I regard this possibility as yet further motivation for investment of research resources in understanding how students respond to the typical survey instruments employed, and by direct implication how students form the beliefs they would report under flawless measurement conditions.

If the correlations are not produced by trivial measurement errors, the panel data models point toward the need for addressing a fundamental question: Does the persistence of incorrect beliefs generate a trajectory of college preparatory commitment decisions that renders educational expectations, as carriers of all such underlying component beliefs, self-fulfilling prophecies?

Summary of Results: Is the Association Causal?

Because there is no evidence that expectations are universally noncausal, best-possible forecasts, and yet some evidence that expectations are serially correlated across time in a way consistent with an underlying dynamic causal process, the educational expectations of some students may be based on relatively stable incorrect component beliefs. And because educational expectations may be systematically incorrect, educational expectations may be self-fulfilling prophecies that compel students to pursue courses of behavior they would have rejected as possible if their educational expectations had been based on component beliefs that were absolutely correct. This conclusion suggests that students' beliefs are neither perfectly noncausal nor inconsistent with a causal claim, and hence at least indirectly supportive of the assertion that students' beliefs do matter for at least some students.

CONCLUSIONS

In this chapter, I have devoted a considerable amount of energy to the analysis of a question that was originally formulated in the 1970s. I have argued that attempting to resolve this question (and, along the way, coming to understand that the available data simply cannot resolve it in any conclusive way) is critical for recognizing the potential of the core mechanism of status socialization theory. In particular, I have argued that the belief formation processes at the core of the model were too quickly downgraded in favor of models that emphasized measurable structural constraints. As I now move forward in subsequent chapters to build on more recent literature on educational attainment, it should be asked whether the motivating empirical question of this chapter is as relevant for the empirical patterns revealed by the most recent data. Does the black-white difference in the expectations-attainment relationship still exist?

The answer to this question is largely irrelevant to the argument I have developed in this chapter, as my aim, again, was merely to prosecute the literature from the 1970s and 1980s using data on the empirical patterns with which prior scholars worked. But, I would not want to imply that these re-lationships have necessarily remained unchanged in the past two decades. In-deed, there is good reason to suspect that some change has occurred. On the one hand, considerable racial inequality remains in the United States, as well as a black-white gap in achievement and attainment. This continuing ra-cial inequality suggests that the same explanatory narratives offered earlier should retain some validity and hence a relative mismatch between the ex-pectations and attainments of blacks may still exist. On the other hand, blacks have gained in socioeconomic well-being since the 1970s, and these gains may have affected the belief-based mechanisms emphasized earlier in this chapter, such that black students' perceptions of the opportunity struc-ture may have moved closer to those of whites (see also Morgan 1998). Ac-cordingly, the explanatory narratives offered earlier may still apply, but only in weaker form. And hence, there may still be a relative mismatch, just one that is now considerably less dramatic.

Some available data can shed light on these trends. The *Monitoring the Future* surveys (hereafter, *MTF*) provide yearly data on the educational ex-pectations of high school seniors, as analyzed in Hauser and Anderson (1991) and Morgan (1998), and these can be compared with trends in col-lege entry. Using the *MTF* data, Figure 3.2 presents trend lines for the pro-portion of white male, white female, black male, and black female high school seniors from 1976 through 2000 who definitely expected to attain a bachelor's degree at some point in their futures. When aligned with the trends in college entry reported earlier in Figure 1.1 (see Chapter 1), the trends in expectations reported in Figure 3.2 suggest that the black-white difference in the expectations-attainment relationship may have changed.

In the late 1970s, black students were at least as optimistic (if not more optimistic) than whites of the same sex about their chances of obtaining bachelor's degrees, even though they were less likely to enter and complete college. This pattern of findings from the 1970s and early 1980s is consis-tent with the literature addressed in this chapter on black-white differences in the expectations-attainment relationship. But, Figure 3.2 also suggests that the mismatch between the expectations and attainments of blacks may have moderated in the 1980s and 1990s. The college graduation expecta-tions of whites increased relative to those of blacks, so that blacks no longer had as relatively optimistic expectations as earlier.[19]

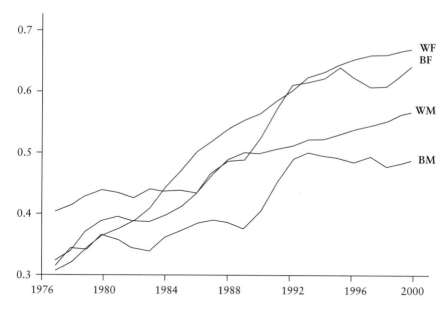

Figure 3.2.   Proportion of High School Seniors Who Definitely Expect to Graduate from a Four-Year College (three-year moving average). WM = white males, WF = white females, BM = black males, BF = black females.

SOURCE: *Monitoring the Future Surveys*, 1976–2001

In order to investigate this possibility further, I reestimated the empirical models from this chapter as completely as possible using the more recent *NELS* data analyzed in Chapter 1 for the high school class of 1992. As I mentioned earlier, the *NELS* does differ in design from the *HS&B* survey analyzed in this chapter, and hence one should not blindly attribute differences in findings for the two surveys to changes over time in empirical patterns in the population. Nonetheless, the *NELS*-based models suggested that for the more recent cohort of high school seniors, these black-white differences have moderated. The analyses of bounds and the panel data models were similar for the *NELS* cohort of students. But, structural equation models, which are the clearest legacy of the literature critical of the Wisconsin model, did not suggest as substantial of a race difference in the expectations-attainment relationship. Limited as they are, these findings further support my contention that some of the core ideas of the Wisconsin model deserve to be taken seriously. There is even less reason now to argue that they should be set aside in pursuit of ostensibly more complete models that can explain away discrepant race differences with mechanisms of pure structural constraint.

Where do we go from here? In order to move forward, sociologists need to build a flexible and explicit model of students' behavior. The model should focus as much on alternative courses of preparatory commitment to further schooling as on consequential enrollment decisions. But, the model should be forward looking, and therefore allow students to adjust their levels of short-run commitment to schooling in response to their beliefs about their own potential futures. After this core model is developed, mechanisms for the evolution of beliefs about generic costs and benefits of education need to be developed. Only then, I will argue, can sociologists engage in what I suspect will emerge as the main agenda for sociology of education thereafter: the incorporation of explicit mechanisms of social influence and structural constraint into this new model of commitment. In the remaining chapters of this book, I attempt to make progress in all of these tasks.

APPENDIX 3.1

No-Assumptions Bound for the Average Causal Effect

$\overline{A}_{i \notin E}^{ea}$ and $\overline{A}_{i \in E}^{ef}$ are bounded on both sides by 0 and 1. The no-assumptions lower bound on the average causal effect is derived by substituting for $\overline{A}_{i \notin E}^{ea}$ and $\overline{A}_{i \in E}^{ef}$ the values of 0 and 1, respectively, into the definition of the average causal effect on the right-hand side of Equation 3.3:

$$[\pi \overline{A}_{i \in E}^{ea} + (1 - \pi)\{0\}] - [\pi\{1\} + (1 - \pi)\overline{A}_{i \notin E}^{ef}] \le \overline{\delta} \tag{3A.1}$$

The upper bound is derived by substitutions of 1 and 0, respectively:

$$\overline{\delta} \le [\pi \overline{A}_{i \in E}^{ea} + (1 - \pi)(1)] - [\pi(0) + (1 - \pi)\overline{A}_{i \notin E}^{ef}] \tag{3A.2}$$

Combining and simplifying Equations 3A.1 and 3A.2 yields the no-assumptions bound:

$$\pi \overline{A}_{i \in E}^{ea} - (1 - \pi)\overline{A}_{i \notin E}^{ef} - \pi \le \overline{\delta} \le \pi \overline{A}_{i \in E}^{ea} - (1 - \pi)\overline{A}_{i \notin E}^{ef} + (1 - \pi) \tag{3A.3}$$

With dichotomous potential outcomes, the bound is by definition of width 1 because the lower bound and the upper bound differ only by two complementary probabilities, $-\pi$ and $1 - \pi$.

Bound for the Average Causal Effect
Assuming Monotone Causal Response

Monotone causal response is an assumption about individual-level potential outcomes. In this context, the assumption is that for every individual i, $A_i^{ea} \geq A_i^{ef}$, which is tantamount to assuming that the individual-level causal effect in Equation 3.1 can take on values of 0 or 1 but not -1. This monotone response assumption tightens only the no-assumptions lower bound, and it does so by requiring the substitution of observable population-level means instead of the more extreme values of 0 and 1 in Equation 3A.1:

$$[\pi \overline{A}_{i \in E}^{ea} + (1 - \pi)\{\overline{A}_{i \notin E}^{ef}\}] - [\pi\{\overline{A}_{i \in E}^{ea}\} + (1 - \pi)\overline{A}_{i \notin E}^{ef}] \leq \overline{\delta} \qquad (3A.4)$$

Combining this tighter lower bound with the unaltered upper bound in Equation 3A.2 and then simplifying yields the bound:

$$0 \quad \leq \quad \overline{\delta} \quad \leq \quad \pi \overline{A}_{i \in E}^{ea} - (1 - \pi)\overline{A}_{i \notin E}^{ef} + (1 - \pi) \qquad (3A.5)$$

Bound for the Average Causal Effect Assuming Monotone
Causal Response and Monotone Causal Selection

Monotone causal selection is a population-level assumption about cross-individual patterns of expectation formation and attainment propensity. In this context, the assumption entails two cross-group inequalities: $\overline{A}_{i \in E}^{ea} \geq \overline{A}_{i \notin E}^{ea}$ and $\overline{A}_{i \in E}^{ef} \geq \overline{A}_{i \notin E}^{ef}$. This monotone causal selection assumption only tightens the no-assumptions upper bound, and it does so by requiring the substitution of observable population-level means instead of the more extreme values of 1 and 0 in Equation 3A.2:

$$\overline{\delta} \leq [\pi \overline{A}_{i \in E}^{ea} + (1 - \pi)\{\overline{A}_{i \in E}^{ea}\}] - [\pi\{\overline{A}_{i \notin E}^{ef}\} + (1 - \pi)\overline{A}_{i \notin E}^{ef}] \qquad (3A.6)$$

Simplifying Equation 3A.6 and combining it with Equation 3A.5 results in the joint bound for the average causal effect assuming both monotone causal response and monotone causal selection:

$$0 \quad \leq \quad \overline{\delta} \quad \leq \overline{A}_{i \in E}^{ea} - \overline{A}_{i \notin E}^{ef} \qquad (3A.7)$$

Derivation for the Bounds Implied by
a Rational Expectations Assumption

Let the set of all information that determines attainment and that can be known at the time expectations are formed be I. Elements of I may include, for example, the main independent variables of status socialization theory—socioeconomic status, ability, and significant others' influence—and structural variables such as the cost and availability of college education. Similarly, let U be the set of unavailable information that determines attainment but that will be revealed after expectations are formed and before attainment is determined. In this context, the elements of U include pieces of information that are contingent on events that have not yet occurred by the time expectations are formed, such as scores on standardized college entrance exams not yet taken. Because I and U mutually exhaust all information that determines attainment, the function $A(I, U)$ completely characterizes attainment.

[Note: Attainment is a function of more than just available information I and individually contingent unavailable information in U. Attainment is also a function of aggregate shocks, implicitly embedded in U but that can be denoted separately by S. These shocks might include shifts in the market-level benefits of college education, changes in college costs, or exogenous events such as an intervening military draft in response to the outbreak of war. Accordingly, even though attainment is a function only of I and U, it is sometimes useful to more completely specify attainment as $A(I, U \notin S, S)$.]

Similar to Manski (1990), if $\Pr_U | I$ denotes the true objective probability distribution of U conditional on discrete combinations of elements in I, the educational attainment probability for all individuals subject to the same set of information, $\Pr(A = 1 | I)$, can be given the explicit expression $\Pr_U(A = 1 | I)$. With this notation, individuals can then be said to have rational educational expectations if the two following necessary conditions are satisfied: (1) individuals know the information in I and the exact function $A(I, .)$ that relates attainment to all known information in I and all knowable information in U that will be realized in the future, and (2) individuals know the exact probability distribution of all relevant future events and therefore the probability distribution of all unknown future information, $\Pr_U | I$.

When individuals have rational expectations, they can form $\Pr_U(A = 1 | I)$ and therefore, by definition, know their true value for $\Pr(A = 1)$. Accordingly, when confronted with a question "Do you expect to graduate from college?" they set their latent probabilistic expectation equal to this value and compare it to a threshold τ. If their value for $\Pr(A = 1)$ is greater than τ, they set E equal to 1.

Manski (1990) shows that even if an outside observer can only observe a subset of I labeled X, in a best-case scenario where there are no aggregate shocks and where students think hard enough in the survey administration context to provide the best possible estimate they are cognitively able to provide, a rational expectations assumption can give a bound for the conditional probability $\Pr(A = 1 \,|\, X, E)$. The crucial idea is this: If expectations conform to a rational expectations assumption, then E is a function of all of the relevant information in I and U that determines attainment but that is not contained in the information X that a researcher observes. In other words, expectations function as an omnibus proxy for consequential pieces of information that determine attainment but that are unobserved by the researcher.

More formally, if $\Pr_I |\, X, E$ is the probability distribution of I conditional on the researcher's observed information X and the respondent-reported rational expectation E, then

$$\int \Pr_U[A(I, U) = 1 \,|\, I] d\Pr_I \,|\, X, E$$

$$= \int \Pr(A = 1 \,|\, I) d\Pr_I \,|\, X, E$$

$$= \Pr(A = 1 \,|\, X, E) \tag{3A.8}$$

by the definition of $\Pr(A = 1 \,|\, I)$ and the law of iterated expectations. Together with the threshold response assumptions stated above, Equation 3A.8 implies the bound:

$$\Pr(A = 1 \,|\, X, E = 0) \quad \leq \quad \tau \quad \leq \quad \Pr(A = 1 \,|\, X, E = 1) \tag{3A.9}$$

which, in the counterfactual notation adopted in the main text can be written:

$$\overline{A}_{i \notin E}^{\text{ef}} \leq \tau \leq \overline{A}_{i \in E}^{\text{ea}} \tag{3A.9a}$$

NOTES

1. I analyzed the same data in Chapter 1, but for comparability with results from the *NELS*, in Chapter 1 I recoded the *HS&B* educational attainment variables to the reflect only the information that would have been available as of 1990. In this chapter, I use the fully informative data up through 1992. But, to keep the

analysis targeted on the central question of the chapter, I limit the sample to white and black students.

2. These unrecognized constraints are both retrospective and prospective.

3. This view of the labor market, though perhaps grounded in a slowly shifting cultural orientation, is nonetheless an incorrect belief about race-specific rates of return to education. Since the 1970s, the racial gap in earnings has been larger among high school graduates.

4. Moreover, if there is relatively more random measurement error in family background reports for blacks, and if measurement error in expectations is invariant by race, then the estimates of the effects of expectations for whites are attenuated relative to those of blacks.

5. Indeed, this last possibility is consistent with the results of Portes and Wilson (1976), especially if one considers the additional variable they include, self-esteem, to be a (rather indirect) proxy for the omitted variables highlighted in the main text. The general line of reasoning followed here is emphasized in a number of methodological pieces (e.g., Berk 1988; Clogg and Haritou 1997), but it has recently found a particularly simple expression in the do(.) function of Pearl (2000).

6. There is an econometric literature that clarifies the nature of this assumption (see Manski 1995, Chapter 7).

7. Although assessing the impact of omitted variables is not beyond the scope of empirical analysis under the structural equations framework, since one can over-identify the model in Figure 3.1 by assuming theoretical values for e and then adopting a full-information approach to parameter estimation (see Bollen 1989), the consequences of omitted variable bias can be examined more completely by embracing a specific counterfactual framework for thinking about causality. This framework also allows for a more intuitive examination of individual-level, causal-effect heterogeneity.

8. I rely on this coding for three reasons. First, it is now generally recognized that years of education do not form a wholly satisfactory metric, as a unit difference of 16 years instead of 15 years is likely more consequential for most outcomes than an equivalent unit difference of 14 years instead of 13 years. Second, the acquisition of a bachelor's degree is, I assume, how high school students evaluate the decision of whether to go to college after high school, which is still the educational transition of greatest analytic interest. Thus, I assume that forward-looking beliefs about the acquisition of variations in 12 versus 14 years or 16 versus 20 years of education are of less interest. Third, confining analytic treatment to a single binary outcome eases the presentation of the counterfactual framework, and is also more consistent with the coding of college plans in both of the most important Wisconsin model articles (Sewell et al. 1969; Hauser et al. 1983). The counterfactual framework is of course applicable to non-dichotomous variables as well (e.g., Manski 1997).

9. Winship and Morgan (1999) provide a review of the relevant foundational literature on counterfactual causality, and, as is especially relevant for this application, Sobel (1998) offers a didactic application of the framework in a reinterpretation of status attainment research. The counterfactual framework is consistent with the characterization that Sewell and his colleagues gave of the Wisconsin model. After discussing the impossibility of regarding the Blau-Duncan model of status attainment as a causal model, Sewell et al. (1969:84) wrote:

> we present theory and data regarding what we believe to be a logically consistent social psychological model. This provides a plausible causal argument to link stratification and mental ability inputs through a set of social psychological and behavioral mechanisms to educational and occupational attainments. One compelling feature of the model is that some of the inputs may be manipulated through experimental or other purposive interventions. This means that parts of it can be experimentally tested in future research and that practical policy agents can reasonably hope to use it in order to change educational and occupational attainments.

10. Because of the obvious terminological confusion between educational expectations and the expectation operator from probability theory, I will use *population average* and *population mean* when in other contexts one might prefer to use the term *expectation* from probability theory.

11. The average effect estimates could be more directly related to the path-model estimates by further stratifying the sample based on additional Wisconsin model variables in X and then averaging over strata in proportion to the distribution of cases across the strata.

12. As the method of bounds was only recently formalized, there is no generally accepted procedure to estimate bootstrapped bounds. I used STATA to draw (with replacement) 1,000 replicated samples of size N and then calculated bootstrapped distributions of the upper and lower bounds using these 1,000 samples from which standard errors can be calculated. The bootstrapped bounds reported in parentheses are the upper/lower end of 95 percent confidence interval for the upper/lower bound.

13. For other binary codings of educational expectations, monotone causal response may be less defensible. For at least some students, increases in one's expectation from "obtain a BA" to "obtain a PhD" may actually decrease the probability of graduating from college if frustration emerges, etc.

14. Assuming that e in Figure 3.1 is equal to different extreme values and then estimating an overidentified structural equations model is analogous to this analysis of bounds.

15. For a sample of students, half of whom have rational latent expectations of .49 and half of whom have rational latent expectations of .51, if the threshold is .5 and there are no intervening aggregate shocks, the product moment correlation between E and A would be only .02.

16. These conclusions are based on theoretical bounds that ignore sampling error. Bootstrapping the conditional means (analogous to what was executed for Table 3.4) would change the conclusions only slightly, suggesting that it may be the case that in the senior year white males without a parent with a college degree have rational expectations and in the sophomore year that black females with a parent with a college degree have rational expectations (i.e., the upper end of the 95 percent bootstrapped confidence interval for the graduation rate among those who expect to graduate is .555 and .544 respectively instead of the theoretical values of .495 and .343).

17. It is an interesting question whether wishful thinking can be thought of as lowering the response threshold in order to protect oneself from the negative self-evaluation one might generate by underestimating one's future potential.

18. Analogous models for expectations reported in 1982, 1984, and 1986 that use all information available by the senior year (including additional test scores and updated significant others' influence) yield the same autoregressive error structure, although the correlations are about 60 to 80 percent the size of those for the models reported in Table 3.5. Moreover, including as *ex post* information in X a variable for educational attainment also yields the same autoregressive structure, although the correlations are between about 50 and 97 percent of the size of analogous correlations from models without attainment in X.

19. Nonetheless, some new optimism may have emerged for black females in the late 1990s. Mirroring to some extent the evolving gender differential in college entry rates among whites, in the 1990s the expectations of white women began to increase relative to those of white men. But, this gender difference also emerged for blacks, even though the rate of college entry for black females did not increase as much as for white females.

PART II

A COMMITMENT-BASED MODEL
OF EDUCATIONAL ATTAINMENT

CHAPTER FOUR

The Generation of Preparatory Commitment from Forward-Looking Beliefs

The decision of whether to enter college immediately following high school is especially consequential in contemporary American society because it is a genuine non-repeatable decision. Delayed college entry yields different payoffs that result in alternative life course outcomes. For a substantial proportion of students on the margin of college entry (that is, those for whom policy interventions are designed to encourage college enrollment; see Kane 1999b; Kosters 1999), the immediate college entry decision is vexing. The alternative choices are clearly in view from early adolescence onward, but there is no simple normative guide for behavior. As a result, everyday commitment to preparation for college instruction varies across high school students, affecting resulting enrollment decisions and the potential gains from college instruction.

A tractable and explicit model is needed for the consequential everyday decisions that prepare individuals to enact and then benefit from alternative courses of future instruction, one that neither reduces students to myopic automatons who simply observe their peers nor inflates them to the status of über decision makers who have rational expectations and effortlessly process all possible information. Rather, the framework must be grounded on a flexible and plausible mechanism that can be used to carefully specify how one's beliefs about alternative potential futures determine one's current behavior. This model should not be regarded as a mere add-on to models of instantaneous enrollment decisions, but rather as an equally fundamental model that determines many of the inputs into models of enrollment decisions.

As shown in prior chapters, according to status socialization theory, students' college plans are shaped by their own expectations and by how their expectations respond to the expectations of parents, teachers, and peers. But this position merely begs the questions: On what basis do students and their significant others form their expectations? Do significant others, for example, transmit accurate information about one's likely success in the educational system? Or do significant others systematically mislead students, so that some students who could succeed in college are discouraged while others who would likely fail are encouraged? How do students then reconcile inconsistent expectations, especially when those formulated through self-reflection conflict with those significant others offer?

The stochastic decision tree model of commitment that I begin to develop in this chapter is designed to enable the explicit modeling of questions such as these. The model presupposes that the everyday decisions of individuals are self-regulated by simple commitments toward the future. Individuals who can easily envision themselves pursuing a specific future course of behavior will have high levels of commitment to that course of behavior and will accordingly put forth more effort in preparation for it. Adopting a weak form of decision evaluation that is justified by the bounded rationality literature on cognitive constraints (and, in recognition of the necessity of relying on a simple decision tree in order to allow for uncertainties in the identification of everyday decisions that one will have to navigate in the interim), the model then provides a plausible and parsimonious mechanism to analyze the way in which individuals formulate forward-looking beliefs about their own behavior, as conditioned by their beliefs about the payoffs to alternative courses of potential behavior.[1]

The remainder of the chapter is organized as follows. As a starting point, I will present three assumptions and in so doing define the concepts of prefigurative commitment and preparatory commitment. Since the stochastic decision tree model that I later propose is an elaboration of an orthodox one-shot decision tree for choice under uncertainty, I then introduce a simple decision tree model of college entry, note its commendable analytic specificity, but then argue that as commonly invoked it cannot serve by itself as a complete framework for modeling preparatory commitment in advance of college entry decisions (and hence is, on its own, an inadequate model of the college entry decision).

I then introduce the stochastic decision tree model and use a set of numerical simulations to demonstrate how it operates, in particular by showing how it allows commitment toward the future course of action "Go to college" to be a function of the amount of processed information available to a high school student and the amount of effort expended to analyze it. Accordingly, I will claim that, among students who eventually enact the same college entry decision, those who are not systematically misinformed but who are nonetheless not well informed will exhibit less effort in the short run and attain lower levels of the returns expected from a college education in the long run. This result provides the crucial link between college entry decisions and the trajectories of achievement typically observed in high school.

AN ALTERNATIVE GUIDE FOR FORWARD-LOOKING BEHAVIOR: PREFIGURATIVE AND PREPARATORY COMMITMENT

The stochastic decision tree model of commitment is grounded on the specific assumption that in the period leading up to the college entry decision:

> A1. Intermediate everyday courses of behavior are self-regulated by the clarity of prefigurative commitments toward alternative future courses of behavior.

For example, the strength of a high school student's prefigurative commitment to the future course of behavior "Go to college immediately following high school" is the ease with which he or she is able to envision entering and ultimately graduating from a college degree program.[2]

In its abstract form, Assumption A1 is strongly supported by the social psychological literature, and in particular by a new literature on control and automaticity (see Pittman 1998; Wegner and Bargh 1998). The selection or adoption of a prefigurative commitment to a future course of behavior, such as "I will enroll in college," is roughly analogous to the selection of an initial control criterion. If the conscious control criterion is sufficiently strong and if there is scope to minimize self-monitoring costs, then the control criterion is transformable over time into a self-regulating and only minimally conscious behavioral mechanism that automates appropriate everyday behavior.[3]

Prefigurative commitment is a decomposable control criterion for current behavior, and its dimensions are specific to each decision context. However, for educational attainment, three underlying dimensions are sufficiently exhaustive: purposive-prefigurative commitment, normative-prefigurative commitment, and imitative-prefigurative commitment.[4] For the non-repeatable

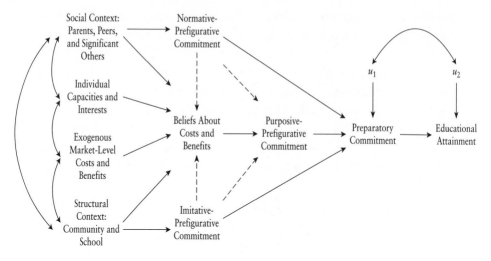

Figure 4.1.   Schematic Representation of the Preparatory Commitment Model of Educational Attainment

decision "Go to college" versus "Do not go to college," these three types of prefigurative commitment are set in response to three forward-looking prediction rules: "I will go to college if I perceive it to be in my best interest to do so," "I will go to college if my significant others perceive it to be in my best interest to do so," and "I will go to college if I expect other students similar to me will also go to college." These three generative dimensions are roughly analogous to the self-reflection, adoption, and imitation mechanisms of status socialization theory (see Haller 1982; Morgan 1998).

Figure 4.1 presents a schematic picture of the relationships that the concept of prefigurative commitment is meant to capture, drawn for comparison with the Wisconsin model, shown earlier in Figure 2.1. The broad set of exogenous factors on the left of the figure affect individuals' later educational attainment in part by the ways in which they structure individuals' commitments to schooling. The central mediating mechanism is therefore the set of prefigurative commitments generated in the course of individuals' schooling, separable into its three sources.

As drawn in Figure 4.1, purposive-prefigurative commitment has quite consciously been placed along its central axis. Although all three dimensions of prefigurative commitment have salience for many decisions, purposive-prefigurative commitment is both the most theoretically interesting (because it has the most power to subsume the other two) and the least developed within the sociological literature on educational attainment. I will therefore focus development of the stochastic decision tree model in this chapter on the construction of purposive-prefigurative commitment, reserving for subsequent chapters the development of possible ways to introduce reinforcing and destabilizing normative and imitative-prefigurative commitment into the model. Thus, I motivate the stochastic decision tree model by assuming that:

A2. Individuals use a decision tree to identify and prefiguratively commit to the future course of behavior that they believe is in their best interest.

Having defined prefigurative commitment as a cognitive attachment to a future course of behavior, the potentially observable course of everyday behavior that positions an individual to realize his or her prefigurative commitment can then be defined as preparatory commitment. A student with maximal preparatory commitment toward the prefigurative commitment "I will enroll in college" will enact all possible behavior that prepares him or her for enrolling in college and then successfully obtaining a college degree. While in high school, such students will take college preparatory classes, complete their homework diligently, focus their attention when taking tests, sign up early for college entrance examinations, and investigate their range of realistic college alternatives.

If prefigurative commitment can be weak or strong, then resulting preparatory commitment may be anywhere from nonexistent to maximally intensive. I therefore assume that:

A3. An individual's observable level of preparatory commitment to a future course of behavior is a direct function of the strength of his or her prefigurative commitment to that course of behavior.

If the payoff to college instruction is a function of the ability to benefit from opportunities for learning, then prior levels of educational achievement are crucial for understanding the impact of educational attainment and for understanding how individuals forecast the likely payoff to entering college at the time they are confronted by a stark enrollment decision. More generally, if, as is the case with many non-repeatable decisions, the payoff to a utility-maximizing affirmative decision is a function of preparatory commitment, then prefigurative commitment determines an individual's future level of well-being, above and beyond simply pushing an individual over a decision threshold, as will be discussed below (see Figure 4.4).

A DECISION TREE MODEL OF EDUCATIONAL ATTAINMENT

The stochastic decision tree with which I propose to model the purposive dimension of prefigurative commitment (and later modify to incorporate other types of prefigurative commitment) borrows the specificity of statistical decision theory, and in particular its basic decision tree foundation. However, I will abandon some common constraining features of orthodox decision theory and its empirical inversion as traditional discrete choice analysis—perfect information processing, redundant belief formation, and permissive revealed preference.[5]

Figure 4.2 presents a standard one-shot decision tree for choice under uncertainty. Although the specific form of the tree is entirely generic, and hence resembles in form nearly all of the models presented in Pratt, Raiffa, and Schlaifer (1995), this specific tree is isomorphic with the set of equations used to model students' enrollment decisions by Manski (1989). For this simple model, a prospective college student must contemplate whether it is in his or her best interest to choose the course of action "Go to college" or "Do not go to college."

Assume that students consider two possible abstract life outcomes—a very good position in life denoted by "High" and a not very good position in life denoted by "Low." These outcomes can be thought of as time-discounted dollar values for expected lifetime earnings (that is, $2,000,000 versus $600,000). Further assume that all students would rather receive High than Low.

Given these preferences, high school students (perhaps with the guidance of their parents, teachers, and peers) must decide which among three alternative paths through the educational system will put them in the best possible position to obtain the life position High rather than Low. Individuals think of these paths as a series of lotteries that are controlled by success parameters π, α, β, and γ that are probabilities between 0 and 1.[6]

According to the model, students recognize that if they choose to go to college they are subject to an intermediate hurdle because college completion is not guaranteed by initial college attendance. Each student's decision tree

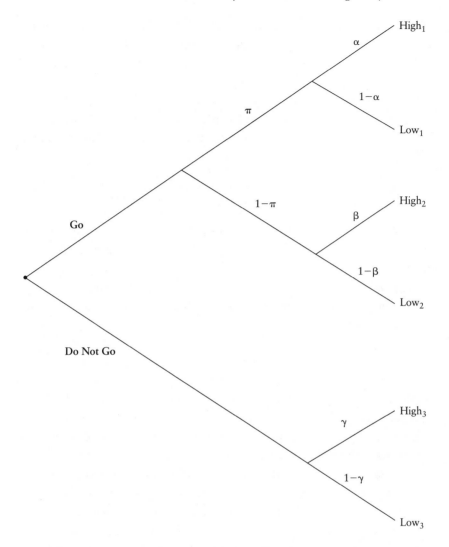

Figure 4.2.   A Simple Decision Tree for the College Entry Decision

has a parameter π that represents each student's subjective belief about the probability of completing college if initially enrolled.[7]

Similarly, students maintain a set of beliefs about the relative likelihood of attaining High versus Low after traversing each of the three possible paths through the educational system. They expect that if they complete college, they will attain High with probability α and Low with probability $(1 - \alpha)$.

If they attempt but do not complete college, then they expect that they will attain High with probability β and Low with probability $(1 - \beta)$. And finally, if they choose to forego college, they expect that they will attain High with probability γ and Low with probability $(1 - \gamma)$.

Rational choice theory offers the prediction that, under specific assumptions about optimization and consistency of choice (see Pratt, Raiffa, and Schlaifer 1995; Sen 1997), prospective college students will choose to go to college if:

$$\pi\alpha[u(\text{High}_1) - u(\text{Low}_1)] + (1 - \pi)\beta[u(\text{High}_2) - u(\text{Low}_2)]$$
$$> \gamma[u(\text{High}_3) - u(\text{Low}_3)] \qquad (4.1a)$$

where $u(.)$ is a utility function that, in its most general sense, assigns subjective value to the alternative payoffs High and Low.[8] If an individual's utility function is process-independent so that $u(\text{High}_1) = u(\text{High}_2) = u(\text{High}_3)$ and $u(\text{Low}_1) = u(\text{Low}_2) = u(\text{Low}_3)$, then both sides of Equation 4.1a can be divided by a common utility difference, $u(\text{High}) - u(\text{Low})$, in order to obtain the simplified decision rule:

$$\pi\alpha + (1 - \alpha)\beta > \gamma \qquad (4.1b)$$

The left-hand sides of these decision rules represent the expected utility of enrolling in college, and the right-hand sides represent the expected utility of not enrolling in college. If the expected utility of enrolling is greater than the expected utility of not enrolling, rational choice theory assumes that a high school student will choose to enroll in college.

After students choose either the upper or lower branch of the tree—and thus either enroll in college or enter the labor force—they are subject to a set of real-life lotteries. The probability of reaching High instead of Low is a function of more than simply a student's decision. Each lottery has a "true" probability, denoted respectively as $\tilde{\pi}$, $\tilde{\alpha}$, $\tilde{\beta}$, and $\tilde{\gamma}$. Actual outcomes are therefore determined in large part by exogenous factors that structure these probabilities. For researchers, claims about the relative sizes of $\tilde{\pi}$, $\tilde{\alpha}$, $\tilde{\beta}$, and $\tilde{\gamma}$ are usually based on assumptions about institutional constraints on educational attainment and the distribution of High versus Low outcomes in society. It is generally assumed that there are positive returns to schooling so that $\tilde{\alpha} \geq \tilde{\beta}$ and that $\tilde{\beta} > \tilde{\gamma}$. However, Manski (1989:307) argues that "analysis is trivial" unless, in the notation used here, for at least some students $\tilde{\beta} < \tilde{\gamma}$ and $\beta < \gamma$. If that were not the case, all students would choose to enter college.[9]

When contemplating college entry decisions, do students maintain reasonable beliefs about the lotteries that they face? In other words, for each individual and for a decision tree such as the one depicted in Figure 4.2, is there a close correspondence between π, α, β, and γ and $\tilde{\pi}$, $\tilde{\alpha}$, $\tilde{\beta}$, and $\tilde{\gamma}$? The traditional assumption among rational choice researchers is that individuals, on average, have correct beliefs about $\tilde{\pi}$, $\tilde{\alpha}$, $\tilde{\beta}$, and $\tilde{\gamma}$. Accordingly, the values of π, α, β, and γ that students rely on when making college entry decisions are assumed to equal (on average) the true probabilities that students will face in their futures. When this strong assumption is maintained, little analytic advantage is gained by preserving a distinction between true values for the parameters of the lotteries and beliefs about them.[10]

When the theoretical correspondence between true parameters and beliefs about them is asserted, grounded on the generally unevaluated assumption that individuals on average have accurate beliefs, a decision tree model can effectively motivate empirical analysis of individuals' observed choice behavior. However, a revealed preference assumption must be invoked first. In particular, one must be able to assume that what individuals are observed to do is precisely what they believed they should do. This assumption may be rather dubious in many applications, as I suspect it is for schooling decisions, for it is generally recognized that what one does is not necessarily what one wanted to do or could have done (see Sen 1982[1977], 1997). The result is that a researcher can only learn, given data about what individuals did, what individuals' preferences and beliefs must have been if the proposed model and its associated assumptions are true.

Nonetheless, to see how this simple model can be used to generate predictions about educational attainment behavior, even without relaxing the constraint that individuals' beliefs are on average correct, consider an abstract version of the most consistent finding on patterns of educational attainment: students from advantaged social backgrounds are more likely to attend college than students from less advantaged social backgrounds. There are at least four ways to use the decision tree model presented in Figure 4.2 in order to generate a predicted distribution that conforms to this common finding.

The *survival rate explanation* asserts that π is a positive function of social background. Students from advantaged social backgrounds may have higher innate or acquired ability to complete college than those from less advantaged social backgrounds. These students may also have a greater capacity to absorb the direct costs that accumulate over the course of college instruction. Students who have larger values for π are more likely to enroll in college, all else equal and if $\alpha > \beta$.

The *social costs explanation* asserts that students from advantaged social backgrounds value the achievement of the outcome High through the pathway of a college education relatively more than other students. In other words, utility functions are heterogeneous and ordered by social background so that, for example, $u(\text{High}_1)$ is greater than $u(\text{High}_2)$ and $u(\text{High}_3)$ for students from the most advantaged social backgrounds while $u(\text{High}_1)$ equals $u(\text{High}_2)$ and $u(\text{High}_3)$ for all other students (and where for simplicity $u(\text{Low}_1) = u(\text{Low}_2) = u(\text{Low}_3)$ for students from all social backgrounds). Boudon (1974) reasoned that students from advantaged social backgrounds may associate more "social benefits" with receiving the outcome High having also obtained a college degree than students from less advantaged social backgrounds. Likewise, students from disadvantaged social backgrounds may associate some "social costs" with achieving the outcome High through a college education, so that for them $u(\text{High}_1)$ and $u(\text{High}_2)$ are less than $u(\text{High}_3)$.

The *rate of return explanation* asserts that the final stage parameters α, β, and γ vary by social background. Students from lower social backgrounds may correctly expect that α is lower for them in comparison to the value of α for students from more advantaged social backgrounds because those whom they observe to have completed college have on average attended poorer quality colleges. More complex background differences in α, β, and γ may exist as well, primarily because education is only one factor that determines the probability of capturing the reward High instead of Low. If students feel that they have other possible routes to achieve advantaged positions, such as family connections, the parameters α, β, and γ will vary with social background in proportion to the distribution of family connections to gatekeepers across the three reward lotteries. For example, α/γ may be larger for students from advantaged social backgrounds if their family connections are only operative if they receive a college degree.

Finally, the *alternative strategies explanation* asserts that students from different social backgrounds attempt to maximize different functions and thus invoke class-specific decision rules. With reference to a slightly more elaborate decision tree than the one presented in Figure 4.2, Breen and Goldthorpe (1997) argue that students from the upper middle class attempt to maximize their chances of entering the upper middle class while students from the lower middle class attempt to minimize their chances of falling into the underclass.

In order to illustrate this last possible elaboration of the basic model presented in Figure 4.2, I reproduce the model of Breen and Goldthorpe (1997) as Figure 4.3 to discuss their argument. The motivation for the model is to explain inequality of educational attainment without having to make assumptions about class-specific norms and values. Elaborating a basic decision tree, Breen and Goldthorpe create three outcomes ordered by desirability: entry into a position in the service class, entry into a position in the working class, and entry into a position in the underclass. In addition, Breen and Goldthorpe accept the claim of Gambetta (1987) that students conceive of educational decisions as staying on in school or leaving school in order to work.

Breen and Goldthorpe make six explicit assumptions about the true entry probabilities into the three classes (and further assume that students have beliefs about them that are on average correct so that maintaining a distinction between parameters such as $\tilde{\alpha}$ and α is not worth the effort). They assume that $\alpha > \beta_1$, $\alpha > \gamma_1$, $\alpha \geq \gamma_1/(\gamma_1 + \gamma_2)$, $(\gamma_1 + \gamma_2) > (\beta_1 + \beta_2)$, $\gamma_2/\gamma_1 > 1$, and $\gamma_2/\gamma_1 > \beta_1/\beta_2$. A substantively important claim inherent in these restrictions is that opportunity costs mount in the course of education in a way such that it is better to leave school rather than fail to achieve having decided to stay (as would be the case in the simple decision tree of Figure 4.2 if $\beta < \gamma$).[11] If it is true that all students are motivated by the desire to avoid downward mobility, Breen and Goldthorpe (1997:284–85) claim that their model guarantees that "children from middle-class backgrounds [in comparison with children from lower-class backgrounds] will more strongly 'prefer' (in the sense of perceiving it to be in their best interests) to remain in school to a further level of education rather than leave."

In order to demonstrate this claim, Breen and Goldthorpe focus on the hypothesized outcomes of representative groups of children whose parents are, respectively, from the service class and the working class. All students have "identical relative risk aversion" such that all students wish not to experience downward mobility.[12] Students from the service class seek to maximize their probabilities of entering the service class. However, students

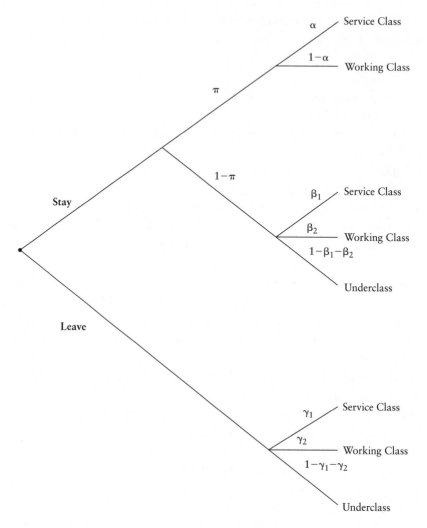

Figure 4.3.   A Single Stay versus Leave Decision Tree.

SOURCE: Breen and Goldthorpe, 1997. Redrawn with permission.

from the working class seek to maximize their probabilities of entering the service class or of entering the working class.

Although stated as a commonality across classes, Breen and Goldthorpe's assumption of identical relative risk aversion can be characterized more simply as a requirement that students from different classes have different decision rules. For comparison with the simplified decision rule from Equation 4.1b based on Figure 4.2, students from the service class choose to go (or stay) if:

$$\pi\alpha + (1 - \pi)\beta_1 > \gamma_1 \tag{4.2a}$$

while students from the working class choose to go (or stay) if:[13]

$$\pi\alpha + (1 - \pi)(\beta_1 + \beta_2) > (\gamma_1 + \gamma_2) \tag{4.2b}$$

From the differences in these two decision rules, and given the six restrictions on the relative sizes of the entry probabilities, Breen and Goldthorpe claim that more students from the service class than students from the working class will stay on in school.[14]

To what extent is the assumption of relative risk aversion a normative argument disguised within a rational choice model? Certainly, it bears some resemblance to the claim of Parsons (1953) that lower class individuals privilege security goals over success goals to a greater extent than their middle class counterparts. The contribution of Breen and Goldthorpe lies not in the wholly original nature of their claims, but rather in the explicitness by which they introduce and develop them. In this regard, the Breen and Goldthorpe model is an important advance for the sociological literature. They convincingly demonstrate that claims based on norms and values (or, in Parsons' case ideal type goals) can be given explicit formulation within an entirely new framework. Whether the decision tree formulation is an improvement over the verbal motivation of Parsons and others can then be determined in further research.

On the whole, rational choice models of educational attainment are more explicit than most other theories of educational attainment, and this is their main strength. Their main weakness arises in practice. Too little effort has been expended evaluating whether the proposed specific micro-processes are reasonable models of behavior.

Given the importance that subjective beliefs about the true decision tree parameters play in determining action in rational choice models (consider each of the four explanations above), it is perhaps surprising that the rational choice literature has developed so extensively since the 1940s without giving much explicit attention to mechanisms of belief formation. The core twentieth-century foundations of the rational choice literature have almost nothing to say about how beliefs about parameters such as $\tilde{\pi}$, $\tilde{\alpha}$, $\tilde{\beta}$, and $\tilde{\gamma}$ (that is, π, α, β, and γ) respond to differences in available information.[15]

Strict Bayesian updating, though rigorously justified as the best normative approach to information processing, reads more like a denial that belief formation is ever important, and for this reason is almost never explicitly invoked in empirical analyses of actual decision making. Surely mean-spreading uncertainty is granted a place in rational choice models, but it is often embedded in the concavity of assumed utility functions and then ignored.

The model I develop in the next section attempts to provide a foundation for a more comprehensive approach. In so doing, I construct a model that is based in part on rational choice theory but that also will allow sociologists to embrace the core mechanism of the Wisconsin model that one's current behavior is conditioned by socially structured beliefs about one's future.

A SOCIOLOGICAL ALTERNATIVE: A STOCHASTIC DECISION TREE MODEL OF COMMITMENT

When thinking about future decisions such as whether to enter college in several years, high school students must also contemplate a series of consequential intermediate decisions. The action "Go to college" can be thought of as a compound outcome of a series of underlying decisions, many of which must be enacted long before the first college tuition bill is due. Moreover, the payoff to obtaining a college degree is a function not just of having enrolled in college but of how seriously one has prepared to master the college curriculum before being exposed to it. Thus, prior preparation can be as consequential for levels of ultimate well-being as whether or not a student is able make an *ex ante* utility-maximizing college entry decision.

Figure 4.4 presents a simple graphical depiction of this claim, where the ultimate payoff is plotted against prior preparation, and where (for this depiction only) it is assumed that all individuals whose prior preparation is greater than a fixed decision threshold enter college. Often, in such analytic situations, one focuses on the mean levels of the payoffs by averaging over those who choose to enter college and those who do not (that is, the levels represented by dashed lines in the figure). I assume that when choices about a non-repeatable decision such as college enrollment are made under uncertainty, the payoff distribution will exhibit patterned heterogeneity across the decision threshold because level of preparation will differ.[16] If this is the case, examination of average differences only is inadequate, both from theoretical and policy-relevant perspectives.

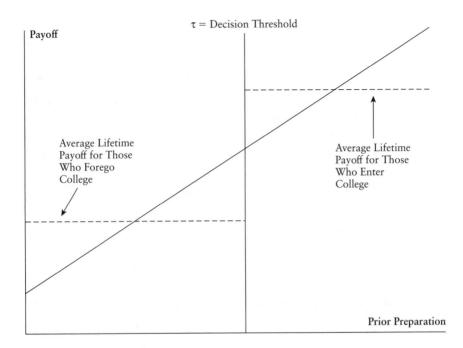

Figure 4.4.   Payoff as a Linear Function of Prior Preparation

Can one model prior preparation, or what I have labeled preparatory commitment, using standard statistical decision theory? Yes, and the accepted procedure for incorporating underlying decisions into an existing decision tree is to add branches for all consequential intermediate decisions. For example, if the intermediate decision is whether to enroll in a trigonometry class in high school, then two alternative decision trees with the structure of the one presented in Figure 4.2 are then specified in toto as expected consequences (and possibly alongside other relevant consequences) for the decision of whether to enroll in the trigonometry class. An augmented decision tree of this form is justified if beliefs such as π or the utility evaluations of High and Low depend on whether one enrolls in the trigonometry class.

Although a single augmentation is easily achieved, further elaboration rapidly overwhelms the simplicity and power of the entire framework. For the decision of whether to go to college, the large number of preparatory commitment decisions that adolescents must navigate in middle school and high school would render their comprehensive decision trees massive and ever-changing as each intermediate decision is considered and then enacted.

A possible solution to the impracticality of complete decision tree augmentation is to limit students' individual time horizons, such as by allowing them to look only one year into the future. This is tantamount to assuming that individuals cannot forecast their futures in any meaningful way and that incentives and institutions determine action almost exclusively as unanticipated constraints on future behavior. Although possibly appropriate for some applications, students clearly are aware of alternative trajectories through the educational system and must think to some extent about their likelihoods of traversing alternative trajectories.

The modifications to the orthodox one-shot decision tree structure that I propose for the modeling of preparatory commitment are inspired by the approach to modeling bounded rationality outlined by Herbert Simon (see Simon 1996 for an overview), as opposed to recent attempts to harness bounded rationality within more traditional modes of rational choice analysis (such as Rubinstein 1998). The modifications incorporate the cognitive constraints of actors, the implicit costs of analyzing available information, and the non-random distribution of information observed in real-world social systems.[17]

Decision Tree Structure

For the college entry decision, I assume that the true comprehensive decision tree of each prospective college student is fundamentally *ex ante* unknowable. Carrying on from the assumptions introduced at the beginning of the chapter, I will assume that:

> A4. The decision tree that individuals use to prefiguratively commit to a future course of behavior is more simple in structure than that which would be required to explicitly model all intermediate decisions that are consequential for the college entry decision.

Equivalently, I will assume that preparatory commitment cannot be modeled as a long series of fully conscious, forward-looking decisions.

For the numerical demonstration of the framework that I offer below, I will use the simple decision tree in Figure 4.2, and hence, when referring to the college choice example, adopt the position of Manski (1989) that for enrollment decisions potential enrollees consider four basic lotteries. For my framework, however, the decision tree serves only as a forecasting tool that students use when self-regulating everyday behavior in the long run—up to the instantaneous enrollment decision.

Belief Distributions

Instead of requiring high school students to construct comprehensive decision trees for all intermediate decisions, I allow the complexity of the everyday decisions that constitute preparatory commitment to be modeled as uncertainty about the parameters of a simple decision tree for a future course of behavior. Thus, I will assume that:

> A5. The parameters of the decision tree that students use to prefiguratively commit to a future course of behavior are fundamentally stochastic.

This assumption is the major departure from standard practice.[18] For the evaluation of an orthodox one-shot decision tree, the usual maintained assumption is that parameters such as π, α, β, and γ in Equations 4.1a and 4.1b are regarded as constants by each student. These constants may vary across individuals, but each individual evaluates a decision rule with point values for its parameters.

Even though a decision rule is always evaluated with point-value beliefs in orthodox rational choice theory, in some cases rational choice researchers allow individuals to entertain more than one possible point value for each decision tree parameter. According to statistical decision theory, for example, a student may recognize that he or she does not know $\tilde{\pi}$, $\tilde{\alpha}$, $\tilde{\beta}$, and $\tilde{\gamma}$ and therefore may attempt to estimate each of them. Under this more complex scenario, students may consult an entire distribution of estimates in their minds, but each student regards this distribution as a distribution of errors from an unknown true constant. In accordance with standard estimation principles, the student would then select point-value beliefs for decision rule evaluation from entire distributions of estimates, which in most cases results in the student selecting the means of the contemplated distributions (that is, when assuming symmetric loss functions; see Lehmann and Casella 1998).

The modification I propose for modeling how students think about a future college enrollment decision is more fundamental. Students recognize that there is no true constant to be estimated because they understand that the decision tree they are consulting is simply a rough approximation to the complex set of real-life lotteries to which they will ultimately be subjected. Thus, students forecast their futures as if any ostensibly true parameters such as $\tilde{\pi}$, $\tilde{\alpha}$, $\tilde{\beta}$, and $\tilde{\gamma}$ have distributions. Accordingly, Assumption A5 stipulates that students maintain entire belief distributions for the parameters of a decision tree, such as π, α, β, and γ in Figure 4.2. As I will show below, students may still wish to determine the most likely values implied by their belief distributions, but because they regard their belief distributions as only rough representations, they are unwilling to exert the analytic or numerical energy necessary to construct maximally precise estimates of the means of their belief distributions.

How are belief distributions constructed and revised? I will address this question in substantial detail in subsequent chapters, but for now I assume that individuals simply store belief distributions in memory based on observations of individuals whom they regard as payoff models. And, in order to generate the analytic and numerical results offered below, I will assume that these belief distributions allow the amount of information available to individuals to be expressed as variances of their belief distributions. Individuals with sparse information at their disposal will have uncertain belief distributions with large variances, and individuals with abundant information will have precise belief distributions with small variances.[19]

For example, consider two high school students contemplating the decision tree presented in Figure 4.2 when forecasting their own future decision of whether to enter college immediately. Student A observes 20 college graduates and 10 college dropouts. In contrast, Student B observes only 2 college graduates and 1 college dropout. The framework I will adopt stipulates that Student A will have more confidence than Student B in eliminating extreme values from his or her belief distributions about his or her subjective probability of graduating from college if enrolled. Student A would consider values such as .66 much more likely than values such as .96 or .36. Student B would likewise consider .66 more likely than either .96 or .36 but would be less willing than Student A to discount the plausibility of .96 or .36. This position is consistent with the dominant literature on belief distributions, which for Bayesian decision theory (see Pratt, Raiffa, and Schlaifer 1995) and information-integration theory in psychology (see Davidson 1995) similarly allows uncertainty and imprecision of beliefs to be a function of the amount of available information.

Decision Tree Evaluation

When contemplating underlying decisions that contribute to a student's preparatory commitment, students set their current level of prefigurative commitment by instantaneously evaluating their stochastic decision trees. As stipulated in Assumption A1, an individual's level of prefigurative commitment is thus analogous to a behavioral control condition that partially automates consistent everyday behavior. In selecting, or reevaluating, a level of prefigurative commitment, how do students evaluate their stochastic decision trees?

By principles of statistical decision theory, the traditional answer (assuming symmetric loss functions and no option values) would be that they calculate the means of their belief distributions, declare them as their best estimates of their point-value beliefs, and use them to solve a decision rule such as Equation 4.1a. Two evaluation methods are consistent with this position: (1) analytically solving for the means by integrating over the density functions of one's beliefs, and (2) randomly sampling a large number of candidate point-value beliefs from one's belief distributions and then averaging over the candidate point-value beliefs. The first method seems entirely unreasonable unless one is prepared to assume either that individuals know calculus or that they maintain degenerate belief distributions. The second method is more feasible, and yet begs the question: How effectively can students numerically solve for the means of their belief distributions? In the numerical simulations of the model offered below, I demonstrate the consequences of answering this latter question in different ways. But before showing the consequences of alternative answers, the extant literature on bounded rationality can be drawn on to narrow the range of plausible answers.

In contrast to computers, humans operate under severe cognitive computational constraints, as has been argued within the rational action paradigm by Herbert Simon since the 1950s. Based on his own research, and his reading of the psychology of concept discrimination, Simon maintained that individuals can store only about seven "chunks" in fast, short-term memory (for example, the seven digits of a U.S. telephone number), but when interrupted in the process of perceiving these chunks individuals can recall only two of them. Relatedly, he maintained that it takes approximately eight seconds to fixate on a new chunk (but perhaps only two or three seconds to fixate on a confirmatory chunk) and transfer it from short-term to long-term memory (see Simon 1996 for an up-to-date summary of his views).

If individuals are subject to substantial cognitive constraints such as these, and hence cannot numerically evaluate density functions in order to quickly recover arbitrarily exact estimates of the means of their belief distri-

butions, individuals must rely on some "fast and frugal" strategies to evaluate their decision trees (see Gigerenzer and Selten 2001). Based on this reasoning, I will assume that:

> A6. Students evaluate their stochastic decision trees by solving a decision
> rule with parameter values that are simple averages of a few randomly sampled
> candidate values drawn from their belief distributions.

In the numerical simulations of the framework offered below, I will vary the
total number of candidate draws that individuals use to evaluate their stochastic decision trees. Drawing directly from Simon's position on the cognitive constraints of the human mind, I (weakly) favor limiting the total number of candidate values drawn by individuals to seven. But, I will also
consider how the patterns of prefigurative commitment change as the number of randomly drawn candidate values increases, partly because it seems
reasonable that individuals may differ in how many candidate draws they
are able and willing to consult.

   In particular, I will allow students to randomly draw candidate parameter values for a decision tree of the structure presented in Figure 4.2 and
then average over these values to form a set of candidate point-value beliefs
$\{\pi', \alpha', \beta', \gamma'\}$. Assuming that utility evaluations are equivalent across paths
and scaled to values of 1 for High and 0 for Low, an individual will set a dichotomous variable E equal to 1 if:

$$\pi'\alpha' + (1 - \pi')\beta' > \gamma' \qquad (4.1c)$$

Otherwise, E will be set equal to 0. E signifies an instantaneous prefigurative commitment to the future affirmative decision "Go to college" (for example, the choice Go in Figure 4.2).[20]

   Over a group of J students with equivalent beliefs, the average level of
prefigurative commitment to future college attendance is simply:

$$\Pr(E = 1) = \frac{1}{J} \sum_{j=1...J} E_j \qquad (4.3)$$

$\Pr(E = 1)$ is therefore equal in expectation to the probability that E will be
evaluated as 1 for a given set of beliefs and prespecified total number of candidate parameter draws selected for decision tree evaluation. $\Pr(E = 1)$ is
equivalent, as shown below, to the probability that the *ex ante* true distribution of expected utility for choosing to go to college is greater than the *ex*

ante true distribution of expected utility for choosing to forego college, conditional on the amount of information processing and evaluation effort a decision maker can marshal. Thus, whereas the binary orientation E represents the instantaneous level of prefigurative commitment that guides each preparatory commitment decision, $\Pr(E = 1)$ represents the average level of prefigurative commitment that is consistent with a set of stable beliefs and a procedure to analyze those beliefs in the process of constructing forward-looking prefigurative commitment. The distinction implies that for two students who at a specific point in time both set E equal to 1, the student whose beliefs imply a lower value for $\Pr(E = 1)$ will be less likely to set E equal to 1 when contemplating subsequent preparatory commitment decisions. $\Pr(E = 1)$ is therefore the more fundamental quantity of interest.

Why would students use this form of decision evaluation? I assume that students generally wish to orient their current behavior to a long-run plan that is in their best interest, but doing so in a way that is as rigorous as stipulated by statistical decision theory is too costly, especially since students themselves must recognize that they cannot form comprehensive decision trees to capture all consequential intermediate decisions. Thus, while students are indeed to some extent myopic, they seek to avoid short-run mistakes in judgment by adopting a relatively frugal process of planning for their futures.[21]

THE GENERATION OF PURPOSIVE-PREFIGURATIVE COMMITMENT

In this section, I offer analytic implications of the stochastic decision tree framework, while at the same time demonstrating its contours with a set of numerical simulations. Throughout the section, I assume that differences in $\Pr(E = 1)$ have consequences for students' final levels of well-being by way of their self-regulated preparatory commitment and the true responsiveness of the payoff distribution to this commitment. I first present an analytic result to establish the baseline value of prefigurative commitment, which applies to the (quite unrealistic) case in which students have too little information to favor any particular range of potential beliefs for the parameters of their stochastic decision trees. I then provide a graphical depiction of 400 numerical simulations for the construction of $\Pr(E = 1)$ under alternative belief distributions about a stochastic decision tree of the structure presented in Figure 4.2. Following the demonstration, I then attribute the patterns observed in the simulations to specific analytic implications of the framework.

Uninformed Beliefs and Prefigurative Commitment

For a derivation of baseline levels of prefigurative commitment, assume that students use the simple decision tree in Figure 4.2 to forecast whether they should expect to go to college immediately following high school. Utilizing the form of decision tree evaluation proposed above, what are the consequences for $\Pr(E = 1)$ of having no information at all on which to base one's beliefs? The following general proposition gives the answer.

> PROPOSITION 1 — *Uninformed Beliefs.* Suppose that Assumptions A1 through A6 hold and that all students share the same utility function. If students have uninformed beliefs and are thus willing to accept as equally likely all theoretically possible values for each decision tree parameter, then they will on average have identical levels of prefigurative and preparatory commitment to alternative future courses of action.
>
> *Proof Sketch for Proposition 1.* Consider the stochastic decision tree with same structure as the decision tree in Figure 4.2, and scale students' utility functions so that the utility of High equals 1 and the utility of Low equals 0, regardless of the path taken through the decision tree. Under this scenario, the belief distributions of students without any information are equivalent to uniform distributions over the 0 to 1 interval.
>
> Accordingly, for each individual, $E[\pi]$, $E[\alpha]$, $E[\beta]$, and $E[\gamma]$ equal .5. And, thus, because $E[\pi]E[\alpha] + (1 - E[\pi])E[\beta] = E[\gamma]$, for alternative candidate decision trees, $\{\pi', \alpha', \beta', \gamma'\}$, $\Pr[\pi'\alpha' + (1 - \pi')\beta' > \gamma']$ equals $\Pr[\pi'\alpha' + (1 - \pi')\beta' < \gamma']$. As a result, $\Pr(E = 1) = \Pr(E = 0) = .5$. This result holds generally for all decision trees where the lottery parameters have the same range for each stage of the decision tree (that is, including decision trees for which the first stage parameters are probabilities that are bounded by 0 to 1 and the final-stage parameters are interval-scaled utility functions that span the entire real line).

According to Proposition 1, for the decision tree in Figure 4.2, the baseline level of prefigurative commitment is .5. In general, with uninformed beliefs, prefigurative commitment will equal $1/n$, where n is the number of future courses of behavior that are contemplated. However, as shown in the next section, for informed belief distributions, prefigurative commitment will diverge from such baseline values.[22]

Informed Beliefs and Prefigurative Commitment

If students have informed beliefs, prefigurative commitment is a function of at least three different dimensions: (1) the amount of processed information (and hence precision of beliefs), (2) the effort expended to analyze processed information, and (3) the core expected utility difference between alternative choices. Before offering the specific proposition and proof sketch that explicates these claims, I provide a series of numerical simulations to demonstrate the basic patterns that they imply for the construction of $Pr(E = 1)$.

Construction of belief distributions for the simulations. With reference to a decision tree with the same structure as the one presented in Figure 4.2, I will adopt beta distributions to encode individuals' beliefs about the probabilities π, α, β, and γ. The continuous beta distribution is the most natural distribution for modeling a probability, since the distribution is bounded by 0 and 1. Nonetheless, the claims that I will develop below do not depend in any important way on this choice of distribution. Any nondegenerate distribution for which expectations and variances can be parameterized independently could be substituted for the beta distribution.

Denoted *Beta(s, f)*, the two-parameter beta density function for an unspecified random variable θ (which could be a parameter such as π, α, β, or γ) is:

$$Pr(\theta) = \frac{\Gamma(s + f)}{\Gamma(s)\,\Gamma(f)} \theta^{s-1}(1 - \theta)^{f-1} \tag{4.4}$$

where the first term is a constant of integration and where it is required that $s > 0$ and $f > 0$. The distribution of θ is the predictive distribution of the expected proportion of successes in an idealized series of independent Bernoulli trials, where the parameter s is the number of successes and the parameter f is the number of failures in a prior series of identical independent trials. The density function can take a variety of shapes: When s equals f, the density function is symmetric with a mean equal to .5; when s and f are greater than 1, the density function is unimodal; when s and f are both less than 1 (but still by restriction greater than 0), the density function is bimodal with spikes at 0 and 1; when both s and f equal 1, the density function is flat and therefore equivalent to a uniform distribution.

The belief distributions used for the following 400 numerical simula-

TABLE 4.1

Distributions of Payoff Models for
the College Entry Decision Tree (see Figure 4.2)

	Very Small Positive Returns (Figure 4.5)	Small Positive Returns (Figure 4.6)	Large Positive Returns (Figure 4.7)	Very Large Positive Returns (Figure 4.8)
Successes for α lottery	1.5	2	3	4
Failures for α lottery	1	1	2	1
Implied mean of α	0.6	0.667	0.6	0.8
Successes for β lottery	1	1	1	3
Failures for β lottery	1	2	3	1
Implied mean of β	0.5	0.333	0.25	0.75
Successes for γ lottery	1	1	1	1
Failures for γ lottery	1	2	4	4
Implied mean of γ	0.5	0.333	0.2	0.2
Assuming Backward Induction:				
Derived Successes for π	2.5	3	5	5
Derived Failures for π	2	3	4	4
Implied Mean of π	0.556	0.5	0.556	0.556
Implied Expected Gain in the Probability of Receiving High Instead of Low When Entering College	.056	.167	.245	.578

tions are based on the heuristic that students observe alternative sets of individuals who serve as labor market models, and that these models can be encoded as the success and failure parameters of beta distributions, s and f. How does this work? Consider the four different distributions of labor market models in Table 4.1, applicable to the decision tree in Figure 4.2. For now, focus on the third column, where the distribution of labor market models indicates that there are large returns to entering college.

For column three, students can be thought of as looking in their immediate structural contexts and observing five models who have chosen to enter college and who have then survived the intermediate lottery parameterized by π and graduated from college. Of these models, three receive the payoff High while two receive the payoff Low. Likewise, the students observe four models who have chosen to enter college but who have failed to graduate from college. Of these models, one receives the payoff High and three receive the payoff Low. And finally, students observe five models who have chosen to forego college, and of these models only one receives the payoff High while four receive the payoff Low.

These labor market models can then be encoded as the parameters of beta distributions, in particular a *Beta*(3, 2) for α, a *Beta*(1, 3) for β, and a *Beta*(1, 4) for γ. Since the mean of a beta distribution is simply $s/(s + f)$, the resulting belief distributions have means of .6, .25, and .2 for α, β, and γ.

As will be shown below, the variances of belief distributions are crucial. For a beta distribution, the variance is $sf/[(s + f)^2(s + f + 1)]$, which decreases as the number of models $(s + f)$ increases. When students observe abundant payoff models, the variances of their resulting belief distributions are small. In accordance with Bayesian decision theory (which will be discussed in substantial detail in Chapter 5), their beliefs can be considered very precise. With beta distributions, when s and f increase by the same constant multiple, the mass of the density function shifts from the tails and accumulates at the mean. Accordingly, in the simulations, I will vary the precision of beliefs by multiplying each of the parameters s and f by the same strictly positive constant, p, a manipulation of beliefs that is analogous to increasing the number of observed payoff models without changing their distributions across branches of the decision tree.

Finally, I will concentrate on differences in the belief distributions for the final-stage reward parameters α, β, and γ. The belief distributions for π will simply be derived by backward induction from the belief distributions for α and β, as described in the simulation algorithm below.

Algorithm for each simulation. Figures 4.5 through 4.8 summarize 400 simulated values of prefigurative commitment, $\Pr(E = 1)$, over three different dimensions—the total amount of processed information available to students (parameterized by the variances of the belief distributions, holding their means constant), the total amount of effort expended to analyze processed information (parameterized by the total number of candidate draws selected for evaluation of Equation 4.1c), and the expected gain for choosing to enter college if efforts to analyze processed information were maximally intensive (parameterized by the means of the belief distributions).

The specific algorithm for each of 400 simulations proceeds in five steps:

Step 1.   Select a set of belief distributions:

A.   Encode the payoff distributions from Table 4.1 as baseline beta distributions:

$$\alpha \sim Beta(s_{\text{High}_1}, f_{\text{High}_1})$$

$$\beta \sim Beta(s_{\text{High}_2}, f_{\text{High}_2})$$

$$\gamma \sim Beta(s_{\text{High}_3}, f_{\text{High}_3})$$

using backward induction to stipulate that

$$\pi \sim Beta(s_{\text{High}_1} + f_{\text{High}_1}, s_{\text{High}_2} + f_{\text{High}_2})$$

B.   Select a constant precision of belief multiplier, p, with which to scale the success and failure parameters of the baseline belief distributions:

$$\alpha \sim Beta(ps_{\text{High}_1}, pf_{\text{High}_1})$$

$$\beta \sim Beta(ps_{\text{High}_2}, pf_{\text{High}_2})$$

$$\gamma \sim Beta(ps_{\text{High}_3}, pf_{\text{High}_3})$$

again, using backward induction to stipulate that

$$\pi \sim Beta(p[s_{\text{High}_1} + f_{\text{High}_1}], p[s_{\text{High}_2} + f_{\text{High}_2}])$$

Step 2.   Let each of J simulated students randomly draw candidate values from the belief distributions specified in Step 1:

A.   One from each of the belief distributions for π, α, β and γ;

B.   And then k additional draws from any of these distributions, where the determination of which belief distribution serves as the source for each additional draw is generated by a multinomial distribution with equal mass of .25 specified for each of the four belief distributions.

Step 3.   Let each simulated student take the simple average of the candidate values for each parameter. The result is a set of student-specific candidate decision trees for each of J students: $\{\pi'_j, \alpha'_j, \beta'_j, \gamma'_j\}_{j=1}^J$.

Step 4.   Let each simulated student use his or her j-specific candidate decision tree, $\{\pi', \alpha', \beta', \gamma'\}$, to evaluate the decision rule in Equation 4.1c.

Step 5.   Average over the J evaluations of the candidate decision trees of simulated students to form an arbitrarily precise numerical estimate of $\Pr(E = 1)$, which summarizes the level of prefigurative commitment associated with the set of beliefs that is specified in Step 1 and the amount of effort expended to analyze the information that is specified in Step 2.

As presented below, variations in the implementation of this algorithm arise from selection of exogenously specified baseline belief distributions, precision of beliefs, p, and the additional number of candidate draws, k. The distributions of payoff models presented in the four columns of Table 4.1

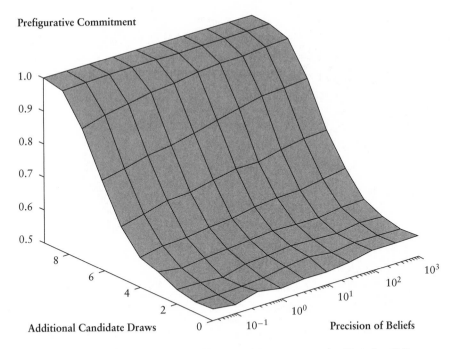

Figure 4.5.   Simulated Values of Prefigurative Commitment for Very Small Returns to Choosing the Decision Go to College

correspond to baseline sets of beliefs where there are very small, small, large, and very large returns to choosing the decision Go instead of the decision Do Not Go. The precision of beliefs parameter p varies over ten logarithmically spaced values, from .0316, to .1, .316, 1, 3.16, 10, 31.6, 100, 316, and finally 1000. Likewise, the additional number of candidate draws k varies over ten values from 0 to 9. Finally, each simulation is performed with J equal to 10,000, which stipulates that 10,000 independent students evaluate identical stochastic decision trees.

Simulation results.   Each of the four surface plots of $\Pr(E = 1)$ in Figures 4.5 through 4.8 correspond to 100 independent implementations of the simulation algorithm, cross-classified by each of the ten prespecified values of p and k. Beyond random simulation noise, which would disappear if J increased to infinity, the four figures differ only in the baseline belief distributions selected from Table 4.1 in Step 1 of the simulation algorithm.

For each of the surface plots of $\Pr(E = 1)$, the right-horizontal axis is the

Prefigurative Commitment

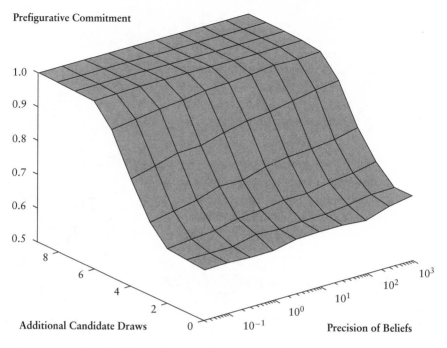

Figure 4.6.   Simulated Values of Prefigurative Commitment for Small Returns to Choosing the Decision Go to College

precision of beliefs, p, scaled logarithmically. The left-horizontal axis is the additional number of candidate draws, k. Moreover, the fourth contour line (when counting along the left-horizontal axis) corresponds to the set of simulations where students make three total additional draws beyond the four requisite draws. This set of simulations corresponds to my reading of Simon's claim that individuals can store only seven chunks of information in short-term memory. Finally, the vertical axis is $\Pr(E = 1)$, scaled from the baseline value of .5 to its maximum of 1.

Three robust patterns emerge from inspection of the figures:

1.   At all 100 points of direct comparison, the surface in Figure 4.5 is either lower than or no higher than the surfaces in Figures 4.6, 4.7, and 4.8. Likewise, the surface in Figure 4.6 is either lower than or no higher than the surfaces in Figures 4.7 and 4.8, and so on. This pattern suggests that $\Pr(E = 1)$ increases as returns to entering college increase, though only weakly so, since $\Pr(E = 1)$ attains its upper bound for a sufficiently large value of k in each of the figures. In particular, as shown in the last row of Table 4.1, the implied ex-

Prefigurative Commitment

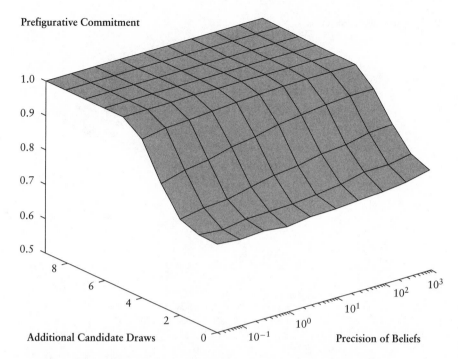

Figure 4.7.   Simulated Values of Prefigurative Commitment for Large Returns to Choosing Go to College

pected gain in probability of capturing High instead of Low when choosing to enter college increases from .056, to .167, .245, and .578 across Figures 4.5 through 4.8. This shift in the expected returns to entering college increases $Pr(E = 1)$ until it reaches its maximum of 1 where it then remains.

2. As shown in all four surfaces, $Pr(E = 1)$ increases with the precision of beliefs, though again, only weakly so since it cannot exceed its upper bound of 1. Increases in the precision of beliefs are equivalent to decreases in the variances of belief distributions. For example, for Figure 4.5, the belief distribution for α is stipulated to be a $Beta(p \times 1.5, p \times 1)$, where p increases from .0316 to 1,000. Accordingly, the belief distribution for α goes from a $Beta(.0474, .0316)$ to a $Beta(1,500, 1,000)$ along the right-horizontal axis of Figure 4.5. This change is analogous to dramatically increasing the amount of information available to an individual without changing the distribution of that information. Thus, the mean of the belief distribution for α remains fixed at .6 while the variance of the belief distribution for α declines from .222 to .000096. Over all four figures, $Pr(E = 1)$ increases weakly in p because the mean candidate draws generated in Step 3 of the simulation algorithm approach the true means of the belief distributions, which themselves imply (to varying degrees)

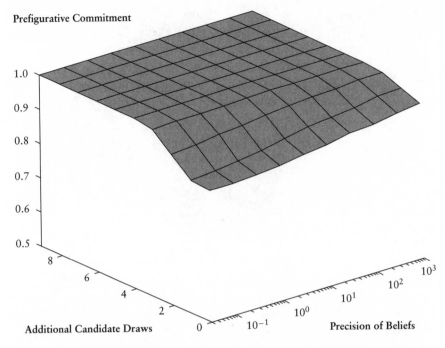

Figure 4.8.   Simulated Values of Prefigurative Commitment for Very Large Returns to Choosing the Decision Go to College

that entering college is in each student's future best interest. In particular, for Figures 4.5 through 4.8 respectively, and with k equal to 0, $\Pr(E = 1)$ increases from .5328 to .5619, .6465 to .6921, .7540 to .7905, and .8845 to .9534 as p increases from .0316 to 1,000. Similarly, for k equal to 3, $\Pr(E = 1)$ increases from .5698 to .5878, .7127 to .8182, .8571 to .9258, and .9905 to .9995.

3.   As shown for all four surfaces, $\Pr(E = 1)$ increases with constant increases in the effort expended to analyze information, in particular the number of total candidate values drawn for construction of a candidate decision tree, $\{\pi', \alpha', \beta', \gamma'\}$. For each surface, simulated values of $\Pr(E = 1)$ increase as k increases from 0 to 9 (and hence the total number of candidate draws increases from 4 to 13) until $\Pr(E = 1)$ reaches the upper bound of 1. For all four figures, the simulated value of $\Pr(E = 1)$ is equal to 1 when k is equal to 9. But, as shown across the figures, the rate at which $\Pr(E = 1)$ approaches 1 in k is a function of both the precision of beliefs and the returns to entering college.

General analytic implications.   The patterns revealed in the simulations suggest the following proposition.

PROPOSITION 2—*Informed Beliefs.* Suppose that Assumptions A1 through A6 hold and that all students share the same utility function. If students have informed belief distributions, prefigurative commitment to the course of action with the largest implied expected utility is

(A) increasing (or nondecreasing) in the common precision of all beliefs,

(B) increasing (or nondecreasing) in the common amount of effort expended to analyze all beliefs, and

(C) increasing (or nondecreasing) in the implied expected utility gain for choosing the action.

Proof Sketch for Proposition 2. Consider a stochastic decision tree with same structure as the decision tree in Figure 4.2, and scale students' utility functions so that the utility of High equals 1 and the utility of Low equals 0, regardless of the path taken through the decision tree.

Proof sketch for part (a):

For mean preserving and proportional increases in the precision of all beliefs (that is, increases in p in the simulations above), $\text{Var}[\pi]$, $\text{Var}[\alpha]$, $\text{Var}[\beta]$, and $\text{Var}[\gamma]$ decline while $E[\pi]$, $E[\alpha]$, $E[\beta]$, and $E[\gamma]$ remain fixed. Because the mean is an efficient estimator of the expectation of a random variable, the expected variance of each element of $\{\pi', \alpha', \beta', \gamma'\}$ is declining, respectively, in the precision of each of the belief distributions for π, α, β, and γ. Thus, as precision increases by the same constant multiple across all four belief distributions, $\text{Var}[\pi'\alpha' + (1 - \pi')\beta']$ and $\text{Var}[\gamma']$ approach 0 and the amount by which any individual's $\pi'\alpha' + (1 - \pi')\beta'$ and γ' differ from $E[\pi\alpha + (1 - \pi)\beta]$ and $E[\gamma]$, respectively, becomes arbitrarily small. Accordingly, if $E[\pi]E[\alpha] + (1 - E[\pi])E[\beta] > E[\gamma]$, then $\Pr[\pi'\alpha' + (1 - \pi')\beta' > \gamma']$ and $\Pr(E = 1)$ go to 1 as beliefs increase in precision.

Proof sketch for part (b):

Given a set of fixed, nondegenerate belief distributions (that is, $E[\pi]$, $E[\alpha]$, $E[\beta]$, and $E[\gamma]$ are constant and where $\text{Var}[\pi]$, $\text{Var}[\alpha]$, $\text{Var}[\beta]$, and $\text{Var}[\gamma]$ are strictly positive and constant), the law of large numbers implies that the expected variance of each element of $\{\pi', \alpha', \beta', \gamma'\}$ is declining in the expected number of candidate draws for each parameter (which equals $1 + k/4$ in the simulations earlier). As the average number of candidate draws increases for each individual, the amount by which any individual's $\pi'\alpha' + (1 - \pi')\beta'$ and γ' differ from $E[\pi\alpha + (1 - \pi)\beta]$ and $E[\gamma]$, respectively, becomes arbitrarily small. Accordingly, if $E[\pi]E[\alpha] + (1 - E[\pi])E[\beta] > E[\gamma]$, then $\Pr[\pi'\alpha' + (1 - \pi')\beta' > \gamma']$ and $\Pr(E = 1)$ go to 1 as the total number of random candidate draws increases.

Proof sketch for part (c):

By the linearity of expected utility theory, if $E[\pi]$ remains fixed, then $E[\pi\alpha + (1 - \pi)\beta]$ is increasing in both $E[\alpha]$ and $E[\beta]$. Accordingly, any increase in $E[\alpha]$ or $E[\beta]$ relative $E[\gamma]$ will increase both $E[\pi\alpha + (1 - \pi)\beta]$ and $\Pr[\pi'\alpha' + (1 -$

$\pi')\beta' > \gamma']$ for all candidate decision trees. Likewise, if $E[\alpha]$ is greater than $E[\beta]$ and both remain fixed, then any increase in $E[\pi]$ will increase both $E[\pi\alpha + (1 - \pi)\beta]$ and $Pr[\pi'\alpha' + (1 - \pi')\beta' > \gamma']$, and so on. For all similar shifts in the expectations of belief distributions, $Pr(E = 1)$ goes to 1 as $\{E[\pi]E[\alpha] + (1 - E[\pi])E[\beta]\} - \{E[\gamma]\}$ increases. Moreover, the rate at which $Pr(E = 1)$ goes to 1 is a direct function of both the average precision of beliefs and the amount of effort expended to analyze beliefs, as shown in the proof sketches of parts (a) and (b) above.

Similarly structured proof sketches can be generated for all decision trees, since the efficiency of the mean as an estimator, the law of large numbers, and the linearity of expected utility theory remain valid for all decision trees. But, if students do not share the same utility function, then Proposition 2 holds only within strata of students who share the same utility function, although a conditional version of Proposition 2 could be offered taking exogenous utility differences into account.

The following four qualifications to Proposition 2 demonstrate the flexibility of the framework:

1. Although part (a) of Proposition 2 claims that prefigurative commitment is increasing in common increases in the precision of all component belief distributions, uneven increases in precision across different belief distributions will not necessarily increase prefigurative commitment. For example, if $E[\pi]E[\alpha] + (1 - E[\pi])E[\beta] > E[\gamma]$, and if the moments of the belief distributions for π, α, and β remain fixed, $Pr(E = 1)$ may be non-decreasing in the precision of the belief distribution for γ. Thus, the underlying analytic structure implied by Assumptions A1 through A6 is more general than the simple Proposition 2 implies. The gross effect of precision of beliefs on prefigurative and preparatory commitment is a function of both the amount and the distribution of imprecision across belief distributions for the branches of a stochastic decision tree, and hence part (a) of Proposition 2 holds only for common increases in precision, p, across all of the component belief distributions. Accordingly, one should not conclude from the arguments above that in order to effectively model prefigurative commitment, all one needs to do is add another term for uncertainty to a generic linear expected utility model (essentially, by building more concavity into the expected utility calculation of choosing to enter college in the backward induction process). As will be shown explicitly in Chapter 5, the relative distribution of precision across the stochastic decision tree is the relevant determinant.

2. As for the first qualification, if analysis effort is not evenly distributed across each of the component belief distributions (that is, if the distribution of effort specified by the multinomial distribution in Step 2A of the simulation algorithm instead assigned different probability mass to additional draws from

alternative beliefs distributions), then prefigurative commitment is not necessarily increasing in the total amount of analysis effort enacted by a decision maker. The gross effect of analysis effort on prefigurative and preparatory commitment is a function of both the amount and the distribution of effort across belief distributions, and hence part (b) of Proposition 2 holds only for common increases in analysis effort across all of the component belief distributions.

3. When the belief distribution for π is formed by simple backward induction, as in the simulations above, $E[\pi]$ will remain fixed only if the distribution of information across α and β remains constant (as is the case only for Figures 4.5, 4.7, and 4.8). Since this may not necessarily be the case, movements of $E[\pi]$, $E[\alpha]$, and $E[\beta]$ in response to shifts in the distribution of payoff models must be tracked simultaneously. Likewise, as discussed in the concluding section to the article, the belief distributions for intermediate lotteries of a stochastic decision tree, such as π, may be entirely independent of the belief distributions for lottery parameters further down the tree, such as α and β. As will be shown in Chapter 5, belief distributions about different stages of the educational attainment process, for many students, would not be entirely independent. Labor market models, for example, are also college graduation and non-graduation models. But, since students may look at relatively young college graduates and non–college graduates (and think about the futures of peers whom they expect to be college graduates and non–college graduates), they most likely form belief distributions for π based on observations of individuals who have not received payoffs in the labor market, or whose lifetime payoffs are unknown.

4. Proposition 2 suggests that $\Pr(E = 1)$ will not reach 1 if k is sufficiently small and the mass of the belief distributions for π, α, β, and γ continue to overlap. This indirect implication in turn implies that for any set of overlapping belief distributions, a low enough level of analysis effort exists that decision makers could enact such that prefigurative commitment would not be universally and maximally intensive. And this claim holds no matter how strongly the distribution of available information suggests that a future course of behavior is in an individual's best interest, as long as belief distributions overlap.

Taken together, the simulations and the analytic implications that are responsible for producing them demonstrate that when the uncertainty of beliefs is allowed to explicitly enter a decision evaluation, preparatory commitment to a future course of behavior such as college entry is sensitive to the amount and type of uncertainty in one's beliefs as well as the effort expended to analyze those beliefs. Thus, even in a world where the returns on investments in higher education are massive, if beliefs are the least bit uncertain, and if students have limited information processing and analysis capacities, some high school students some of the time will perceive it to be in their future best interest to forego a college education. In these episodic and contrarian instances, they will adjust their current behavior accordingly. Since final levels of well-being are a function of preparation for college, even among those who ultimately do not attend college, such information-induced behavioral orientations in high school are important considerations, both for models narrowly concerned with educational achievement in high school, but also for models of the effects of college education on life course outcomes.

CONCLUSIONS

I have proposed in this chapter a stochastic decision tree model of commitment for analyzing preparatory commitment among adolescents toward the future course of behavior "Go to college." Alongside a set of simulations and analytic results, I have argued that students' prefigurative and preparatory commitment are functions of how clearly their stochastic decision trees identify a preferred course of future action. In particular, students whose beliefs are based on abundant information are more likely to clearly identify and then commit to a favored course of action. A primary implication of the framework is that individuals with accurate but sparse information on the potential benefits of a college education may not prepare themselves adequately to attain what they suspect is in their best interest. And even if they do enter college, they may not be well positioned to harvest all of the returns of having made such a utility-maximizing decision because of a lack of prior preparation.

Before turning to belief formation processes in Chapter 5 and then developing elaborations of the model that allow for the incorporation of normative and imitative sources of prefigurative commitment in Chapter 6, I conclude this chapter with some indirect but context-appropriate evidence for the adoption and further development of the stochastic decision tree model.

When seen as a cognitive attachment, prefigurative commitment shares essential features with the concept of an attitude in the social psychology literature. Attitudes toward an object, which can be a type of behavior, are a function of (1) an individual's positive and negative evaluations of possible component characteristics of the object and (2) probability judgments of whether each component characteristic is genuinely reflective of the object. Numerous studies show that individuals who lack information are unable to maintain strong probabilistic judgments and are more likely to have ambivalent attitudes (see Eagley and Chaiken 1998). This literature is broadly supportive of the claim that prefigurative commitment is a joint function of the accuracy and amount of available information (see also Davidson 1995; Petty and Krosnick 1995).

Despite this general evidence, the suitability of the framework must be evaluated for each domain in which it is invoked. For preparatory commitment to the course of action "Go to college," there is some relevant evidence. Educational expectations—answers to questions such as "How far in school do you think you will get?"—represent the only commonly available measure of students' subjective beliefs about their future educational attainments. Morgan (1998) presents trend lines for the family-background-adjusted educational expectations of high school seniors from 1976 to 1990 and trend lines for the same years of the rate of return on years of educational attainment for young labor market participants. Across race, sex, and time, educational expectations roughly trace the same pattern as rates of return, lending some support to the assumption that students form attachments to levels of educational attainment that they would judge to be in their best interest. Albeit weakly, these patterns support the contention that prefigurative commitment is a function of the labor market returns that contribute to plausible belief distributions for parameters such as α, β, and γ of the specific stochastic decision tree considered in this chapter and hence support for part (c) of Proposition 2.[23]

If prefigurative commitment is a function of precision of beliefs, and if educational attainment is a function of prefigurative commitment by way of preparatory commitment, then there should be negative correlations between perceived uncertainty during adolescence and forecasts of future educational attainment as well as educational attainment as an adult. It can be shown with many data sources, such as the *High School & Beyond Survey*, that internal locus of control (Rotter 1982[1966]) is positively related to both educational expectations and educational attainment. Such correlations provide some indirect support for the assertion that ceteris paribus prefigurative commitment is a function of precision of beliefs and that these effects may propagate through levels of preparatory commitment all the way to educational attainment and eventual labor market position.

Finally, there is also some indirect evidence that preparatory commitment may be a function ceteris paribus of precision of beliefs, if it is the case that increases in the amount of available information increase the precision of beliefs. First, Morgan and Sørensen (1999) present evidence that mathematics achievement among high school students is positively related to the network connections of a school community to independent sources of information, as proxied by the number of connections parents have to adults outside of the school community. Such network bridges generate horizon-expanding environments that have the potential to increase student effort and preparatory commitment to the utility-maximizing future course of behavior "Go to college."

Second, Kane (2001) shows, from a sample of Boston area high school students, that central city students and suburban students exhibit different levels of what I would label preparatory commitment. The suburban students were nearly three times as likely to have taken either the SAT or ACT, and were twice as likely to have applied to college in the fall of their senior year. And yet, both types of students appear to have the same beliefs, on average, about the costs and benefits of college. Both groups overestimated the direct costs of college, and, on average, both groups overestimated the labor market benefits of completing college (see discussion earlier in Chapter 2). The earnings expectations are perhaps telling and supportive of the stochastic decision tree model. Comparing median responses for earnings expectations at age 25, city students expected a gain of $21,100 (from $28,900 to $50,000 per year). For suburban students, the medians were almost identical suggesting a gain of $20,000 (from $30,000 to $50,000 per year). Kane (2001) estimated that in the local labor market, the true earnings difference was only about $10,000, from $23,000 to $33,000.

But, there was one important difference, which, at the population level, is akin to the difference in the precision of beliefs that drives commitment differences in the simulations reported earlier. For city students, the tenth percentile for earnings expectations after completing college was $20,000 while for suburban students it was $30,000.[24] In short, about the worst that suburban students expected they could do following college graduation was to receive the typical earnings of a high school graduate. And yet, some city students apparently felt that it was conceivable that, even if they completed college, they might earn less than the typical high school graduate. Such crossover in beliefs about the payoffs to alternative trajectories through the educational system, according to the stochastic decision tree model developed in this chapter, leads to lower levels of preparatory commitment for enrolling in college.

The next step in developing the stochastic decision tree model is to specify explicit mechanisms of belief formation and belief revision that are responsive to information differences. In constructing models of belief formation in Chapter 5, I will argue that one first must declare that the traditional belief formation and belief revision mechanisms based on Bayes' theorem are the gold standard for such processes (which is the implicit assumption beneath the belief construction procedures detailed in the descriptions of the simulations of this chapter).

NOTES

1. As shown in Morgan (2002), the framework itself is quite general and can be used to model preparatory commitment to alternative courses of action for all non-repeatable decisions with outcomes that are properly seen by decision makers as uncertain (i.e., decisions for which no direct learning-by-doing is possible and for which payoffs are generated by an independent and only partly observable stochastic process).

2. My concepts of prefigurative and preparatory commitment differ from the sort of forward-looking strategies for guaranteeing self-control and overcoming weakness of will which, in the work of Elster and others (see Elster 1984, 2000), have acquired the label of precommitments. Rather, my notion of commitment resonates with an older sociological tradition, as best exemplified by Parsons' notion of "the transition from acceptance to commitment" (Parsons 1951:332). For the college choice example, I maintain that accepting the simple guide for action, based on an accurate set of beliefs, that obtaining a college degree may be in one's future best interest does not also imply that one will exhibit the commitment necessary to realize what is known to be in one's future best interest.

3. See the automatization mechanism in Wegner and Bargh (1998:465).

4. Recall the extended quotation from Haller (1982), which is quite similar to this definition. I merely wish to allow for more flexibility than does Haller.

5. Although I abandon such elegance for genuine modeling reasons, it is worth noting that some of the pioneers of discrete choice analysis are also finding good and very general justifications for relaxing these foundational assumptions (see McFadden 1999, 2001).

6. Although seemingly very limited, this setup of the alternative returns to different pathways through the educational system is actually very general. One could

easily add intermediate destinations, such as "Middle." Or one could replace High, Low, and the associated success parameters α, β, and γ with rankings on a separate continuous distribution of rewards. This distribution could be an optimally weighted joint distribution of discounted lifetime earnings, nonmonetary rewards of jobs (as, for example, captured by the index of job desirability of Jencks, Perman, and Rainwater 1988), and general status and quality of life gains associated with increases in educational certification. In this case, rather than maintaining different values for α, β, and γ, one would allow the quantiles of the outcome distribution to vary across the three pathways (and, in line with the following argument, base expected utility calculations on three different expected values of the continuous distribution function of rewards).

7. Keep in mind that this is a model of decision making and thus precedes the behavior that it models. The parameter π is not, for example, the conditional probability of completing college among those who actually enroll in college. Rather, π is the subjective belief that each individual—including those who ultimately choose to forego college—maintains for his or her own personal probability of graduation from college if initially enrolled.

8. Although not explicitly addressed in this presentation, I do not wish to exclude the possibility that option values (as for the college choice example was first modeled by Weisbrod 1962 and Comay, Melnik, and Pollatschek 1973) could be embedded in the utility function explicitly (i.e., by including components above and beyond the valuation of High versus Low) or could be factored into the means of belief distributions about the final-stage lottery parameters. The first type of modification would prevent the simple elimination of the utility function as I move from Equation 4.1a to Equation 4.1b, but it would not otherwise complicate analysis. The second form of revision, which I would prefer, does not change the model in any fundamental way, other than changing the meaning of High and Low (which are nothing other than nominal labels in any case).

9. As shown below, the stochastic decision tree model that I propose yields nontrivial predictions even in such cases.

10. There is a hidden assumption here as well. In order for individuals to have accurate beliefs about the parameters of a decision tree, it must also be the case that their decision trees are accurate representations of the real-life set of lotteries that they will face. Thus, there can be no branching points that are ignored for the sake of simplicity (or that cannot be integrated out by collapsing an option into a relevant parameter for a prior branching point).

11. This restriction is not unique to the model of Breen and Goldthorpe (1997). Manski (1989) builds a model on top of the same restriction.

12. This assumption is not related to the assumption of aversion to uncertainty that many rational choice analyses of risk maintain.

13. Breen and Goldthorpe propose slightly different alternative decision rules based on the odds of staying over leaving.

14. In the final portion of their argument, Breen and Goldthorpe then make

the assumption that the primary effect of Boudon (1974) operates (i.e., students from lower social backgrounds have lower ability and fewer resources) so that while there are no class differences in α, β, and γ, there are important class differences in π. Not surprisingly, their model shows that the greater propensity of students from the service class to stay on in school increases as the (accurately perceived) difference in π across the service and working classes increases.

15. Pioneering rational choice theorists were aware that beliefs are important (since utility functions are merely functions of component beliefs), but they became convinced that it is prohibitively difficult to measure individuals' beliefs. Axioms of revealed preference were thus regarded as tremendous breakthroughs, since decisions could be analyzed by observing behavior without having to look inside actors' heads.

16. The payoff distributions for each decision may indeed cross the threshold, if one also assumes a stochastic component to the choice function.

17. I see no reason at this point of theoretical development of the proposed model to entirely abandon expected utility theory in favor of prospect theory (Kahneman and Tversky 1979), any of its subtle variants (see Camerer 1995), or aspiration adaptation theory (Selten 2001). Such drastic modifications may be called for in the future, but for now only modest departures from orthodox statistical decision theory suffice.

18. Related stochastic utility and random preference models have been proposed in economics and psychology, (see Becker, DeGroot, Marschak 1963; Hey and Orme 1994; Loomes and Sugden 1995; Machina 1985). The main idea of this literature is that disturbance terms should be added to core fixed utility functions so that observed choices can be modeled as a function of errors in preferences, broadly construed. None of the proposed models are concerned with forecasts of a decision yet to be made, and hence with the idea that preparatory commitment is a function of the clarity of forecasts of the future. And thus, although they are related to my proposals, they have no straightforward connection with my stochastic decision tree model of commitment.

19. I take a very broad definition of information. It includes more than just the amount of exogenous information available about the opportunity structure, as it also includes information about one's future behavior. For the latter, consider two students. One is absolutely certain that she will take trigonometry, and the other is, for any number of reasons, less certain of whether or not she will take trigonometry. I would argue that, for a variety of reasons, the first student is likely to have more certain beliefs about the payoff to college than the second student.

20. In this setup, prefigurative commitment is to the course of behavior "Go to college." But, since an increase in prefigurative commitment to the course of behavior "Go" is exactly equivalent to a decrease in prefigurative commitment to the course of behavior "Do not go," one could obtain the same results offered below by flipping around the parameterizations and modeling prefigurative commitment to the course of behavior "Do not go."

21. More generally, students recognize that their stochastic decision trees are rough approximations to the future lotteries to which they will be subjected. Moreover, most students likely believe that each preparatory commitment decision is, in isolation, relatively unimportant. For both of these reasons, the opportunity costs of exerting heroic levels of computational power to formulate and then rigorously evaluate the most fine-grained decision tree possible are simply too high.

22. I will continue to assume that utility functions and beliefs are so finely calibrated that no ties occur in the process of evaluating decision rules. Hence, I use strict inequalities for all decision rules, as is also the case for the college choice example analyzed by Manski and Wise (1983). Using weak inequalities and allowing for ties would merely force trivial modifications to the propositions and simulations.

23. That educational expectations are always shown to be a function of test scores supports the contention that prefigurative commitment is also a function of at least the mean of the belief distributions for π.

24. Likewise, the 25th percentile was $30,000 for city students versus $40,000 for suburban students. In contrast, the 75th and 90th percentiles were virtually identical ($67,500 versus $70,000 and $100,000 versus $100,000).

CHAPTER FIVE

The Evolution of the Beliefs
That Determine Commitment

How do forward-looking beliefs, including forecasts of one's own future behavior, condition current behavior? In Chapter 3, I argued that observed
educational expectations may have a causal effect on educational attainment
if they are imperfect forecasts of one's own future behavior. And yet, so little
information is available on how educational expectations are formed, this
claim cannot be substantiated. In order to move forward and collect better
data, sociologists need to develop theoretical mechanisms of belief formation and belief revision that can be called on to guide this pressing agenda.

In Chapter 4, I laid down the basic structure of a new set of theoretical
mechanisms for modeling educational attainment. However, in order to focus on the structure of the proposed stochastic decision tree, I simply asserted that belief distributions exist and then used simulations to examine
the consequences of differences in the precision of beliefs on short-run prefigurative and preparatory commitment toward alternative consequential future courses of action. In this chapter, I take a step backward and develop
plausible mechanisms for belief formation and belief revision processes.

The mechanisms I will propose are based on Bayesian learning theory.[1]
Before introducing these mechanisms, I will present Bayes' theorem and demonstrate its usefulness in settings other than educational attainment. The rhe-
torical strategy of the first section is to present belief formation and revision
for an example that is familiar to academic researchers: To which journal
should I submit my manuscript? This strategy is a thinly veiled attempt to
convince the reader that Bayesian learning is a plausible representation of
how people form and revise beliefs about courses of action that are important to them. I will then move on to a canonical example from the literature,

139

invoking a fictitious casino visitor. Finally, I will offer the conjecture that high school students implicitly invoke similar mechanisms when combining their prior beliefs with new information about the structure of educational and occupational opportunity that they confront in their futures.

In the second section, I will present simple Bayesian learning for a stochastic decision tree and use numerical simulations to demonstrate how such learning may vary across types of students. Although the initial simulations will focus on the processing of accurate information, I will then introduce inaccurate information into the framework.

A BENCHMARK FOR BELIEF REVISION: BAYES' THEOREM

Bayesian learning theory is an application and extension of the classical rules of conditional probability to the forecasting of parameters that are crucial for making a decision in the presence of uncertainty. Readers who are already well acquainted with Bayes' theorem can skip ahead to the next section with little consequence.

Consider two sets of mutually exclusive and collectively exhaustive events, $\{A_1, A_2, \ldots, A_n\}$ and $\{B, \neg B\}$ over the same total probability space. If the event B occurs (rather than $\neg B$), the fundamental rule of conditional probability:

$$Pr(A_i, B) = Pr(A_i \mid B)Pr(B) = Pr(B \mid A_i)Pr(A_i) \qquad (5.1)$$

gives two ways to calculate the probability that any of the events A_i occurs along with B: (1) multiply the probability that A_i occurs when B occurs by the probability that B occurs, or (2) multiply the probability that B occurs when A_i occurs by the probability that A_i occurs. Nominally, Bayes' theorem is simply a reorganization of the last two terms of Equation 5.1, such that:

$$Pr(A_i \mid B) = \frac{Pr(B \mid A_i)Pr(A_i)}{Pr(B)} = \frac{Pr(B \mid A_i)Pr(A_i)}{\sum_{i=1}^{n} Pr(B \mid A_i)Pr(A_i)} \qquad (5.2)$$

where, as shown in the third expression, $Pr(B)$ is calculated by summing its conditional probabilities, $Pr(B \mid A_i)$, in proportion to the probability distribution of the conditioning events, $Pr(A_i)$.

For a Bayesian analyst, the preference for Equation 5.2 over Equation 5.1 is twofold. First, the fundamental assumption of Bayesian decision theory is that it is easier to formulate and analyze beliefs if they are encoded in conditional and unconditional probability statements rather than joint probability statements.[2] Second, if one wants to analyze how the occurrence of B affects the probable occurrence of one or more events A_i, then one can usually simplify calculations by ignoring the denominator of Equation 5.2, recognizing that $\Pr(A_i|B)$ is proportional to $\Pr(B|A_i)$ times $\Pr(A_i)$.

Bayesian Updating of Probabilities for Discrete Events

Consider the example depicted in Table 5.1 where a young sociologist attempts to decide whether to submit a manuscript for review to a prestigious general sociology journal or instead to a specialized sociology journal (that is, a high-quality journal that, by virtue of its smaller circulation, is a less prestigious venue for one's research). The young sociologist has published several articles in the specialized journal, comparable in quality to the manuscript she now must decide where to submit. As a result, she feels confident that she can get her article published in the specialized journal. However, since she wants the article to be published soon, she must decide whether it is worth her effort, and the potential time delay to publication, by first trying to get the article published in the more prestigious general journal. The decision she directly contemplates is whether to submit the article for review to the general journal.

The American Sociological Association publishes manuscript acceptance rates every year for the general journal and these figures are fairly consistent across years. They indicate that only about 15 percent of initial submissions to the general journal are eventually published there. Because the young sociologist sometimes reviews articles for the journal, she knows well how bad some of the submissions to the journal are. As a result, she decides that her chances of acceptance are better than those of the typical submission. Through some introspection, she decides that the probability is .05 that her article will be immediately accepted, subject only to a few revisions in order to satisfy the editor. (The event D in the probability statements in Table 5.1 represents the eventual editorial decision.) Through further introspection, she estimates that the probability is .35 that she will be invited to resubmit a revised manuscript for further review. However, she feels that ultimately if asked to resubmit the paper, she would be more likely than not to eventually receive an editorial decision of acceptance. Thus, she decides that the probability that her manuscript will be accepted after navigating the revise-and-resubmit process is .25 (while the probability that it will

TABLE 5.1

Using Bayes' Theorem to Decide Whether to Submit
an Article to a General or Specialized Sociology Journal

Possible Outcomes of Submitting to General Journal	PRIOR PROBABILITY FOR THE EDITOR'S DECISION $\Pr(D)$	CONDITIONAL PROBABILITIES THAT A COLLEAGUE WILL RECOMMEND SUBMISSION TO THE GENERAL JOURNAL GIVEN THE EDITOR'S EVENTUAL DECISION			POSTERIOR PROBABILITY FOR THE EDITOR'S DECISION $\hat{\Pr}(D) = \dfrac{\Pr(R = y \mid D)\Pr(D)}{\Pr(R = y)}$
		$\Pr(R = y \mid D)$	$\Pr(R = n \mid D)$	$\Pr(R = y \mid D)\Pr(D)$	
Immediate acceptance	.05	.40	.60	.02	$.02/.26 = .077$
Eventual acceptance	.25	.40	.60	.10	$.10/.26 = .385$
Immediate or eventual rejection	.70	.20	.80	.14	$.14/.26 = .538$

ultimately be rejected through the same process is .1). Finally, by subtracting from 1 these three probabilities of .05, .25, and .1, she recognizes that she has implicitly estimated the probability that her manuscript will be immediately rejected as .6. She considers this a reasonable value, for there is a good possibility that the referees and the editor will jointly decide that the article is not of general interest to the discipline, regardless of any thoughtful judgment of its merit. Adding this probability to her estimated probability of .1 for rejection via the revise-and-resubmit process, she notes that her prior probabilities for the three editorial decisions, as displayed in the first column of Table 5.1, are .05 for immediate acceptance, .25 for eventual acceptance, and .7 for immediate or eventual rejection.

Because she intends to ask a senior colleague for comments on the manuscript anyway, she decides to ask her colleague to also indicate whether she should submit the manuscript to the prestigious general sociology journal. The senior colleague has served on the editorial board of the general journal and is therefore more familiar with the process of editorial decision making. The author, from past experience and from talking to other colleagues about the judgment of the senior colleague, formulates the conditional probabilities in the second and third columns of Table 5.1. She estimates that, if the article is destined to be accepted (either immediately or via the revise-and-resubmit process), then the probability that the colleague will recommend submission to the general journal is .4. And, if the article is destined for either immediate or eventual rejection then the probability that the colleague will recommend submission is only .2.

One can think of these conditional probabilities as long-run averages of the past behavior of the colleague and thus as an indication of the colleague's wisdom and expertise. For example, of all the articles that in the past the colleague was asked by various junior colleagues to judge and which were eventually accepted, the senior colleague gave the right advice 40 percent of the time. However, among those manuscripts that were immediately or eventually rejected, the senior colleague gave the right advice 80 percent of the time. Clearly, even for a senior colleague, it is much easier to predict rejections than acceptances for the prestigious general journal.

Now suppose that the senior colleague suggests to the young sociologist that she should submit the manuscript to the general journal. How should she revise her prior beliefs about the probability of acceptance in order to take account of the judgment of her colleague? Bayes' theorem provides the optimal answer to this question. First, she should multiply the estimated conditional probability of the senior colleague's recommendation to submit the manuscript, $Pr(R = y \mid D)$, by her prior probability of the conditioning event, $Pr(D)$. Having obtained the three numbers in the fourth column of Table 5.1, she then follows the division operation indicated in Equation 5.2. She divides each of the three numbers, $Pr(R = y \mid D)Pr(D)$, by the sum of all three, equal to $Pr(R = y)$, in order to obtain revised probabilities of the alternative editorial decisions that sum to 1.

As these final probabilities are conditioned on evidence, they are referred to as posterior probabilities to distinguish them from the prior probabilities maintained in advance of considering the evidence. The young sociologist's posterior belief about the probability of acceptance, conditional on the senior colleague's suggestion to submit the article to the general journal, is therefore .462 (that is, .077 + .385). She should still believe that it is more likely than not that her manuscript will be rejected, but she should have substantially more confidence in potential acceptance.[3]

There is one final point to be made for this example, in order to demonstrate why a decision maker is often justified in calculating only the numerator of Equation 5.2. If the young sociologist is only interested in knowing the relative likelihood that her manuscript will be accepted rather than rejected, she can skip the last step shown in Table 5.1 and instead calculate the odds of acceptance over rejection. For example, her prior odds of acceptance are $(.05 + .25)/.7 = .429$ whereas her posterior odds of acceptance are $(.02 + .10)/.14 = .857$.

No young sociologist would likely perform such a careful analysis of the chances that his or her manuscript would be accepted for publication in the *American Sociological Review*, although I suspect that some young statisticians and economists might do so for their flagship journals.[4] Nonetheless, sociologists do make submission decisions by estimating the likelihood that their manuscripts will be accepted by various journals. And in doing so, they take account of their prior experience with the relevant journals, publicly available information on typical acceptance rates, their judgments of the quality of their own work, the submission suggestions of their colleagues, and their knowledge of how their colleagues typically react to the manuscripts of other scholars.

If this is so, then sociologists implicitly invoke calculations such as those suggested by Bayes' theorem, even though they may not strictly obey the probability calculations. In practice, some sociologists may be unwilling to move as far away from their prior beliefs toward their colleagues' recommendations as Bayes' theorem requires. Nonetheless, Bayes' theorem gives a standard against which possible behavioral departures can be measured. In studying the ways in which students formulate beliefs about their potential futures and update them in response to new evidence, such a standard is needed, and I therefore propose to use Bayes' theorem in that context as well.

Bayesian Updating of Probabilities as Continuous Distributions

In Chapter 4, I introduced the beta distribution as a convenient distribution for parameters, such as probabilities, that are bounded by 0 and 1. As will now become apparent, I also chose the simple beta distribution to facilitate the presentation of Bayesian learning in this chapter.

As in Chapter 4, allow θ to be a random variable that is bounded by 0 and 1 so that it can represent a probability. Assume that θ has a nondegenerate distribution over the entire probability space (that is, is nowhere absolutely 0), and suppose θ is specified as a beta distributed random variable, denoted in the last chapter as a *Beta*(s, f) in Equation 4.3. In order to assess only the relative likelihood of different values of θ and to simplify calculations, ignore the constant of integration in Equation 4.3 and instead use the simpler unnormalized beta prior density function:

$$\Pr(\theta) \propto \theta^{s-1}(1 - \theta)^{f-1} \tag{5.3}$$

where the symbol $\propto$ is defined as "proportional to."

For a learning context, suppose that a relatively experienced gambler walks into a casino with \$1,000. Being the lucky 1,000th visitor of the day, the manager of the casino approaches the guest and gives her the opportunity to place a bet that the flip of his penny will yield Heads. The payoff is double or nothing, and the guest must bet at least \$500 but no more than \$1,000. However, the manager also indicates that the penny is fake. It is weighted so that when tossed it does not yield equal long-run frequencies of heads and tails. Fortunately, the manager will allow the guest to pay \$50 for the privilege of flipping the coin 10 times in order to help decide whether or not to place a bet on the single toss that will count. The guest decides to hand over the \$50 and give the penny a test run.

Because the casino is still in business, the guest assumes that the probability that the fake penny will yield heads is probably less than .5. Nonethe-

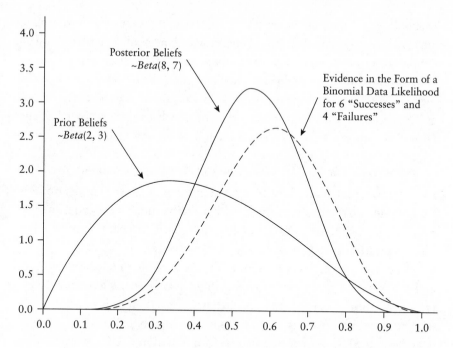

Figure 5.1. Updating a Beta Prior Distribution with a Binomial Data Likelihood

less, since the guest surmises that she is the celebrated 1,000th visitor of the day, she wonders whether perhaps the casino wants to produce a winner for publicity benefit. If the latter is the case, she concludes that the coin is likely rigged to guarantee a winner. Through further such introspection, she decides that her beliefs about the probability that the coin will yield Heads are adequately summarized by the *Beta*(2, 3) density presented in Figure 5.1. The mean, mode, and variance of this distribution are .4, .333, and .04, respectively. She is fairly uncertain of the true value of θ, but she is more pessimistic than not.

She flips the penny 10 times and obtains the sequence HHTHTHTHHT. Because the outcomes of the coin flips are independent events, she ignores the ordering and notes that the penny has come up Heads 6 times and Tails 4 times. In order to decide whether to place a bet on the next flip of the fake penny, she must now combine the evidence from her 10 experimental flips with her prior beliefs.

A naive gambler, given the 10 flips, would assume that the best possible guess that the true probability that the penny will yield Heads on the next toss is .6, and would then rely only on this value to determine whether the bet is worth taking. However, the lucky 1,000th visitor is more reasonable and recognizes that 10 flips are not very many test cases. As a result, in approaching the decision, she would likely be unwilling to completely let go of her prior beliefs. In particular, she would wonder, in light of the new but limited evidence, how likely it is that the true probability is still her initial best guess of .4 based on what she considers to be reasonable prior beliefs about the casino's reputation and past behavior.

In full form, Bayesian theory is a formalized set of rules that, subject to a set of foundational axioms (Savage 1954), guide a decision maker to (1) combine optimally one's prior beliefs and evidence in the form of data and then (2) use one's updated beliefs and preferences over outcomes in order to enact an optimal decision. Again, I will only describe the first process in this section, saving the second for later.

With a probability distribution of prior beliefs in hand, the decision maker must represent the 10 trials as a data likelihood that can be combined with the prior distribution. The appropriate probability distribution across success and failure of n independent coin flips (known more generally in statistical terminology as Bernoulli trials) is the two-parameter binomial distribution whose probability mass function is:

$$\Pr(y = 1, \ldots, n \mid \theta, n) = \frac{n!}{y!(n - y)!} \theta^y (1-\theta)^{n-y} \qquad (5.4)$$

where the fixed parameter θ is the probability of success and the fixed parameter n is the number of independent trials. The scaling factor $\frac{n!}{y!(n - y)!}$ ensures that probabilities of all possible sets of outcomes (that is, proportions of successes and failures across the n trials) sum to 1.

If θ is unknown, as in this case, but the gambler observes a set of outcomes from independent trials, she can form a data likelihood for θ by holding the parameters y and n fixed and allowing θ to take on a distribution over all values between 0 and 1. In the present context, the 10 flips of the fake penny can therefore be encoded in a binomial data likelihood with y and n fixed at 6 and 10 but with θ varying over its whole parameter space from 0 to 1, as shown by the dashed line in Figure 5.1.[5]

The maximum likelihood estimate of θ, $\hat{\theta}_{ml}$, is that value of θ between 0 and 1 that yields the largest value for the right-hand side of Equation 5.4. It is easy to see that $\hat{\theta}_{ml} = y/n$ for a binomial likelihood equation. However, other values of θ are still possible and not all of these other values are equally likely. The data likelihood implies that values such as .2 are very unlikely, but values such as .5 and .7 are only slightly less likely than the maximum likelihood estimate of .6.

According to Bayesian theory, the best estimate, from the perspective of the decision maker, of the true value of θ is not the simple maximum likelihood estimate of .6. Rather, the estimate of θ that the decision maker should most strongly rely on is the mean of a posterior distribution of beliefs that incorporates information from both the data likelihood and the distribution that represents her prior beliefs.[6]

From the formulation of Bayes' theorem in Equation 5.2, the posterior distribution is calculated by multiplying the prior distribution in Equation 4.3 by the data likelihood version of Equation 5.4, yielding a posterior probability distribution of θ:

$$\Pr(\theta) = \frac{\Gamma(s + f + n)}{\Gamma(s + y)\Gamma(f + n - y)}\theta^{s-1}(1 - \theta)^{f-1}\theta^{y}(1 - \theta)^{n-y}$$

The posterior distribution depends on the s and f parameters from the prior distribution and the y and n parameters from the data likelihood. Ignoring the scaling factor, the posterior can be rewritten and then simplified:

$$\Pr(\theta) \propto \theta^{s-1}(1 - \theta)^{f-1}\theta^{y}(1 - \theta)^{n-y}$$
$$\propto \theta^{s+y-1}(1 - \theta)^{f+n-y-1} \tag{5.5}$$

With reference to Equation 5.3, Equation 5.5 is easily recognizable as an unnormalized *Beta*$(s + y, f + n - y)$ distribution.

Applying the updating Equation 5.5 to the example at hand, if the casino visitor's prior beliefs are adequately summarized by a *Beta*$(2, 3)$ distribution as in Figure 5.1, then her posterior beliefs after observing 6 Heads and 4 Tails should be properly summarized by a *Beta*$(8, 7)$ distribution, also presented in Figure 5.1. This posterior distribution of beliefs about θ has mean, mode, and variance of .533, .539, and .0156. The mean of the posterior distribution of θ is a compromise between the mean of the prior distribution of .4 and the maximum likelihood estimate of .6 suggested by the data. Moreover, the variance of the posterior distribution is less than half of the variance of the prior distribution, indicating that the series of coin tosses has reduced the uncertainty of the visitor's beliefs.

If the axioms of decision theory are accepted, this compromise between the means and the narrowing of the variance is optimal, as determined by the relative amount of information contained in both the prior distribution and the data likelihood. If the visitor had been permitted to gather more information by flipping the coin 20 times, and if she had obtained the same proportions of Heads and Tails (that is, 12 Hs and 8 Ts in any order), then the mean, mode, and variance of the resulting *Beta*(14, 11) posterior distribution would be .560, .565, and .0095 respectively. The posterior distribution would be even more concentrated, and its mean would be weighted more toward the maximum likelihood estimate suggested by the data.[7]

This simple illustration of Bayesian updating of beliefs demonstrates its two main features: (1) the mean of a posterior distribution is an optimally weighted average of the mean of the prior distribution and the most likely value suggested by the observed data, and (2) the variance of the posterior distribution shrinks as more information is assumed in the prior distribution or observed and encoded in the data likelihood. The first point was clear from the journal submission example, but the latter point is more clear in this example. Figure 5.1 should provide the basic intuition, and the next variant on the same example should remove any lingering confusion.

Bayesian Updating with a Nonconjugate Prior Distribution

As presented above, the combination of the beta prior distribution with the binomial data likelihood shows how simple the calculations for Bayesian updating can be. Indeed, the updating process is so simple with the use of such closely related distributions that it is sometimes hard to see why Bayes' theorem is the justification for the multiplication performed in Equation 5.5. To show more clearly the connection to Bayes' theorem, consider the following variant on the casino example of last section.

Suppose that the casino manager informs the 1,000th visitor that the coin is weighted to yield Heads with either probability .3 or probability .6. Further assume that the visitor enacts the same process of introspection but arrives at the following probability mass function for her prior beliefs:

$$\Pr(\theta = .3) = .667$$
$$\Pr(\theta = .6) = .333$$
$$\Pr(\theta \neq .3 \text{ or } .6) = 0 \tag{5.6}$$

Notice that the mean of this distribution is .4 (that is, .667 × .3 + .333 × .6 = .4), thus matching the mean of the *Beta*(2, 3) distribution utilized above to represent prior beliefs with a continuous distribution.

After the casino visitor observes 6 Heads and 4 Tails, she must again form a posterior distribution for her beliefs. For this example, she need only consider the two possible values for θ stipulated by the casino manager, just as for her discrete prior distribution. She can form the posterior distribution for the two possible values of θ using Bayes' theorem in the same way as shown in Table 5.1:

$$\hat{Pr}(\theta = .3) = \frac{(.3)^6(1 - .3)^4(.667)}{(.3)^6(1 - .3)^4(.667) + (.6)^6(1 - .6)^4(.333)} = .227$$

$$\hat{Pr}(\theta = .6) = \frac{(.6)^6(1 - .6)^4(.333)}{(.3)^6(1 - .3)^4(.667) + (.6)^6(1 - .6)^4(.333)} = .773 \qquad (5.7)$$

Contrary to the beliefs encoded in her prior distribution, her beliefs that incorporate evidence favor the alternative hypothesis that θ is .6 and suggest that the bet may therefore be worth taking.[8]

As with the continuous distribution example presented last section, one can calculate the means and variances of the distributions to demonstrate that the posterior distribution is a compromise between the prior distribution and the data. The mean of the prior distribution is .4. In contrast, the mean of the posterior distribution is .532 and is thus shrunk toward .6. Indeed, it is almost exactly equivalent to the mean of the posterior in the continuous distribution example presented earlier. And, while the variance of the prior distribution is .01999, the variance of the posterior distribution is only .01840.[9]

Making a Decision in the Presence of Uncertainty

Bayesian decision theory is more than simply a set of rules for assessing uncertainty by combining prior information with newly acquired evidence. Rather, it is a complete framework for making a decision. In fact, Bayesian decision theory subsumes all of what is referred to as subjective expected utility theory in Chapter 4.

At this point, a detailed presentation of the full framework is of little benefit and can be found elsewhere (for example, Pratt, Raiffa, and Schlaifer 1995, Chapters 6 and 19; Chernoff and Moses 1959, Chapters 4 through 6).

In the remainder of this chapter and thereafter, I draw mostly on the belief revision mechanism of Bayesian decision theory that is presented in this section.[10]

BELIEF REVISION PROCESSES FOR THE PARAMETERS OF A STOCHASTIC DECISION TREE

I now turn to mechanisms of belief formation and belief revision, using the rules of conditional probability as expressed in Bayes' theorem. I will show how Bayesian updating can be used to specify plausible learning mechanisms for the parameters of the stochastic decision tree developed in the last chapter. Again, I will rely on numerical simulations to demonstrate the implications of the framework. Formal propositions could be developed, since the ideas introduced here are relatively simple extensions of Propositions 1 and 2 of Chapter 4 (and which follow directly from the four qualifications to the propositions detailed there). But, as will soon become obvious, such formalization of relatively simple results provides no new insight and can be easily managed by those readers inclined to extend the proof sketches of Chapter 4.

I will again adopt beta distributions to encode individuals' beliefs about the four parameters of the simple stochastic decision tree identified there: π, α, β, and γ. For this reason, the Bayesian learning depicted in Figure 5.1, where a beta prior distribution is updated with a binomial likelihood, is similar to the mechanism that I will now adopt for modeling the formation and revision of beliefs about the parameters of the stochastic decision tree.[11] Nonetheless, the core ideas of this chapter will hold under any set of probability distributions for arguments similar to those invoked for the proof sketches of the propositions in Chapter 4.

Uninformed Beliefs with No Subsequent Learning

Suppose that at some initial starting point students have virtually no information on the parameters of their stochastic decision trees. In this case, the belief distributions of the stochastic decision tree parameters could be defined as *Beta*(.01, .01) distributions. The density function of each distribution is U-shaped with spikes at 0 and 1, is symmetric, and has an expectation of .5. Such a distribution is a plausible representation of uninformed beliefs about the probability that a future event will be a success instead of a failure.[12]

Suppose that these uninformed students nonetheless attempt to analyze their stochastic decision trees as in Chapter 4.[13] They wish to set a level of prefigurative commitment that can then serve as a forward-looking guide to automate current everyday behavior. I will continue, in this chapter, to model this evaluation process as the selection of a value of either 1 or 0 for a variable E, where a 1 signifies an instantaneous prefigurative commitment to the future affirmative decision "Go to college" (for example, the choice Go in Figure 4.2). And, as in Chapter 4, I will continue to assume that students decide on the value of E by selecting candidate parameter values for their decision trees, averaging over these values to form a set of candidate point-value beliefs $\{\pi', \alpha', \beta', \gamma'\}$, and then evaluating the decision rule in Equation 4.1c. Accordingly, a student will again set E equal to 1 instead of 0 if and only if $\pi'\alpha' + (1 - \pi')\beta' > \gamma'$.

Finally, suppose that students' cognitive constraints are substantial, such that they typically draw only seven candidate parameter draws when evaluating their stochastic decision trees. This is equivalent to fixing k at three in the simulations reported in Chapter 4, which corresponds to my reading of Simon (1996) that individuals can store only approximately seven pieces of information in fast, short-term memory, which is where I assume inputs for an instantaneous evaluation of a stochastic decision tree must be stored as a decision rule is contemplated.

To set a baseline for no learning, using the basic simulation algorithm of Chapter 4, suppose that 10,000 students attempt to evaluate their stochastic decision trees over 100 points in time, but, for now, that over time they do not receive any new information. As a result, they maintain uninformed belief distributions, and, at all points in time, their belief distributions for π, α, β, and γ remain *Beta*(.01, .01) distributions. Under this scenario, the average level of prefigurative commitment, $\Pr(E = 1)$, will remain at .5 (or, in actuality, because of the strict inequality in Equation 4.1c, at a value just below .5). This simulated time path for $\Pr(E = 1)$ is presented as the bottom line in Figure 5.2, where the random fluctuation of $\Pr(E = 1)$ reflects the variation observed across the finite number of simulated students.

If students maintain uninformed belief distributions and hence do not rely on any information that suggests pursuing a college degree is either in their best interests or against their best interests, ceteris paribus they will simply choose with equal probability whether to engage in behavior that

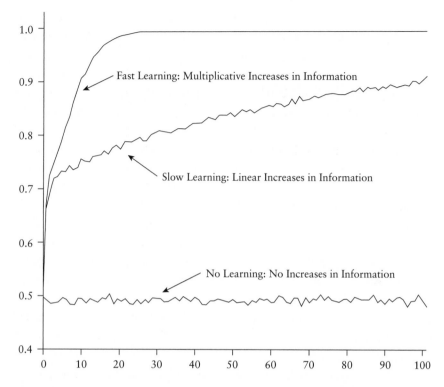

Figure 5.2.   The Evolution of Commitment in a Labor Market Where the Payoff to a College Education Is Large

prepares them for college instruction. As for Proposition 1 of Chapter 4, the baseline level of prefigurative commitment is one of almost complete indifference. And yet, in this case, the baseline is thought of as an initial state of beliefs before which any learning about the parameters of the decision tree has occurred. Individuals will move away from this baseline, in one direction or the other, only if their beliefs evolve in response to information that suggests college is in their best interests or is not.

The Processing of Accurate Information

Suppose now that students gradually process information from a labor market where there are high returns to obtaining a college degree. In particular, assume that the information distribution is the same as in the third column of Table 4.1, such that the expected value of obtaining a highly prestigious position in life increases substantially if one obtains a college degree. In particular, the expected increase in the probability of obtaining High instead of Low for the decision tree in Figure 4.2 is .245 for this assumed labor market. The parameters listed in the third column of Table 4.1 suggest that three out of every five college graduates would be observed in the position High instead of Low, whereas only one out of every four college dropouts and only one out of every five high school graduates would be observed in the position High instead of Low. If students had an abundance of information and unbounded abilities to analyze it, they would recognize that the best possible guesses for α, β, and γ are .6, .25, and .2.

Finally, assume that the true probability of graduating from college for each student is .556, which, again, as for the simulations of Chapter 4, is the mean of a *Beta*(5, 4) distribution. This distribution is the backward-induced belief distribution for π from the belief distributions for α and β, as specified in Step 1A of the simulation algorithm of Chapter 4. In this chapter, I will drop this constraint in some subsequent simulations and hence allow the belief distribution for π to evolve independently of the belief distributions for α and β.

Now, consider the same process of analyzing beliefs about the parameters of the stochastic decision tree as before, but allow students to process accurate information about this labor market and update their beliefs 100 times. As shown in Figure 5.2 for two groups of students subject to different rates of learning, the time path for $\Pr(E = 1)$ ascends from its value just below .5 toward 1. For fast learners, the increasing information pushes $\Pr(E = 1)$ up to 1 after approximately 30 rounds of updating, while for slow learners $\Pr(E = 1)$ has still not reached 1 after 100 rounds of updating.

In this example, the precise difference between slow learners and fast learners is arbitrary, but the relative rates at which $\Pr(E = 1)$ approaches 1 is a general qualitative result for all similar parameterizations. For the simulations reported in Figure 5.2, slow learners process linear increases in information; that is, they acquire the same amount of information in each subsequent time period and update their belief distributions to incorporate this new information using a variant of the updating process depicted in Equation 5.5. For example, for the parameter α, slow learners update as follows:

$\alpha_{t=1} \sim Beta(.01, .01)$

$\alpha_{t=2} \sim Beta(.04, .03)$

$\alpha_{t=3} \sim Beta(.07, .05)$

$\alpha_{t=4} \sim Beta(.10, .07)$

$\alpha_{t=5} \sim Beta(.13, .09)$

. . .

$\alpha_{t=101} \sim Beta(3.01, 2.01)$

Across all beliefs, the new information arrives in proportion to the distribution of information in the third column of Table 4.1, but each new dose of information is small. For this simulation, the dose in each round of updating is the relevant element of the third column of Table 4.1 divided by the total number of rounds of updating. For α, the doses in each round of updating are .03 and .02 for the beta success and failure parameters.

For fast learners, in contrast, each dose of new information is initially small but increases in time. For the parameterization I will adopt here, the increases in dosage size are linear, such that the initial belief distribution for α for fast learners is updated multiplicatively as follows:

$\alpha_{t=1} \sim Beta(.01, .01)$

$\alpha_{t=2} \sim Beta(.04, .03)$

$\alpha_{t=3} \sim Beta(.13, .09)$

$\alpha_{t=4} \sim Beta(.28, .19)$

$\alpha_{t=5} \sim Beta(.49, .33)$

. . .

$\alpha_{t=101} \sim Beta(300.01, 200.01)$

Again, across all belief distributions, the new information arrives in proportion to the distribution of information in the third column of Table 4.1. But, for fast learners, the doses of new information are increasing in each round of updating, as a linearly increasing multiple of the doses of new information received by slow learners. For α, the doses for fast learners are equal to $.03(2t - 1)$ and $.02(2t - 1)$ for the beta success and failure parameters, where t is the time counter for the simulation.

This stipulated difference between slow and fast learners is somewhat arbitrary, as the growth function of new information for slow and fast learners could be altered.[14] I selected this parameterization so that, at each point in time t, fast learners have acquired a total of $(t - 1)$ times as much new information as slow learners. This allows slow and fast learners to acquire the same amount of information in the first round of updating, but then the amount of information acquired by fast learners increases relative to that of slow learners in each subsequent time period. For example, after the second round of updating (that is, t equal to 3), fast learners have acquired twice as much information. And, after the hundredth round of updating (that is, t equal to 101), fast learners have acquired 100 times as much information.

As a result, for both groups $Pr(E = 1)$ jumps from below .5 to .66 after the first round of updating because both groups, on average, have processed the same amount of new information. That new information accurately implies that college has a large pay off in the reference labor market. And, yet, thereafter the time paths of $Pr(E = 1)$ diverge, as fast learners acquire relatively larger amounts of information in each subsequent time period.

To show more carefully what drives this difference, Figures 5.3 and 5.4 present simulated time paths for the expected values of π, α, β, and γ across both fast and slow learners, along with the same time paths of $Pr(E = 1)$ from Figure 5.2. Both groups, on average, accurately estimate the returns to college completion in the labor market. But, there is less bounce in the expected time paths of fast learners (that is, the average value of each parameter across simulated students), since each simulated fast learner is more likely to have estimated values for π, α, β, and γ (based on only a few candidate parameter draws) that are closer to the implied means of their belief distributions. As a result, averaging over all simulated students, the time paths for the expected values of each parameter more quickly smooth out for fast learners, as they are able to much more quickly eliminate extreme values from their belief distributions.

The consequence of this difference is that fast learners are more quickly able to construct unambiguous belief distributions about the payoff to a college education. Even after 100 rounds of updating, approximately 10 percent of slow learners believe, in random contrarian moments, that their stochastic decision trees imply that college is not a worthwhile investment in their futures. The difference between fast and slow learners is not produced

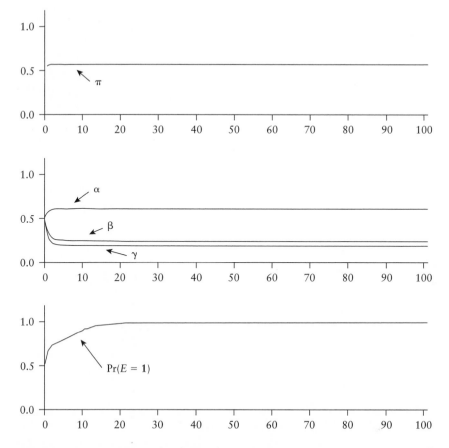

Figure 5.3. Fast Learning for the Stochastic Decision Tree Parameters (see Figure 5.2)

by disinformation, but rather it is produced by an external process that determines how fast prospective college students learn to eliminate extreme values from their beliefs about their future life chances.

This pattern of results is, therefore, exactly analogous to those of Chapter 4. Indeed, the simulation is equivalent to modeling the fourth contour line from the right-horizontal axis of Figure 4.7 with a few fairly subtle conceptual modifications. The notion of increases in the precision of beliefs has been replaced by a specific learning process based on Bayes' theorem. The claim introduced in this chapter, and demonstrated in the simulation re-

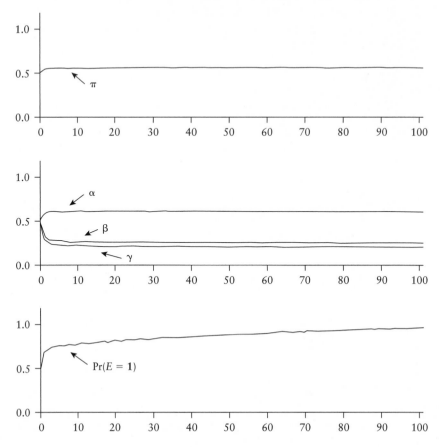

Figure 5.4.   Slow Learning for the Stochastic Decision Tree Parameters (see Figure 5.2)

ported in Figure 5.2, is that individuals travel along the fourth contour line of the surface in Figure 4.7 as they acquire information. But, they travel at different rates, and these rates can be conceptualized as rates of learning if one accepts the foundational axioms of Bayesian theory.

The major challenge, of course, is to figure out a way to model and then empirically examine whether students who exhibit low levels of preparatory commitment resemble slow Bayesian learners rather than fast Bayesian learners. Before developing a framework for such modeling, in the next section I offer a similar set of simulations where I vary the accuracy of the information that is processed.

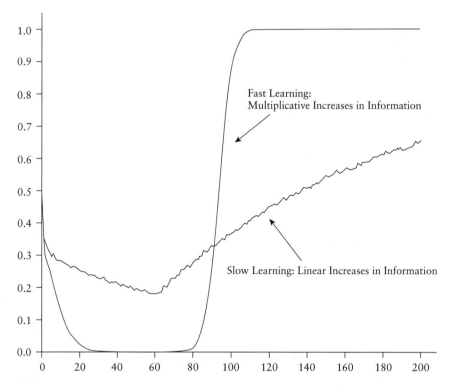

Figure 5.5.   The Evolution of Commitment in a Labor Market Where the Payoff to a College Education Is Large but Initial Information (for $t < 61$) Implied the Opposite

The Processing of Inaccurate Information

Suppose that the same two groups of slow and fast learners instead start off by processing inaccurate information. In particular, for the first 59 rounds of updating, as shown in Figure 5.5, they process information that suggests that the mean values of π, α, β, and γ are .4, .4, .2, and .6 instead of .556, .6, .25, and .2, respectively. That is, up through the 60th time period, students process information that suggests that a college degree will hurt their chances of attaining a highly prestigious position in life. After this initial period, both sets of students then process the same accurate information as for the simulations reported in Figures 5.3 and 5.4.

As shown in Figure 5.5, the fast Bayesian learners more quickly process the initially inaccurate information, and their expected level of prefigurative

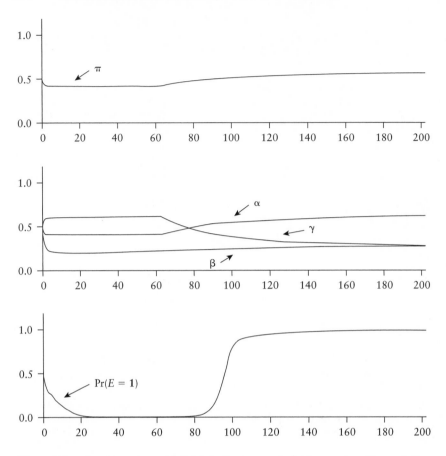

Figure 5.6.   Fast Learning with Initially Inaccurate Information (see Figure 5.5)

commitment plummets to 0 in only about 30 rounds of updating. In contrast, the prefigurative commitment of slow learners declines, but relatively more slowly over the same time period. By the 59th round of updating, slow learners have expected levels of prefigurative commitment just below .2.

From the 60th round of updating onward, all students are again processing accurate information, and the expected level of prefigurative commitment for slow Bayesian learners begins to increase as in the simulation reported in Figure 5.2, but from a lower level. And, yet, for fast learners, $Pr(E = 1)$ remains for a while at 0 before then crossing the time path for slow learners and rising rapidly to 1. Figures 5.6 and 5.7 show the underlying

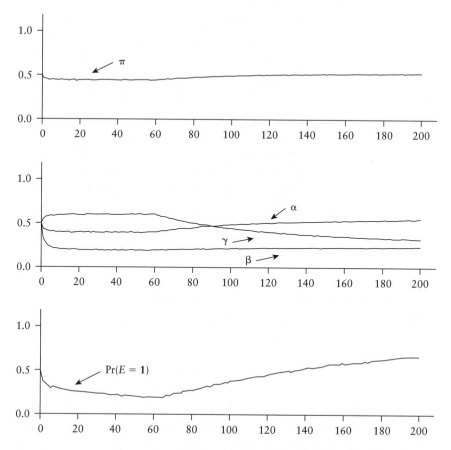

Figure 5.7.   Slow Learning with Initially Inaccurate Information (see Figure 5.5)

time paths for the expected values of each stochastic decision tree parameter, along with the time path for $\Pr(E = 1)$ from Figure 5.5 for reference.

Why is there a lag in the apparent responsiveness of the expected level of prefigurative commitment for fast Bayesian learners, followed by a relatively swift jump to 1? By the 60th time period, the belief distributions of fast learners are very precise, with little overlap and with the vast majority of probability mass sitting near their means. As a result, the accurate information from the 61st time period onward must mix with these very precise distributions.[15] Thus, although the implied means of the belief distributions of fast Bayesian learners are shifting between the 60th and 80th rounds of updating, it takes until the 80th round for the distribution of the expected utility of college completion to begin to cross the distribution for the expected utility of not completing college. The belief distributions then pass each other quickly, and $\Pr(E = 1)$ goes to 1 as the precise belief distributions of fast learners unambiguously imply that education is in each individual's best interest.

For slow learners, however, there remains some uncertainty well after the 80th time period, such that the initially inaccurate information has not yet been overwhelmed by the new information. Indeed, since slow Bayesian learners are not characterized by a quick descent to 0 in the first 30 rounds of updating, they remain in a zone of ambiguity throughout all 200 rounds of updating. Later in this chapter, I will discuss the simulations reported in Figure 5.5 as reflecting the elegance but inherent rigidity of the Bayesian learning framework.

Why Would Individuals Differ in their Rates of Bayesian Learning?

If slow Bayesian learning is thought of as the baseline, why would some individuals be fast Bayesian learners? There are at least three plausible reasons.

1. Differences in the Amount of Available Information.   In the simulations offered so far, I have at times made glancing references to the possibility that individuals differ in the amount of readily available information in their local environments. If so, it may simply be the case that fast Bayesian learners are those who receive more information in every period of time. As a result, they learn to eliminate extreme values from their beliefs more quickly than their slow Bayesian counterparts. A ceteris paribus change of environment could therefore turn a slow Bayesian learner into a fast Bayesian learner.

Clearly, we have far too little information on the distribution of information across alternative environments to determine whether exogenous differences in the amount of available information could generate differences in rates of learning about the parameters of a stochastic decision tree. I will offer some proposals for new directions in the modeling of information and data collection in Chapter 7.

2. Differences in the Propensity to Search for Information.   Individuals may respond differently to the same amount of available information. Some students may receive passively the new information in their environments, whereas others may seek out confirmatory information every time they receive a new piece of information. If so, the latter group of students will accumulate information at a faster rate, as the information flow itself generates a feedback effect that may appear to a student as a form of self-discovery.

And, although there may be a static personality difference between some students—such that some are receptors whereas others are seekers—it may be that the main difference is a temporal one. Students who are primarily receptors may experience catalytic events that prompt them to become seekers. If so, then these catalytic events would be a primary focus of research.

Events that prompt students to become seekers could be as simple as a change in environment, although in this case something other than an increase in available information would have to change. A dynamic version of the significant others' influence mechanism of the Wisconsin model could account for such a change. Only when data is available to chart the evolution of such belief distributions will sociologists know whether such catalytic events exist.

3. Differences in the Amount of Information Sharing. While arguing that sociology should privilege rational action theory when developing explanatory models, John Goldthorpe (2000:132) writes that "sociologists should aim to treat the information available to actors as a product of the social relations in which they are involved." If one regards social structure as a product of social relations, in the sense that it is a residue of past action and the institutions that have resulted from such action, then modeling exogenous differences in the amount of available information in students' environments may satisfy Goldthorpe's plea. And yet, his plea is relevant even more to modeling at the micro level.

The process of peer influence, which has always been at the heart of the significant others' influence mechanism of the Wisconsin model, could be conceptualized as a type of information sharing. Students who maintain many connections to like-minded students (that is, students whose beliefs are similar in their central tendencies) may feel as if they have more information at their disposal than students who maintain few connections to like-minded students. In Chapter 6, I will elaborate this basic claim, introducing the obvious complexities that emerge when students are members of cross-cutting social circles.

In sum, learning in the Bayesian tradition captures two related processes: (1) a compromise between the central tendencies of prior beliefs and new information, and (2) a down-weighting of the plausibility of values that are extreme with respect to both prior beliefs and new information. My contention is that the first process is consistent with much that has been written in the sociological literature on educational attainment, but that the second has been largely ignored, even though, as I have just argued, the reasons to suspect that some students resemble fast instead of slow Bayesian learners are not necessarily inconsistent with the sociological hypotheses encapsulated in the Wisconsin model.

Explanations for race differences in achievement, for example, are frequently based on arguments about perceptions of the opportunity structure, as discussed in Chapter 3. In none of this literature has the independent role of uncertainty of beliefs been analyzed, nor the social processes by which such uncertainty of beliefs can be altered. In the next section, I demonstrate some ways in which the literature could be developed in this regard, again using classic black-white differences in educational achievement as an example.

BLACK-WHITE DIFFERENCES IN
EDUCATIONAL EXPECTATIONS REVISITED

Consider black-white differences in the relationship between educational expectations and attainment, as analyzed in Chapter 3. Although blacks often report college plans just as ambitious as those of whites, they are less likely to realize their own expectations. Their college entrance rates are lower, and in the short run their preparatory commitment for college instruction lags behind that of whites.[16]

The stochastic decision tree framework suggests an explanation for this discrepancy, which has achieved the label of a paradox within some strands of the sociology of education literature (see Mickelson 1990). Suppose that black and white high school students are asked to agree or disagree with the statement: "I expect to go to college." To answer this question, suppose that they take a small step outside of themselves, ask the question: "Is college in the best interest of someone like me?" They then consult the stochastic decision tree that represents their beliefs.[17]

In this scenario, students are now outside of their everyday experiences, as they have been asked to become an informant on their futures.[18] In so doing, they adopt a different mode of stochastic decision tree evaluation. They no longer wish to set an instantaneous level of prefigurative commitment, but rather they average over their past levels of prefigurative commitment, and in particular calculate the number of times in the past that they have committed themselves to preparation for postsecondary schooling, which is equivalent to the number of times they have set E equal to 1 in the past. If beliefs are relatively stable over the time period consulted, this assessment of past levels of commitment will be equal to the value of $\Pr(E = 1)$ for the stochastic decision tree that students are referring to when confronted by the survey question.

If all students maintain similar fixed response thresholds, such that they will answer yes if $\Pr(E = 1)$ is greater than .5, then the responses of black and white students may resemble each other, even though black students on average may have lower levels of prefigurative commitment and therefore, in everyday behavior, may be less committed to postsecondary schooling. And, if blacks and whites have different loss functions when responding to the survey question (as for the differential response threshold explanation from Chapter 3), and hence have a lower threshold that $\Pr(E = 1)$ must cross in order to respond affirmatively to the question, then even less of a race difference may be detected in the supposed ambitions revealed by educational expectations.

Accordingly, one could adopt the stochastic decision tree framework and assert that, although whites and blacks, on average, have similarly accurate beliefs about the labor market benefits of postsecondary schooling, white students have more information and hence are more likely to quickly process information when updating their beliefs about their stochastic decision trees. If so, then blacks are more likely to have lower levels of prefigurative and preparatory commitment because the evolution of their beliefs is more similar to those of slow Bayesian learners than those of fast Bayesian learners, as presented in Figure 5.2. Nonetheless, the responses they offer to questions on their educational futures do not reflect this difference in prefigurative commitment because the underlying race difference in prefigurative commitment does not cross the relevant response threshold.[19]

Although I favor this simple explanation, I will show in Chapter 6 that the stochastic decision tree framework can enable specifications of alternative mechanisms for the generation of black-white differences in achievement.

These are not necessarily inconsistent with the claim that blacks, although not necessarily misinformed, are nonetheless not as well informed as whites.

In this section, as in other chapters, I have applied these general ideas to puzzling race differences that have remained unexplained in the literature. The ideas, however, are more general, and hence could be used to develop explanations worthy of empirical investigation for many of the questions raised in Chapter 1. For example, learning about the existence of Pell Grants should increase prefigurative commitment among credit constrained students by raising optimism about the probability of graduating from college. If such a belief response does not occur for at least some students, then either (1) no students are credit constrained, or (2) perceptions of the opportunity structure, at least in this narrow sense, do not have effects on short-run commitment behavior.

LIMITATIONS OF BAYESIAN LEARNING MODELS

At the beginning of this chapter, I introduced Bayesian learning in an application that should be familiar to most academic researchers: To which journal should I submit my recently completed manuscript? My hope was that this example would convince some readers that they were Bayesian learners all along but did not realize it. Although the case is harder to make for adolescents contemplating their futures, it is plausible that students would have the same reaction were they given a narrative explanation for how they may be making some of their own decisions. For high school students, the application would have to be something considerably more Colemanesque, such as: "What is your football team's probability of winning a championship?" or "What is the probability that you will obtain a date with a member of the homecoming court?"

There are, however, some serious objections to Bayesian learning as a descriptive model of behavior. In this section, I will discuss some inherent analytic limitations and relevant experimental findings. And, I will then raise the issue of whether there are any credible general alternatives to Bayesian learning.

Analytic Limitations of Bayesian Learning

The elegance of Bayesian learning theory is its main limitation. For the beta distributions above, if a student updates his or her prior belief distribution with new information, his or her posterior belief distribution will represent, in its central tendency, a compromise between the prior distribution and the new information. His or her posterior will also have smaller variance than his or her prior. The latter consequence is quite general and is the crucial result that generates my claims about movements in prefigurative commitment. And yet, this ever-declining variance property can represent a modeling limitation.

Suppose a student updates his or her prior with new information, but thereafter does not receive any more new information. In this case, according to Bayesian theory, his or her beliefs will remain exactly the same for every future time period. This may be problematic, from a descriptive perspective, if one assumes that beliefs have a natural tendency to flatten out in the absence of a constant flow of confirmatory evidence. There is no such thing as a general information decay parameter in the Bayesian learning paradigm. That is, there is no provision within Bayesian theory for a baseline level of Bayesian forgetting, which represents a serious limitation of the framework.

This constraint arises in another context, already foreshadowed for the fast learners depicted in Figure 5.5. If a student updates a prior distribution with one set of information for a sufficient amount of time, then his or her posterior distribution may become very precise. And yet, if the student then begins to process an entirely different set of information, that information may have little or no effect on his or her beliefs until enough new information has been accumulated to balance out the information already acquired from the older set of information.

In some sense, this pattern is the main attraction of the Bayesian learning framework; actors do not simply surrender their prior beliefs when confronted with new information. But, in some modeling contexts, it may be that the exact compromises stipulated by Bayes' theorem between one's prior and new information are too rigid. One can get around the rigidity by specifying alternative rates of information acquisition, or, as hinted earlier, by introducing a baseline rate of Bayesian forgetting. There is, however, no denying that Bayes' theorem is rigid and hence potentially limiting in its modeling capacities.

Objections from Experimental Research: Individuals Are Not Proper Bayesians

Two common objections to Bayesian learning as a descriptive model of belief revision have been stressed: Individuals ignore base rates (Kahneman and Tversky 1972); individuals are conservative and do not fully absorb new information into their beliefs (Edwards 1968). In Bayesian language, these findings imply that individuals maintain poor priors and do not update their priors as fully as Bayes' theorem requires.

Especially when it is properly noted that all such experiments were designed with the sole goal from the outset of disproving Bayes' theorem as a legitimate descriptive model of behavior, I do not regard either of these objections as damning. From a subjectivist viewpoint, which is the dominant Bayesian position, prior beliefs are simply those that individuals maintain. Whether prior beliefs are in accord with what a researcher can estimate as a true frequency is irrelevant. It is unsurprising to a Bayesian analyst that subjects in a psychological experiment tend to ignore base rates in hypothetical scenarios with which they have had little personal experience.

For example, in the classic experiment of Kahneman and Tversky (1972), psychology students are posed with the following scenario:

> A cab was involved in a hit-and-run accident at night. Two cab companies, the Green and the Blue, operate in the city. You are given the following data:
>> (a) 85 percent of the cabs in the city are Green and 15 percent are Blue
>> (b) a witness identified the cab as Blue
> The court tested the reliability of the witness under the same circumstances that existed on the night of the accident and concluded that the witness correctly identified each one of the two colors 80 percent of the time and failed 20 percent of the time. What is the probability that the cab involved in the accident was Blue rather than Green?

If the prior probability mass for Blue cabs is .15, as suggested by part (a) of the setup, the correct posterior probability derived from Bayes' theorem is .41. In response to the question, most subjects give probabilities much higher. The standard explanation for this finding is that individuals ignore the base rate (that only 15 percent of cabs are Blue) and therefore that individuals are not Bayesian learners.

This clever example is illuminating, but does it really mean that individuals never use anything like Bayes' theorem in updating their own beliefs? Since few undergraduates have ever thought about the distribution of cabs in a city, nor been witnesses in courtrooms, it seems odd to expect students to easily solve for the proper posterior probability. The problem is not that students fail to incorporate the new information properly but rather that they have no personal stake in formulating a reasonable prior distribution in such an artificial situation.

A similar argument can be made against the finding that individuals are not as responsive to new information as Bayes' theorem requires. What individuals perceive as a data likelihood may not be the same data likelihood that a researcher specifies. Indeed, evidence of conservatism in beliefs can be interpreted as support for Bayes' theorem (and against the relevance of the finding that prior beliefs do not accurately reflect base rates). Individuals take their prior beliefs seriously and do not give them up entirely when confronted with new information.

Although it was fashionable in the 1970s and 1980s in psychology and experimental economics to denigrate Bayes' theorem, the conclusion I draw from the experimental literature is much less strong: In carefully designed experiments, subjects can be shown to be poor Bayesians when they revise their beliefs, especially if the experiment is as artificial and confusing as the Blue/Green cab example presented earlier. Whether or not students are poor Bayesians when they revise their beliefs is simply unknown and must be examined. An evaluation of whether Bayes' theorem is a useful model of information processing and belief revision for students is a good starting point for the empirical evaluation of the stochastic decision tree model I have proposed and for alternatives to this model that others may find more promising.

Are there credible general alternatives to Bayesian learning? Bayes' theorem is the gold standard for belief revision, but it is not the only available formal model of belief revision. Most of the alternatives have their origins in behavioral psychology (see Bush and Mosteller 1955, 1959; Spiegelhalter and Cowell 1992). If students are not Bayesian learners in this context, they may be Thorndike learners, Thurstone learners, or Bush-Mosteller learners. Alternative possibilities abound. What I propose is simply that we establish Bayesian learning as a working hypothesis, on the argument that we ought to privilege simple ideas that are plausible and have been found useful in many domains of research. Of course, in the process of building models of belief formation processes, and evaluating them with empirical data, it may well be the case that Bayesian learning will fall from grace. That would be genuine progress. At present, rejecting Bayesian learning because it seems too complicated or has been the target of experimental critique would be premature.

CONCLUSIONS

The theory of Bayesian learning provides building blocks to represent promising sociological hypotheses as carefully specified mechanisms. In the parameterizations adopted in this chapter, the rate of learning is generally more consequential than the expected values of the belief distributions.[20] Although plausible for actors who are confronting decisions far in their futures, rates of learning would not necessarily dominate over potential shifts in expected values of belief distributions. The larger point of the simulations, if not the point of this entire book, is that ignoring the independent contributions of precision of beliefs is consequential, while embracing the potential consequences of such differences can enable more subtle theoretical claims that, if confirmed, may improve explanations of educational achievement and attainment.[21] Nonetheless, Bayesian models of belief updating will only show their promise if they are embedded in more complete models of the social processes that determine them. In Chapter 6, normative and imitative sources of commitment are reintroduced.

NOTES

1. A few words of caution about the Bayesian foundation of the proposed mechanisms are in order. Bayesian decision theory is a formal system of applied mathematics for the modeling of uncertainty (see Berger 1985; Pratt, Raiffa, and Schlaifer 1995). This chapter is in no way an attempt to enter the debate on the appropriateness of Bayesian data analysis techniques (see Carlin and Louis 1996; Gelman, Carlin, Stern, and Rubin 1995; Leonard and Hsu 1999) that are seen by many researchers as a controversial alternative to dominant statistical practices based on the classical frequentist theory of statistics.

2. For example, a Bayesian would argue that the only way for a high school sophomore to formulate a reasonable belief about his or her personal probability of gaining admittance to Yale is to first formulate beliefs about events such as scoring in the top decile on the SAT and then multiply these probabilities by beliefs about the probability of being admitted if such events occur. In other words, a Bayesian analyst always regards any joint probability statement as fundamentally a conditional probability statement multiplied by the probability that a set of conditioning events occurs.

3. Whether this additional confidence is enough to convince her to submit the manuscript to the general journal will be a function of both the posterior probability and her personal loss (or utility) function representing the subjective value that

she attaches to acceptance and rejection from both the general and specialized journals.

4. See Oster (1980) for a colorful example of how much analytic effort one can devote to submission decisions.

5. The data likelihood in the figure is equal to n times the binomial probability from Equation 5.4 with $y = 6$ and $n = 10$, evaluated at 1,000 equally spaced values of θ between 0 and 1.

6. Purists will note that in this introduction to Bayesian updating, I implicitly maintain a symmetric loss function (e.g., a standard frequentist squared-error loss function).

7. For one further comparison, if the original 10 coin flips had yielded 9 Hs and 1 T, the posterior $Beta(11, 4)$ distribution would have mean, mode, and variance of .733, .769, and .0122.

8. The binomial constant of integration is not displayed in Equation 5.8 because it can be factored out of the numerators and denominators and thus cancels.

9. To see how important prior information can be, especially with a discrete distribution for beliefs, recalculate Equation 5.7 with the opposite prior: .333 for $\theta = .3$ and .667 for $\theta = .6$. The resulting posterior probabilities, given the evidence from the original 10 coin flips, are .068 for $\theta = .3$ and .932 for $\theta = .6$.

10. But for completeness, I would like to answer the question: What action should the hypothetical casino visitor take in the last example? Recall that prior to the 10 experimental flips, the visitor felt that her probability of winning the bet was only .4. However, after taking account of the evidence offered by the 10 experimental trials, the visitor's belief about the probability of winning increased to .532.

Now suppose that the casino manager only allows the 1,000th visitor to bet $500 that the next flip of the coin will be Heads. Since the visitor has $950 remaining, she is able to make such a bet. But before doing so, she must assess the relative consequences of winning versus losing. Assigning subjective value to the outcomes of alternative possible courses of action is known as setting a loss function, which is simply the negation of a utility function in subjective expected utility theory. In this case, the loss function is simple, taking only two values.

First, assume that subjective loss is equal to monetary loss. Under this assumption, her loss when the casino wins would be $500 while her loss when she wins would be $-$500 (that is, a gain of $500). The prior expected loss of the bet is ($500)(.6) + (−$500)(.4) = $100 while the posterior expected loss is ($500)(.468) + (−$500)(.532) = −$32. Thus, prior to the 10 experimental flips, the casino visitor would have felt justified in turning down the bet, for she would expect to lose money by deciding to take the bet. However, after the 10 flips, the casino visitor might feel uneasy passing up the $500 bet, for it is more likely than not that she would be passing up the opportunity to make $500.

Now, consider a slightly different scenario that generates a more complex asymmetric loss function. Suppose that the casino manager will only allow the visitor to place a $950 bet. In this case, a loss of $950 represents all of the money that she brought to the casino. Such a loss would prevent her from engaging in further gambling, and assuming that she enjoys gambling, a loss of $950 dollars would likely be more distressing than a gain of $950 would be gratifying. Thus, the loss function for this decision cannot be represented by simple monetary loss. Instead, a new scale of loss is needed that is an appropriate nonlinear transformation of monetary value. Such a loss function would not be symmetric relative to the midpoint of monetary loss at $0.

Suppose that a loss function $L(.)$ is found where $L(\$950) = 1.5$ and $L(-\$950) = -1$. The posterior expected loss for a bet of $950 dollars, under this alternative scenario, is $(1.5)(.468) + (-1)(.532) = .17$. Thus, even though the visitor is more likely than not to feel that she is likely to win the bet, the expected loss of the bet is positive (and thus greater than the 0 implicit loss associated with not taking the bet). The casino visitor would therefore decide not to take the bet because the prospect of losing all of her money is too devastating to take a chance with such limited information about possible success.

11. The updating mechanism is similar to but not exactly the same as a beta prior updated with a binomial likelihood. For the simulations reported later, the new information is represented in each round of updating as a scaled down binomial likelihood, where analogs to the binomial parameters y (that is, successes) and n (that is, total number of trials) are not generally integers. In this sense, the new information is in the form of a second beta distribution, and the updating is simply a beta prior multiplied by another beta distribution. Although a small abuse of Bayesian traditions, the proportionality of the posterior is preserved. Purists, for whom this mechanism may appear to be overly simplified, can simply regard the time paths presented later as interpolated time paths between rounds of standard beta updating with binomial likelihoods. For example, the slow Bayesian learners from Figure 5.2 begin with a $Beta(.01, .01)$ prior for α in the first time period but then update this prior in the 101st time period with a binomial likelihood where y is 3 and n is 5. The resulting posterior is a $Beta(3.01, 2.01)$, and all of the points in time between the first and 101st time periods can simply be ignored. In contrast, fast Bayesian learners simply accomplish the same updating more quickly. Their $Beta(.01, .01)$ prior for α is updated with the same binomial likelihood where y is 3 and n is 5, but the updating occurs in the 11th time period. As result, the fast Bayesian learners have a posterior in the 11th time period that is a $Beta(3.01, 2.01)$, while slow Bayesian learners have not yet updated their prior.

12. Other plausible starting points could be chosen for the belief distributions, such as a uniform $Beta(1, 1)$ distribution, or an alternative U-shaped distribution, such as a $Beta(.5, 5)$, which has a special place in Bayesian theory as the well-behaved Jeffrey's prior for a beta distribution. Although a different starting distribution would affect the rate at which commitment reaches its extreme values, none of the qualitative conclusions of the chapter would change.

13. If it seems unnatural to assume that such totally uninformed students

would maintain a two-stage stochastic decision tree, then one may alternatively suppose that such students maintain only a two-branched tree with two parameters, the probability of attaining High if entering college and the probability of attaining High if not entering college. The main claims of this chapter will hold under this simpler tree as well. Indeed, as suggested for Proposition 1 in Chapter 4, virtually any tree structure can be used to establish a baseline level of no commitment to any future course of action.

14. In order to generate the patterns in Figure 5.2, two stipulations must hold: (1) for both groups, the density of new information across branches of the decision tree is the same, and (2) the amount of new information acquired in each round of updating is greater for fast learners than for slow learners.

15. Under the parameterization adopted here, fast learners are actually processing much larger quantities of accurate information from the 61st time period onward, since the doses of information for fast learners are still defined to be $(2t - 1)$ times the doses of accurate information for slow learners.

16. Black students are less committed to schooling and score lower on typical standardized tests given in high school, even though their educational expectations are nearly as high as those of whites. And, even though a large portion of the gap can be attributed to race differences in family background, a stream of literature remains (see Jencks and Phillips 1998) that argues that a black-white gap in performance in high school remains substantial even after adjustments for family background are performed.

17. In Morgan (1998), I refer to this sort of self-reflection as the construction of a rational fantasy.

18. Within Giddens' stratification model of agency (see Giddens 1984 and also Chapter 1), this is a complex shift. At its most simple level, students are simply asked to reveal their motives, and I assume that they do so, in this action context, by consulting their beliefs about costs and benefits. But, in the process of engaging in such externally induced investigations of their motives, students further depart from the practical consciousness that guides everyday action (and which, I argue in this book, is part and parcel of the monitoring of prefigurative commitment with a stochastic decision tree). Instead, the students enter fully into their discursive consciousness, attempting to rationalize action as much as reflexively monitor it.

19. Or, one could assert that the traditional differential socialization argument is correct, but that the variable used to measure significant others' influence does not reveal the relevant process. Instead of capturing the catalytic events that prompt whites to seek out confirmatory information or reflecting the peer relations that boost the relative amount of information that whites feel is available to them through their social connections, the significant others' variable simply measures the expectations of the student that his or her significant others maintain.

20. Consider one additional group of students. Students in this group have overly optimistic beliefs, such that the expected values of π, α, β, and γ are .556, .8, .5, and .2 instead of .556, .6, .25, and .2 respectively. This group of students

has the same beliefs about the probability of graduating from college if initially enrolled, and yet feels on average that one's probability of attaining High is much higher if one attends college. These students' beliefs, in their central tendencies, imply a massive increase of .467 (i.e., $\{[(.556)(.8) + (1 - .556)(.5)] -.2\}$) in the probability of attaining High. For such overly optimistic students, it could be shown that the time path of $\Pr(E = 1)$ goes to 1 faster than for all other groups of at least partially slow learners, and yet still approaches 1 slower than for uniformly fast learners. Thus, even though the beliefs of the fast Bayesian learners depicted in Figure 5.2 have beliefs that, on average, predict a lower expected utility of completing college, their expected levels of prefigurative commitment are much higher by virtue of their higher rate of information processing.

21. But, if one wished to instead ignore the precision of beliefs (either out of a quest for parsimony or another motivation), one need only consider the updating of very precise distributions. This would be equivalent to modeling differences in the back-right edges of Figures 4.5 through 4.8.

CHAPTER SIX

Incorporating Imitative and Normative Sources of Commitment

When introducing the stochastic decision tree model of commitment in Chapter 4, I focused attention on the purposive dimension of prefigurative commitment. But, I also noted the importance of imitative and normative sources of prefigurative commitment. In Figure 4.1, I suggested that these other dimensions of commitment affect preparation for college and may play a role in shaping purposive-prefigurative commitment as well. In this chapter, I begin to specify the connections between belief formation and the alternative dimensions of commitment.

First, I consider the prospects for a model based primarily on students' myopic imitation of the college entry behavior of prior students. Then, as in Chapter 5, I continue to argue that social influence processes can be modeled as a type of information sharing. But, I will also embrace the claim inherent in the basic adoption mechanism of the Wisconsin model: some students, regardless of the independent information they receive, may simply adopt the beliefs suggested to them by their significant others. Finally, I suggest a further set of proposals for modeling beliefs about the fairness of the educational system, which are particularly important when attempting to explain racial differences.

To understand the mode of theoretical development I engage, first recall that the purposive dimension of prefigurative commitment arises in response to the prediction rule: "I will go to college if I perceive it to be in my best interest to do so." This dimension of prefigurative commitment may be reinforced or undermined by the normative and imitative dimensions that arise in response to the additional prediction rules "I will go to college if my significant others perceive it to be in my best interest to do so" and "I will go to college if I expect other students similar to me will also go to college." Incorporating these additional dimensions of prefigurative commitment can be accomplished in two ways, one external to the structure of the model presented in Chapters 4 and 5 and one internal to its explicit mechanisms.

One could model normative-prefigurative commitment as external coercion. For example, a student might reason: "Regardless of whether or not I think that going to college is in my best interest, I will go to college because my parents say that I must do so." In this case, preparatory commitment is a response to the normative influence of parents and is determined secondarily by the prefigurative commitment arising from an evaluation of a stochastic decision tree. Similarly, imitative-prefigurative commitment could be modeled externally as a pure contextual effect. A student might reason: "Regardless of whether or not I think that going to college is in my best interest, I will go to college if I observe other students similar to me going to college." Students from disadvantaged social origins, for example, observe many fewer students entering college immediately following high school than other students. For this reason alone, students from disadvantaged social origins may be less likely to expect to attend college and thus less likely to prepare themselves to do so.[1]

Although external to the decision evaluation mechanism I proposed in Chapter 4, incorporating normative and imitative sources of prefigurative commitment in these ways is consistent with much past sociological scholarship. Thus, in the schematic Figure 4.1, I allowed normative and imitative sources of prefigurative commitment to have their own direct causal effects on preparatory commitment for college. It may be that future empirical analysis will determine that these normative and imitative processes are dominant and should be at the center of a model of educational attainment. For now, no evidence suggests that this is the case.

I therefore offer an alternative and complementary approach, one that is internal to the structure of the stochastic decision tree model as developed in the last two chapters. For this approach, one would first stipulate that purposive-prefigurative commitment is the primary controlling guide for forward-looking behavior but then specify lower-order mechanisms for the generation of the parameters on which forward-looking decision evaluation is based. In particular, one would specify that the beliefs with which students formulate purposive-prefigurative commitment using a stochastic decision tree are subject to lower-order normative and imitative pressures that themselves must be explicitly modeled.

It seems undeniable that students' belief distributions are shaped in response to the views and actions of their significant others. Students' beliefs about the probability of graduating from college if initially enrolled are a function of the views and actions of their parents, teachers, siblings, and peers. Supportive parents are able to convince their children that they will receive adequate financial support. Teachers are able to convince students that they are smart enough to survive college instruction. Relatedly, students may see their older siblings and friends thriving in college environments and may thus eliminate low values as permissible probabilities for their own likelihood of graduating from college if enrolled. In principle, the same sort of social influence processes may operate for beliefs about the returns to alternative pathways through the educational system.

In order to develop models that incorporate imitative and normative dimensions of prefigurative commitment, one should proceed in four basic steps: (1) develop an explicit model of the hypothesized normative and imitative processes; (2) derive predictions for the parameters of students' stochastic decision trees and other measured variables that one is willing to assert are associated with them; (3) collect data on students' stochastic decision trees and the other measured variables suggested in Step 2; and (4) evaluate the predictions and, if they are supported, consider retaining the model of the normative or imitative process just developed.

At this point, without data on students' stochastic decision trees, only the first two steps can be carried out completely. And yet, using the other measured variables identified in Step 2, some informative empirical analysis is possible. I will sketch the basic strategy in the next three sections, first for a model of imitative behavior, then for a model of social influence, and finally for a model of adjustment to beliefs about the fairness of the educational system.

MODELING IMITATION

What if students do not use stochastic decision trees and instead invoke myopic imitation-rules as guides for their own future behavior, such as: "I will prepare myself to go to college if students who are one grade ahead of me but otherwise exactly equivalent to me have gone on to college"? If students think in this seemingly simplistic manner, then one might stipulate that students' levels of preparatory commitment are not primarily a function of purposive-prefigurative commitment (that is, $\Pr(E = 1)$ as computed with reference to a stochastic decision tree). Instead, students' preparatory commitment (and then resulting enrollment decisions) are entirely dependent on their observations of the current behavior of older students. No cost-benefit analysis of future courses of action is necessary, as students implicitly assume that older cohorts of students have done these calculations for them (or, even more simply, that the decisions of all older cohorts of students were at some point, before the imitation-rule took hold, based on a reasonable analysis of the proper course of behavior).

Although it should be fairly straightforward to determine whether such simplistic imitation-rules prevail, I am unaware of such an evaluation. It is quite possible that there are no evaluations because there are good a priori reasons to doubt the explanatory power of imitative behavior in this context.[2] Looking for guiding patterns in older cohorts of students sounds simple in theory, but it is considerably harder in practice for students to implement. In all schools, no matter how socioeconomically advantaged or disadvantaged, college preparation and attendance patterns vary. For the imitation-rule outlined earlier, students must first select for subsequent observation and imitation those older students who are similar to them on all characteristics.[3] Because there is likely no "perfect match" (and behavior among the set of older students one might deem "close enough" may vary), students cannot form a simple binary guide for their current preparatory commitment behavior.

Since it would therefore seem unreasonable to assume that students can formulate simple commit or do-not-commit rules based on direct observation, one might then decide to model preparatory commitment assuming that students infer their own probability of entering college by implicitly modeling the observed behavior patterns of older cohorts. If so, then students must recognize the variation in college entry and the preparatory commitment patterns that generate it, and it would then seem unreasonable to assume that they would be uninterested in determining what generates the aggregate behavior pattern. If so, they are likely to then construct some form of a simple decision tree in order to understand the behavior of older students. And, if so, after having constructed such a model in search of an understanding of others, students would presumably conclude that they might as well use it to directly model their own future behavior as well.

Based on this argument, I do not see simplistic imitative behavior as a serious alternative to the consultation of a stochastic decision tree as a forward-looking guide for current behavior. To a modeler, imitation is beguiling in its apparent simplicity, but it is not as simple for students to deploy in action as it may at first seem. Nonetheless, as I indicated earlier, it would be worthwhile to attempt to evaluate the tenability of such an imitation explanation. To do so, one would ask students to (1) estimate the college entry rates of recent high school graduates, (2) estimate the college entry rates of recent high school graduates very similar to them, and (3) estimate their likelihood of entering college in the future. Then, one would ask students to formulate a stochastic decision tree and estimate distributions for its parameters. If students' observable commitment behavior, along with their forecasts of their own future behavior, are more strongly associated with their subjective estimates of local college entry rates than with the purposive-prefigurative commitment implied by their elicited beliefs about a stochastic decision tree, then this would be compelling evidence that imitation should be placed squarely at the center of models of educational attainment.

MODELING SOCIAL INFLUENCE

The significant others' influence (SOI) mechanism of the Wisconsin model represents a solid and memorable piece of sociological theory. Unfortunately, the technology of path-models and regression analysis stripped it of any subtlety. To develop a model of social influence via peer networks that can help to conceptualize normative and imitative processes, I draw foundational literature from elsewhere, returning to the SOI mechanism in the course of development.

DeGroot (1974) proposed a model of convergence to a group consensus that has many attractive features, especially when used to model analogous probabilistic reasoning about stochastic decision trees. When attempting to reach agreement on the value of a parameter, individuals in a group form their own prior beliefs. Before they share their beliefs in collective deliberation, they also form importance weights that reflect their relative confidence in the forecasting abilities of each other. DeGroot's model specifies the evolution of the debate, as it is reflected in shifts of individuals' own beliefs.

For his model, the prior beliefs of n individuals are encoded in an n by 1 vector f_t. Each individual's set of n confidence weights is normalized to sum to 1 and then stacked as rows in an n by n matrix $\mathbf{P}$. With these two simple inputs, DeGroot maintained that vectors of updated opinions can then be obtained for any point in time by iteratively multiplying the vector of prior beliefs by the weight matrix: $f_{t+1} = \mathbf{P}f_t$. Depending on the structure of $\mathbf{P}$, iterated updates will either converge to a consensus value for the parameter for all group members or, if not, to alternative values championed by competing coalitions (see also Abelson 1964).

DeGroot's model is simple, and it is also based on intuition similar to that invoked for the SOI mechanism of the Wisconsin model. According to the interpretation of the Wisconsin model that I developed in Chapter 2, individuals forecast their own future behavior through self-reflection and then combine their self-reflection with the forecasts of their significant others. Through this combination, they form updated expectations of their own future behavior. But, I wish to develop now a model for the component beliefs on which expectations are based, rather than a model for educational expectations themselves (based on the argument put forward in Chapter 3 that educational expectations are not informative enough). And, using DeGroot's model, I will allow the weights embedded in his influence matrix $\mathbf{P}$ to be entirely unspecified. Analogous weights for the Wisconsin model are path coefficients attached to variables that measure the forecasts of significant others. I have seen no convincing claims that survey data, when paired with least squares or maximum likelihood formulae, reveal weights that warrant causal claims about social influence processes. Thus, I see the unspecified nature of DeGroot's matrix $\mathbf{P}$ as an attractive feature.

There is a stream of the sociological network literature that has also drawn on DeGroot's model (see Marsden and Friedkin 1994 for a review), and which, quite usefully, attempts to develop a rationale for the weight matrix $\mathbf{P}$ for sociological applications. Friedken and Johnsen (1990) posit the theoretical model:

$$\mathbf{y}_{t+1} = \alpha \mathbf{W} \mathbf{y}_t + \beta \mathbf{X} \mathbf{b} \tag{6.1}$$

where $\mathbf{y}_t$ is an n by 1 vector of initial opinions and $\mathbf{y}_{t+1}$ is an n by 1 vector of opinions after one iteration of social influence. $\mathbf{W}$ is an n by n matrix that captures the closeness of actors on some dimension of influence potential (analogous to DeGroot's transition matrix $\mathbf{P}$), based at least heuristically (and sometimes explicitly) on classic measures of closeness or equivalence in social network analysis (see Wasserman and Faust 1994). $\mathbf{X}$ is an n by k matrix of exogenous determinants of opinions, generally assumed to exert constant effects across all time periods that are summarized by the k by 1 parameter vector **b**. Finally, α and β are empirically derived weights that scale the relative importance of the endogenous social influence process and the exogenous determinants in **X**.

The social influence model of Equation 6.1 has some nice theoretical properties. It embeds the dynamics of DeGroot's model in concepts and measures familiar to most sociologists. Opinions are seen as a weighted linear average of standard regression-like independent variables and the opinions held by others. If the opinion is whether individuals should expect a student to attend college, this model is consistent with the Wisconsin model, and yet holds out the possibility that the weights that determine the patterns of social influence are themselves determined by a meaningful social process, reflected in a social network structure.

Nonetheless, the model in Equation 6.1 does not incorporate DeGroot's general notion that individuals in a group average beliefs that are full distributions rather than simple point estimates (in part, I presume, because DeGroot does not emphasize this feature when he presents his own model). In the context considered here, variances of forecasts of parameters are important. An appropriate Bayesian core of a sociological social influence model—one that preserves DeGroot's conception of a group consensus as a weighted combination of forecasts that are distributions of the future—would take form (with beta distributions) as:

$$\Pr(\theta)_{i,t+1} \propto \theta^{(\mathbf{w}_i \mathbf{s}_i - 1)}(1 - \theta)^{(\mathbf{w}_i \mathbf{f}_i - 1)} \tag{6.2}$$

where θ is an unspecified parameter (in this context, some parameter of a stochastic decision tree) and where $\Pr(\theta)_{i,t+1}$ is a beta posterior distribution for θ for each individual i.

Individuals maintain prior beliefs as beta distributions so that the success and failure parameters, s and f, vary across individuals. For Equation 6.2, these parameters are stacked in n by 1 column vectors **s** and **f**. And, as for Equation 6.1, an n by n matrix **W** of influence weights exists, defined in any number of ways depending on the context (that is, closeness in the network structure, subjective beliefs about the relative wisdom of one's significant others, and so on). Whatever the stipulated meaning of the weights, the value in the jth column of the ith row of **W** indicates the influence that the ith individual attaches to the views of the jth individual. Accordingly, the $\mathbf{w}_i$

in Equation 6.2 are defined as 1 by n row vectors of social influence weights extracted from **W**, each of which sums to 1 across j.

For this model, an individual with prior beliefs that are adequately represented by a beta distribution will have posterior beliefs that are a weighted function of his or her prior beliefs and those of his or her peers, the latter weighted in proportion to his or her closeness to or confidence in each of them.[4] If additional predictors, as in **X** for Equation 6.1, are assumed to determine beliefs, these effects can be partialled out of the belief distributions with standard empirical methods (and, at any point in time, if the effects are assumed to be constant fixed effects, as in Equation 6.1).

If such a model captures basic social influence processes that operate across peer networks, what implications does it have for the evolution of commitment that I have argued is generated by the parameters of individuals' stochastic decision trees? In contrast to the example in the next section, there is no unique implication for movement in either the means or variances of the belief distributions for π, α, β, and γ. Any such movement would depend on the structure of **s**, **f**, and **W**, which I have left entirely unspecified.

The only general implication of this social influence model is the expected emergence of clustering as individuals progress from middle school through high school. If peer groups are more stable than not, the belief distributions of peer groups should generally become more homogeneous in time, resulting in increasingly similar trajectories of commitment. More importantly, if this model captures the underlying influence process, one should see this convergence weighted toward the initial belief distributions of the most influential members of each peer group.

Again, since appropriate data are not yet available, it is impossible to verify these predictions, even though they are more or less consistent with the literature in the sociology of education. Virtually all research on peer cultures in American secondary education has confirmed Coleman's (1961) findings in *The Adolescent Society*. Schools contain leading crowds whose behavior and opinions shape the values and norms of their schools. Many students esteem these popular students, adopting their beliefs, opinions, and modes of behavior. Those students who rebel against the prevailing status system of the adolescent society, including the dominant opinion leaders of their schools, form countercultures by cultivating alternative peer groups with distinct status hierarchies. All peer groups, therefore, implicitly maintain alternative social influence weighting schemes, resulting in a clustered but probably still largely connected mapping for entire schools.

Moreover, students' beliefs about a stochastic decision tree parameter are responsive to more than just their closeness to these peers, as identified by their corresponding rows of the **W** matrix and the central tendencies of peers' beliefs. The variances of peers' beliefs also matter. For example, members of a cohesive but less than perfectly bounded countercultural peer group may still be influenced by the solidly informed beliefs of the leading crowd, even though the leading crowd is, by the specification of **W**, relatively socially distant. The degree to which the leading crowd will still have influence will be a negative function ceteris paribus of the certainty of the beliefs prevalent in the countercultural peer group.

Again, without data on how students view their stochastic decision trees, it is impossible to determine whether such subtle weighting of the opinions of others can be empirically validated. But, one can evaluate second-order predictions for measured variables that are correlated with the inputs and outputs of the presumed stochastic decision tree and with the social influence patterns in an assumed matrix **W**. Adjusting for exogenous predictors of poorly functioning schools and average levels of family background in communities, the density of friendship networks across schools should be positively associated with levels of commitment, as greater amounts of information should be shared across peer networks (assuming, of course, that the adjustment for exogenous differences in the quality of schools and communities has been effective, such that the average quality of shared information is partialled out). The basic idea is that the **W** matrix, when representing the network connectedness of students within a school, should spread information around the school as the proportion of nonzero elements increases. In highly connected schools, students are able to draw on abundant information to eliminate extreme values from their belief distributions. This prediction is supported by the results from high school students reported in Morgan and Sørensen (1999), if one is willing to assume that mathematics achievement gains between the tenth and twelfth grades reflect preparatory commitment to postsecondary schooling.[5]

In principle, the model of peer influence in this section could be generalized to more encompassing types of social influence, by including all adults and peers whose beliefs about a stochastic decision tree parameter would be regarded by a student as influential. One would augment the **W** matrix, allowing individuals to form new vectors of importance weights that include all significant others deemed worthy of consultation (or, impossible to ignore).

MODELING BELIEFS ABOUT THE FAIRNESS OF THE EDUCATIONAL SYSTEM

In prior sections of this chapter, commitment has been modeled as a function of students' immediate environments (for example, reference groups of older cohorts and current networks of valued peers). Generalized beliefs about the openness of the opportunity structure and the fairness of the educational system can also shape commitment. In some cases, these beliefs cannot simply be conceptualized as alternative beliefs about the payoff to a college education and hence cannot be entered directly into the stochastic decision tree model of Chapter 4. In this section, with reference to black-white differences in achievement in high school, I will demonstrate the value in modeling such processes directly and only thereafter looking back at possible connections to the stochastic decision tree model.

The Black-White Gap in Achievement and the Disidentification Explanation[6]

Even though black-white differences in test scores have narrowed substantially over the past few decades, a sizable gap remains even after adjustments for family background. Recent attempts to explain the persisting gap have focused on parenting practices, teacher expectations, and the structural characteristics of schools and school systems (see Hallinan 2001 and Jencks and Phillips 1998 for reviews of this literature). None of these explanations has proven sufficient for explaining the racial gap in achievement, particularly among middle class students.

Claude Steele has offered a new explanation, attracting a good deal of scholarly and public interest. Supported in part by results from a series of compelling laboratory experiments, Steele argues that the relatively poor test performance of black adolescents is partly a subconscious response to groundless but pervasive stereotypes of inherent black inferiority. Labeled "stereotype threat," this mechanism has found support in the experimental work of other psychologists (see Steele, Spencer, and Aronson 2002 for citations). Steele further argues that the piecemeal effects induced by stereo-type threat are steadily amplified by black students' *disidentification* with educational success, a protective process through which the motivation to achieve declines because conceptions of overall self-worth are gradually sep-arated from performance in school (Steele 1992, 1997).

There is much value in the theoretical ideas and experimental findings of Steele and his colleagues. In the remainder of this section, however, I will reinterpret the disidentification portion of his framework using the literature from the sociology of education. This interpretation enables an evaluation using survey data and also demonstrates the potential utility of using the sto-chastic decision tree framework for modeling race differences in achievement.

A Summary of the Disidentification Explanation in Its Original Form

As initially delineated by Steele and his colleagues (see Steele 1992, 1997; Steele and Aronson 1995), the disidentification explanation of race differ-ences in achievement is an extension of past research in social psychology on black-white differences in the relationship between self-esteem and educa-tional achievement (Demo and Parker 1987; Porter and Washington 1979, 1993; Rosenberg 1979). These earlier studies showed that (1) self-esteem and academic achievement are correlated among white students and among black students and (2) black students have levels of self-esteem at least as high as those of white students, even though black students, on average, do not perform as well in school. In an attempt to explain this apparent para-dox, Rosenberg (1979:267) drew on William James' principle of selective valuation and asserted that "we not only seek to excel in those areas on which we have staked ourselves but we tend to stake ourselves on those ar-eas in which we excel." According to this line of thinking, black students are able to maintain self-esteem, in spite of lower educational achievement, by selectively valuing performance in nonacademic domains.

Steele's disidentification explanation is another variant of James' prin-ciple of selective valuation, but one that is based on a more specific gen-erative process. This process is grounded on Steele's assumption that black students from all levels of the socioeconomic spectrum are haunted by the specter of confirming stereotypes of inherent black inferiority. These threat-ening stereotypes interfere with everyday educational performance in school, especially on important tests, because black students try too hard to avoid the low performance that "makes the stereotype more plausible as a self-characterization in the eyes of others, and perhaps even in one's own eyes" (Steele and Aronson 1995:797). Stereotype-threatened test takers spend "more time doing fewer items more inaccurately—probably as a result of alternating their attention between trying to answer the items and trying to assess the self-significance of their frustration" (Steele and Aronson 1995: 808). Stereotypes do not directly lower the motivation or performance expectations of test takers. Instead, stereotypes activate a subconscious mechanism wherein stereotype anxiety, which is manifest in self-evaluative pressure, impairs test-taking efficiency.

Over time, black students adapt to their predicament, and this adaptation results in disidentification. In order to maintain positive self-images, students inoculate their global self-esteem against performance evaluations in schooling. In so doing, they disidentify with educational achievement in general in order to claim a psychic victory that preserves self-worth. Unfortunately, however, disidentification does not offer a costless victory because it undermines the motivation and commitment necessary for continued educational achievement. Thus, unlike stereotype threat, disidentification directly lowers motivation and one's own performance expectations, further depressing future achievement.

What is the mechanism that links poor test performance (perhaps in response to stereotype threat) to full-blown disidentification with schooling? In reviewing the literature on stereotypes and social stigma, Crocker, Major, and Steele (1998) suggest that an intermediate psychological state develops in which students adopt coping strategies to reconcile their performance disappointments with their valuation of schooling. Crocker et al. (1998:528) state that:

> [One] way the stigmatized may deal with threats to personal and collective self-esteem posed by their predicaments is to psychologically disengage their self-esteem from their outcomes in a particular domain or context. When one disengages one's self-evaluation in a domain from one's outcomes in the domain, those outcomes become less relevant to one's self-esteem. We use the term disengagement to refer to the initial disconnecting of one's self-esteem from one's outcomes in a particular stigma-threatening situation—the first reaction. And we use the term disidentification to refer to the more chronic adaptation—in response to the chronic threat of stigmatization in a domain—of dropping, or not taking on the domain as a personal identity, as a long-term basis of self-esteem.

In this characterization, disengagement[7] from performance evaluations is an intermediate stage through which students pass on their way to full-blown disidentification.[8]

A Direct Model for Movement Between Identified and Disidentified States

I will now develop a slightly more formal analytic model that grounds Steele's disidentification explanation on core mechanisms from the sociological literature, and I will then relate it to the stochastic decision tree model developed earlier. In developing the model, I take Coleman's (1981:9) strategy to use a mathematical model that "generally conforms to the ideas one has of the substantive process." And, I adopt some of the same mathematical tools (for example, Markov chains; see Norris 1997) that Coleman adopted when analyzing data on the adolescent society (see Coleman 1964a, Chapters 12 and 13; Coleman 1964b). I first develop the simplest possible Markov model for movement between identified and disidentified states. I then invoke identity theory from sociology, connect it to the literature in the sociology of education, and develop a structural model that generates achievement and global self-esteem patterns, conditional on one's disidentification status.

Stereotype threat generates second-order achievement declines, according to Steele and his colleagues, by setting off a disidentification response among stereotype-threatened students. The state-space diagram of Figure 6.1 represents the basic Markov model on which I will elaborate. In line with Steele's theorizing, students in the state $DIS = 0$ are identified with schooling and can be suitably characterized by the following idealized self-appraisal narrative:

> Hypothetical identified student: "Doing well in school is important to me. When I receive a good grade or a high test score, I am happy, and I want to share my good feelings with my parents and friends. When I receive a poor grade or a low test score, I feel depressed, and I try to avoid telling my parents and friends about my poor performance."

In contrast, students in the state $DIS = 1$ are disidentified with schooling and are characterized by the following alternative idealized self-appraisal:

> Hypothetical disidentified student: "Doing well in school is not very important to me. When I receive a poor grade or a low test score, I don't really care. I am

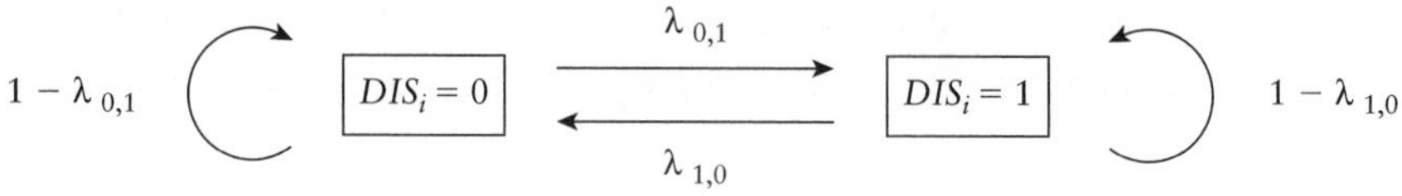

Figure 6.1.　A Markov Model for Movement Between Identified and Disidentified States

> not ashamed of it, and I do not hide my results from my parents or friends. When I receive a good grade or a high test score, I suppose I feel a little bit happy, but not really."

Students oscillate between these polar states, as they define their identities and plan for their education in the future by consulting their stochastic decision trees. Although some students remain solidly in either state, a substantial proportion of high school students are at risk of shifting from one state to the other, and then perhaps back again. Such shifts would necessarily be consequential for educational achievement, perhaps by way of the preparatory commitment decisions that I have argued are to some degree regulated by students' stochastic decision trees and that I will discuss later in this section.

The state-space depicted in Figure 6.1 is Markovian when constraints are placed on patterns of movement. In particular, the probability of moving from one state to another state (for example, from the identified state to the disidentified state, $DIS = 0$ to $DIS = 1$) remains constant for all time periods, so that knowledge of the distribution across states at time period t depends only on the distribution across states in time period $t - 1$ and knowledge of the time-invariant transition rates between the alternative states. Movement between states is determined by two transition rates, $\lambda_{0,1}$ and $\lambda_{1,0}$, which are probabilities between 0 and 1. They are attached to the arrows between the two states in Figure 6.1, but they are also specified as elements in a two-by-two transition matrix:

$$\lambda = \begin{bmatrix} 1 - \lambda_{0,1} & \lambda_{1,0} \\ \lambda_{0,1} & 1 - \lambda_{1,0} \end{bmatrix}$$

that generates the time path for distributions across the two states. The sequence of resulting distributions is the Markov chain.

Table 6.1 simulates Markov chains for this system, assuming the existence of two different sets of hypothetical white and black students. The

TABLE 6.1

A Simple Markov Model for the Evolution of Disidentification

A. WHITE STUDENTS (OR BLACK STUDENTS NOT SUBJECT TO STEREOTYPE THREAT)

Transition Matrix λ			Distribution at $t = 0$ s(0)	Distribution at $t = 1$ λs(0)	Distribution at $t = 3$ λs(2)	Distribution at $t = 5$ λs(4)	Distribution at $t = \infty$ λs(∞)
$\begin{bmatrix} .95 & .25 \\ .05 & .75 \end{bmatrix}$		$DIS = 0$	.950	.915	.873	.853	.833
		$DIS = 1$	.050	.085	.127	.147	.167

B. BLACK STUDENTS SUBJECT TO STEREOTYPE THREAT

Transition Matrix λ			Distribution at $t = 0$ s(0)	Distribution at $t = 1$ λs(0)	Distribution at $t = 3$ λs(2)	Distribution at $t = 5$ λs(4)	Distribution at $t = \infty$ λs(∞)
$\begin{bmatrix} .80 & .10 \\ .20 & .90 \end{bmatrix}$		$DIS = 0$	.950	.765	.545	.437	.333
		$DIS = 1$	.050	.235	.455	.563	.667

transition matrices for white and black students differ, as shown in the first column of Table 6.1. For white students, the values for $\lambda_{0,1}$ and $\lambda_{1,0}$ stipulate that between time $t - 1$ and time t, the probability that an identified student will move to the disidentified state is .05 while the probability that a disidentified student will move to the identified state is .25. For black students, the probability of moving from the identified to the disidentified state is higher (.20 instead of .05), and the probability of moving from the disidentified to the identified state is lower (.10 instead of .25). Thus, for the Markov chains reported in Table 6.1, stereotype threat generates two distinct effects: (1) it causes a larger proportion of students to become disidentified, and (2) it causes a smaller proportion of students to become identified again. And, as implied in the discussion earlier, the alternative transition matrix of black students is a direct response to the existence of stereotype threat.

The two different transition matrices imply race-specific time paths for the distribution across identified and disidentified states, as shown in the fourth through seventh columns of Table 6.1. For both groups of students, the initial distribution at time $t = 0$ is the same. Ninety-five percent of students are identified with schooling, and 5 percent of students are disidentified with schooling.[9] The distribution across states at $t = 0$ is a pre-stereotype-threat equilibrium distribution, and the distribution across states at $t = \infty$ is a long-run equilibrium distribution toward which the Markov chain of probability distributions would converge. The distribution across states at time t is easily calculated by stacking the probabilities at time $t - 1$ in a column vector, $s(t - 1)$, and then pre-multiplying the vector by the transition matrix.

For the hypothetical numbers chosen for the simulation of Table 6.1, the proportion of white students who are identified declines steadily from .95 to .853 by $t = 5$, and then declines further to its equilibrium value of .833. Thus, if $t = 1$ were the eighth grade and $t = 5$ were the senior year of high school, approximately 15 percent of white students would typically be observed on any particular day in the senior year in the disidentification state rather than the identification state. For black students, however, the alternative transition matrix generates a much higher percentage of disidentified students over the same time period. The proportion of black students who are identified declines much more substantially from .95 to .437 by $t = 5$, and then further to the equilibrium value of .333. By the end of high school, more than half of all simulated black students would be observed in the disidentification state on any particular day. Although these proportions are arbitrary, it will always be the case that the percentage of students who will end up disidentified with schooling will be greater for blacks than for whites if $\lambda_{0,1}$ is higher for blacks and $\lambda_{1,0}$ is lower for blacks.

Can the transition rates be estimated from available data? Unfortunately, no. There is no known measure of disidentification. All that is in the available survey data are measures of global self-esteem and separate measures of academic self-concept. For this reason, Steele and his colleagues initially defined disidentification with reference to the strength of relationships across cross-sections of white and black students between achievement and global self-esteem (see Steele 1992, 1997), and at times between academic self-concept and achievement (see Crocker et al. 1998). Thus, even though the Markov model is a useful framework, a supplementary model is needed to translate the disidentification process summarized in Table 6.1 into a set of relationships between global self-esteem and academic achievement.

A Structural Model for the Evolution of Achievement and Self-Esteem

Although selective valuation—as elaborated in sociology by Morris Rosenberg in his theory of self-esteem—is one departure point for developing a mechanistic model of the disidentification process, one that is apparently favored by Steele and his colleagues, its variable-centered, psychometric-construct approach is insufficiently complete to capture the dynamic social processes that sociologists of education generally posit when developing explanations for achievement differences in American secondary education. At least since Hollingshead (1949), Coleman (1961), and Stinchcombe (1964), the literature on endogenous peer effects in the sociology of education has been centrally concerned with the interactive behavior patterns of heterogeneous but networked populations of adolescents.

I therefore will now develop a structural model for shifts in the relationship between achievement and self-esteem by first asserting a correspondence between identification with schooling and the probability of engaging in achievement-oriented behavior. I then construct a four-equation threshold model for the relationship between the probability of engaging in such behavior and both achievement and global self-esteem.

I first draw on the form of identity theory developed by Sheldon Stryker (see Stryker and Burke 2000), incorporating his latest thoughts on the potential of identity theory to reinvigorate the study of self-esteem (see Ervin and Stryker 2001).[10] With its origins in structural symbolic interactionism, Stryker's identity theory is an attempt to operationalize Mead's basic framework of "society shapes self shapes social behavior" by developing Stryker's more elaborate dictum "commitment shapes identity salience shapes role choice behavior" (see Stryker and Burke 2000:285–286). In particular, individual selves are composed of multiple identities, each of which is attached to a socially defined role structure of appropriate behavior. Role choice behavior is then a function of both affective commitment (feelings of positive sentiment toward particular identities) and interactional commitment (network ties to significant others who enact behavior consistent with particular identities). As defined in Stryker's dictum earlier, commitment then shapes an individual's identity salience hierarchy, which in turn generates a role-choice function that automates everyday behavior.

For a model of identification/disidentification with schooling based on Stryker's identity theory, one must first stipulate the competing identities to which high school students' selves are committed. This model of high school students' selves must be sufficiently deep, in that it must allow for variation in identity salience hierarchies. But, for the present purposes, it cannot be so finely articulated that it is mathematically intractable. Thus, consistent with the traditional characterization of the adolescent society offered by Coleman (1961), I will assume that all high school students entertain simultaneously a student identity and an adolescent identity. Accordingly, students must choose among behavior patterns consistent with respective student and adolescent roles. Student role behavior is varied, ranging from time spent doing homework to effort exerted in class, including the sort of "good citizenship" that ingratiates oneself with teachers. Adolescent role behavior ranges from conventional status striving, as in the car-and-date-obsessed adolescent culture of Coleman (1961), to the slightly deviant "tabooed pleasures" of Hollingshead (1949:315), and even includes the alienated "short-run Hedonism" of Stinchcombe (1964:16).[11]

Identity theory specifies how individuals choose from among their behavioral options, as a function of one's affective and interactional commitment to the alternative patterns of behavior that characterize the roles one entertains. Stereotype threat, I surmise, generates a shift in affective commitment for black students, away from the student identity. If this shift is bolstered by interactive commitment to the adolescent identity, as would be the case if many other students were responding to stereotype threat as well, a collective devaluation of the student identity might emerge alongside a redefinition of the adolescent identity as one that is inherently in contradiction with the student identity. Such collective identity shifts would be consistent with the emergence of an oppositional culture, as emphasized by Fordham and Ogbu (1986).[12]

Now, denote the probability of engaging in behavior consistent with the student role as $\Pr(S)$. Accordingly, I assume that for every individual i, each decision of whether to engage in a possible instance of achievement-oriented behavior is a draw from a binomial distribution with probability equal to $\Pr(S)_i$. Assuming that academic achievement is a direct function of $\Pr(S)$, a simple threshold model can be asserted, such that the achievement of individual i at time t is:

$$ACH_{it} = ACH_{it-1} + \alpha_t^{ID} + \varepsilon_{it} \qquad \text{if} \qquad \Pr(S)_{it} \geq \tau_t \qquad (6.3a)$$

and

$$ACH_{it} = ACH_{it-1} + \alpha_t^{DIS} + \varepsilon_{it} \qquad \text{if} \qquad \Pr(S)_{it} < \tau_t \qquad (6.3b)$$

where $\alpha_t^{ID} > \alpha_t^{DIS}$ for all t and ε_{it} is normally distributed with mean 0 and variance σ_t^2.[13] Disidentified students are less likely to engage in achievement-oriented behavior consistent with the student identity. The restrictions placed on Equations 6.3a and 6.3b ensure that achievement grows more quickly for identified students, since between time period $t - 1$ and t, the amount by which achievement increases is smaller for students who are disidentified at time t.

Consider how similar this structural model of achievement is to the preparatory commitment framework I outlined earlier. $\Pr(S)$ determines achievement just as prefigurative commitment determines preparatory commitment. Indeed, the Equations 6.3a and 6.3b are analogous to dividing the distribution of purposive-prefigurative commitment across a threshold and then asserting that preparatory commitment and resulting achievement vary across the threshold as well. I will return to this similarity later, and, perhaps unsurprisingly, argue that the decision tree framework represents a more general unifying framework.

Returning to the targeted sociological literature on the black-white achievement gap, past researchers have sought to model variants of Equations 6.3a and 6.3b directly. Although this analysis strategy is a viable and a quite useful exercise, the disidentification explanation enables an alternative but complementary analysis strategy. Since the available data, such as the *NELS* data analyzed by Cook and Ludwig (1997) and Ainsworth-Darnell and Downey (1998), do not contain absolutely all of the information necessary to model all possible types of behavior that might suitably be categorized as more consistent with the student identity than the adolescent identity, results that claim to have modeled comprehensively the relationships between achievement and anti-school behavior are vulnerable to the criticism that the available surveys simply do not adequately capture genuine anti-school behavior. After all, the most truly creative and hence particularly effective anti-school behavior is, almost by definition, impossible for academic researchers to know in advance when developing survey instruments.

The appeal of the disidentification explanation is that global self-esteem should reflect all of these hard-to-measure behaviors. To show how, specify each individual's time-dependent global self-esteem as:

$$EST_{it} = \delta_t^{ID} \varepsilon_{it} + \eta_{it} \qquad \text{if} \qquad \Pr(S)_{it} \geq \tau_t \tag{6.4a}$$

and

$$EST_{it} = \delta_t^{DIS} \varepsilon_{it} + \psi_{it} \qquad \text{if} \qquad \Pr(S)_{it} < \tau_t \tag{6.4b}$$

where (1) ε_{it} is the component of achievement not attributed to relative gains/ declines for identified/disidentified students, as specified in Equations 6.3a and 6.3b, where (2) $\delta_t^{ID} - \delta_t^{DIS}$ is equal to some positive (possibly time varying) constant c for all t, and where (3) η_{it} and ψ_{it} are normally distributed with identical means and with similar, though not necessarily identical, variances.[14] Thus, as stipulated in Equations 6.4a and 6.4b, the linear relationship between self-esteem and achievement is weaker in every time period for those in the disidentified state.[15]

Although one cannot directly observe the thresholds that determine whether at any point in time a students' achievement and self-esteem are determined by Equations 6.3a and 6.4a rather than Equations 6.3b and 6.4b (or by possibly intermediate equations between them), one can use the Markov model developed earlier to derive over-time implications for the cross-sectional relationship between measurable variables for achievement and global self-esteem.

If, at any point in time, black students are more likely to be disidentified, as in the Markov model simulated for Table 6.1, the proportion of students whose achievement and self-esteem are determined by Equations 6.3b and 6.4b rather than Equations 6.3a and 6.4a will be greater for black students than for white students. If this is the case, then four implications immediately follow from the simple structural model, assuming that basic differences in family background have been partialled out of the data that are used to measure achievement and global self-esteem: (1) average achievement should be lower for blacks than for whites; (2) the achievement gap should grow over time; (3) global self-esteem should be more weakly related to achievement among black students than among white students; and (4) the relationship between global self-esteem and achievement should decline for black students, and any such decline should be greater than any similar decline for white students.

The first two implications are strongly supported by the literature on the black-white test score gap, as comprehensively documented in Jencks and Phillips (1998). However, neither of these implications is uniquely tied to the disidentification explanation. The third and fourth implications were collapsed into implication 3 in Morgan and Mehta (2004), and the data conclusively reject them for high school students. As shown in Table 4 of Morgan and Mehta (2004), at no point between the eighth and twelfth grade is the cross-sectional relationship between achievement and global self-esteem weaker for blacks than for whites. We therefore concluded in Morgan and Mehta (2004) that there is little support in the available survey data for the main implications of the disidentification explanation for black-white differences in achievement.

Nonetheless, we did find some compelling black-white differences. When black students formulate self-evaluations of their own academic competence, they are less sensitive to external performance evaluations. And, in particular, as shown in Table 2 of Morgan and Mehta (2004), the relationship between academic self-concept and academic achievement was weaker in the cross-section for blacks than for whites.[16] We therefore offered in the discussion section of the article a variety of explanations for why black students are not relatively more disidentified with academic achievement than whites and yet still are more likely to doubt the validity of performance evaluations of their academic achievement. In the remainder of this section, I recast these speculative interpretations, using an elaborated Markov model and some features of the stochastic decision tree framework.

Discounting Performance Evaluations and the Process of Disidentification

As discussed earlier, after developing a model of disidentification based on the relationship between self-esteem and achievement, Steele and his colleagues then posited the existence of a mediating disengagement process. Achievement declines in response to stereotype threat were said to result first in the discounting of performance evaluations and then thereafter in a realignment of self-esteem with self-evaluations in nonacademic domains (see the quotation from Crocker et al. 1998 earlier).

To incorporate the discounting of performance evaluations into the analytic model of the disidentification process, I first elaborate the two-state Markov model presented in Figure 6.1. As shown in Figure 6.2 and then simulated in Table 6.2, I cross-classify the criterion for disidentification with a separate criterion for discounting performance evaluations (that is, $DPE = 0$ versus $DPE = 1$) in order to form four separate states. Students in each state are characterized by elaborated self-appraisal narratives:

> Hypothetical identified student who remains sensitive to performance evaluations: "Doing well in school is important to me. When I receive a good grade or a high test score, I am happy, and I want to share my good feelings with my parents and friends. When I receive a poor grade or a low test score, I feel

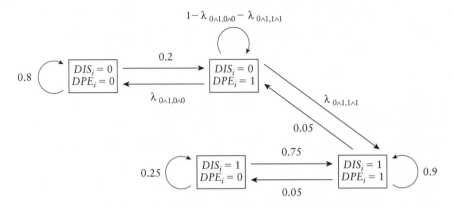

Figure 6.2. A Markov Model for Movement Between Identified and Disidentified States, with Supplementary States for Discounting of Performance Evaluations

depressed, and I try to avoid telling my parents and friends about my poor performance."

Hypothetical identified student who discounts performance evaluations: "Doing well in school is important to me. When I receive a good grade or a high test score, I am happy. But, when I receive a poor grade or a low test score, I generally feel that there is something wrong with the test. It is widely known that students like me do not do well on many tests, because the tests are unfair."

Hypothetical disidentified student who remains sensitive to performance evaluations: "Doing well in school is not very important to me. When I receive a poor grade or a low test score, I don't really care. I am not ashamed of it, and I do not hide my results from my parents or friends. When I receive a good grade or a high test score, I suppose I feel a little bit happy, but school is just not important enough for me to go around bragging about getting an A. I just don't care enough to try do well on tests."

Hypothetical disidentified student who discounts performance evaluations: "Doing well in school is not very important to me. When I receive a poor grade or a low test score, I don't really care. I am not ashamed of it, and I do not hide my results from my parents or friends. Tests just don't matter. Everyone knows that students like me do not do well on them, because the tests are unfair."

For brevity, many of the transition rates in Figure 6.2 are fixed at reasonable values similar to those for the transition matrix assumed for blacks in the second panel of Table 6.1. However, the critical transition rates out of the state where individuals remain identified with achievement but discount the relevance of performance evaluations remain unspecified in Figure 6.2.

TABLE 6.2
A Markov Chain for the Evolution of Disidentification
Where the Discounting of Performance Evaluations
Represents a Slippery Slope Toward Disidentification

Transition Matrix λ					Distribution at $t = 0$ $s(0)$	Distribution at $t = 1$ $\lambda s(0)$	Distribution at $t = 3$ $\lambda s(2)$	Distribution at $t = 5$ $\lambda s(4)$	Distribution at $t = \infty$ $\lambda s(\infty)$
				$DIS = 0$ $DPE = 0$	.950	.760	.550	.402	.056
.8	.2	0	0	$DIS = 0$ $DPE = 1$	.0	.193	.147	.120	.056
.2	.05	0	.05						
0	0	.25	.05	$DIS = 1$ $DPE = 0$	.0	.003	.010	.023	.056
0	.75	.75	.9	$DIS = 1$ $DPE = 1$	.050	.045	.293	.455	.833

Table 6.2 presents a transition matrix and associated Markov chain, assuming that the state $DIS = 0$ and $DPE = 1$ serves as a slippery slope toward disidentification, as suggested by Steele and his colleagues in Crocker et al. (1998). The second row of the transition matrix stipulates that students who are identified with achievement but who discount performance evaluations at time $t - 1$ have a probability of .2 of becoming identified and no longer discounting the relevance of performance evaluations at time t. However, they have a much larger probability of .75 of becoming disidentified with achievement, while also discounting the relevance of performance evaluations. Thus, they have only a .05 probability of remaining in the precarious coping state where they continue to value achievement but discount the relevance of performance evaluations.

As shown in the Markov chain reported in columns three through seven of Table 6.2, even though 95 percent of students are identified with achievement and sensitive to performance evaluations at $t = 0$, by $t = 5$ nearly half of all students become disidentified with schooling. And, for the equilibrium distribution toward which the chain would eventually converge, nearly 83 percent of students are disidentified with schooling.[17]

Based on the results presented in Morgan and Mehta (2004), which suggest that black students are more likely to discount performance evaluations but not more likely to disidentify with achievement, I see no evidence in the available survey data that the discounting of performance evaluations generally leads to full-blown disidentification. Rather, as we speculated in the discussion section of Morgan and Mehta (2004), it may be that black students remain identified with achievement in school because they do not trust the performance evaluations, which they see as evidence of prejudice against their group. Consider the next two alternative specifications of the four-sate Markov model that demonstrate how the discounting of performance evaluations might help to prevent full-blown disidentification.

Table 6.3 presents transition matrices and Markov chains, assuming that the state $DIS = 0$ and $DPE = 1$ serves as either a weak buffer or an absorbing buffer against disidentification. For the weak buffer model reported in panel A, the state where $DIS = 0$ and $DPE = 1$ for $t - 1$ remains a precarious one, but unlike the slippery slope model, the probability of restoring one's faith in tests is greater than the probability of then disidentifying with achievement by time period t. In this way, the precarious state functions as a buffer zone. Many individuals who temporarily lose faith in the validity of tests eventually have their faith restored, probably after having attained a good score on a subsequent test and not wanting to accept that the better score is just luck. For the weak buffer model, more than 80 percent of students remain identified with schooling through time period 5, while even in the equilibrium distribution nearly half of all students remain identified with schooling.

For the absorbing buffer model reported in panel B, the state $DIS = 0$ and $DPE = 1$ has substantial holding power. Given the initially high distribution of identified students, the vast majority of students remain identified through time period $t = 5$, even though if the process were allowed to converge to equilibrium, almost half of students would eventually disidentify with schooling. I see this, intuitively, as the more appealing of the two models specified in Table 6.3. Accordingly, I see the intermediate state that Crocker et al. (1998) imply is merely a transient state, as a more important state in which many students are to be found.

Implications for Modeling Black-White Differences with the Model of Commitment

If this buffering interpretation of the results of Morgan and Mehta (2004) is correct, such that black students discount performance evaluations in order

TABLE 6.3
A Markov Chain for the Evolution of Disidentification Where the Discounting of Performance Evaluations Represents a Buffer Against Disidentification

A. A WEAK BUFFER AGAINST DISIDENTIFICATION

Transition Matrix λ				Distribution at $t = 0$ $s(0)$	Distribution at $t = 1$ $\lambda s(0)$	Distribution at $t = 3$ $\lambda s(2)$	Distribution at $t = 5$ $\lambda s(4)$	Distribution at $t = \infty$ $\lambda s(\infty)$
				$DIS = 0$ $DPE = 0$	.950	.760	.710	.653	.356
.8	.7	0	0	$DIS = 0$ $DPE = 1$	.0	.193	.161	.152	.102
.2	.05	0	.05						
0	0	.25	.05	$DIS = 1$ $DPE = 0$	.0	.003	.005	.010	.034
0	.25	.75	.9	$DIS = 1$ $DPE = 1$	.050	.045	.125	.185	.509

B. AN ABSORBING BUFFER AGAINST DISIDENTIFICATION

Transition Matrix λ				Distribution at $t = 0$ $s(0)$	Distribution at $t = 1$ $\lambda s(0)$	Distribution at $t = 3$ $\lambda s(2)$	Distribution at $t = 5$ $\lambda s(4)$	Distribution at $t = \infty$ $\lambda s(\infty)$
				$DIS = 0$ $DPE = 0$	.950	.760	.511	.368	.108
.8	.05	0	0	$DIS = 0$ $DPE = 1$	.0	.193	.421	.526	.432
.2	.9	0	.05						
0	0	.25	.05	$DIS = 1$ $DPE = 0$	.0	.003	.003	.005	.029
0	.05	.75	.9	$DIS = 1$ $DPE = 1$	.050	.045	.065	.101	.432

to remain identified with achievement in school, then black students are engaging in a process to maintain levels of commitment to schooling that is independent of the basic operation of the stochastic decision tree that I have
outlined earlier. And yet, even though this process originates in more general belief formation processes about the fairness of the educational system
and its evaluative standards, one should expect to see this process reflected
to some extent in black-white differences in beliefs about the parameters of

the stochastic decision tree. If so, this opens up the possibility that the stochastic decision tree framework can be used to further examine and then extend the buffering explanation.

Two basic patterns of black-white differences in beliefs about the parameters of a stochastic decision tree are consistent with the process underlying the buffering explanation: (1) relative increases in the variances of the belief distributions for π, α, and β and (2) decreases in the mean of the belief distribution for π (and perhaps also in the means of the belief distributions for α and β). Consistent with the simulations of Chapter 5, these differences can be conceptualized as the result of alternative belief formation processes that evolve as individuals move away from the state of being fully identified with schooling toward one in which they are still identified with schooling but nonetheless have learned to discount performance evaluations. With reference to the slow and fast Bayesian learners simulated for Figure 5.2, consider the two possible groups of students simulated for Figure 6.3.

The first group processes the same accurate information as the students simulated for Figure 5.2, which suggests that the expected values of π, α, β, and γ are still .556, .6, .25, and .2, respectively. But, these new simulated black students are designated as slow learners about the beliefs relevant to college—π, α, and β—and fast learners about the beliefs relevant to high school, γ. Accordingly, the simulated time path of $\Pr(E = 1)$ goes to 1 faster than for uniformly slow learners but much slower than for uniformly fast learners (as shown in Figure 5.2).[18] And, as a result, this simulated group of students may have lower levels of preparatory commitment and hence lower achievement, and yet still feel substantially more likely than not that they should prepare themselves to go to college.

The second group of simulated students is more pessimistic than the first, but they are still not solidly disidentified with schooling. If they were, their levels of $\Pr(E = 1)$ would drop considerably below .5. Instead, the second group of students is comprised of slow Bayesian learners who have moderately risk averse beliefs. Their beliefs suggest that the expected values of π, α, β, and γ are .333, .6, .2, and .2 instead of .556, .6, .25, and .2 respectively. In contrast to all prior groups of simulated students, these students see college as a risky venture in two respects. First, on average, they feel that the probability of graduating from college if enrolled is quite low. Second, on average, they also feel that attending college does not have a payoff unless one grad-

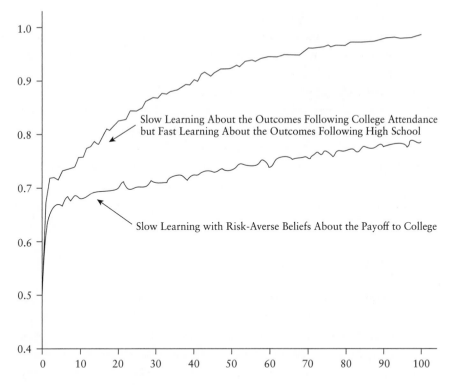

Figure 6.3.   The Evolution of Commitment for Two Types of Students Who Discount Performance Evaluations

uates. As shown in Figure 6.3, the time path of $\Pr(E = 1)$ for this group goes to 1 even more slowly than for the slow learners simulated for Figure 5.2.

Characterizing these two groups of students as types of slow Bayesian learners is not as natural as in Chapter 5, since the discounting of performance evaluations is a response to beliefs about the fairness of the system rather than a slower rate of information acquisition. Nonetheless, the resulting evolution of beliefs is compelling. Students who discount performance evaluations would be less likely to hold precise beliefs about their likelihood of doing well in college and then subsequently in the labor market, as they would be more likely to wonder about the fairness of performance evaluations of college professors and white-collar bosses. Moreover, for each dose of information received, they would respond more tentatively when updating their beliefs.

In sum, the simulations presented in Figure 6.3 are meant to show that the consequences of the discounting of performance evaluations are conditional on beliefs about the value of further schooling.[19] The results of Morgan and Mehta (2004) suggest that black students remain identified with achievement and continue to strive for postsecondary education, even though they are less likely to trust external performance evaluations. Thus, since we did not find evidence that blacks disproportionately succumbed to the most serious form of disidentification, the generally positive trajectories of commitment suggested in Figure 6.3 seem reasonable.[20] Blacks are likely to continue to report that achievement is important to them, but they nonetheless may feel uncertain enough about their futures to suffer some short-run declines in preparatory commitment and the achievement that is a function of it.

CONCLUSIONS

In this chapter, I have indicated that the modeling of imitative and normative sources of commitment, and hence imitative and normative causes of educational attainment, remains an important goal of sociological attempts to explain patterns of educational attainment. And, although I have conceded that in the future the modeling of such processes may prove to have very little connection to the stochastic decision tree framework that I laid out in prior chapters, I have also argued that no such judgment can be made at present. For now, there is value in modeling these processes in ways that are consistent with the stochastic decision tree framework, and in this chapter I have presented modeling ideas for imitation processes, social influence via peer networks, and adjustment to beliefs about the fairness of the educational system in order to demonstrate how this can be accomplished.

In Chapter 7, I revisit the justification for a new model of educational attainment and then conclude by laying out a research agenda for an evaluation of whether the stochastic decision tree framework should be a foundational component of such a model. As suggested at many points in prior chapters, a main goal of the research agenda is to develop new methods with which to measure students' beliefs, and I will accordingly make a case for collecting data on students' beliefs about their stochastic decision trees.

NOTES

1. I will argue in the next section that this imitation mechanism requires the invocation of myopia assumptions that strip it of genuine causal power.

2. One should not forget that immediate college entry following high school is a non-repeatable decision for a major life course transition. Although sideways-looking models of imitative behavior are powerful in some contexts, such as in modeling fads and other contagious behavior, they are of limited utility when individuals are acting in contexts where there is a genuine payoff for engaging in forward-looking assessments of alternatives.

3. If not in all characteristics, then students must select older students who are equivalent at least in all respects relevant to patterns of educational attainment. But, if students have no model in their heads of who should go to college, and hence engage only in myopic imitation, then selecting only a limited set of criteria on which to search for matching students seems impossible, for they should have no conception of what criteria are relevant for patterns of educational attainment. Thus, it would seem that for imitation-rule following to prevail in strict form, students would need to find matches on all characteristics, which is, of course, impossible in any school or community of the size typical of those in the United States.

4. This model is similar to the legacy of DeGroot's model in Bayesian statistics (see Clemen, Jones, and Winkler 1996; Lindley 1985; West 1988).

5. Similarly, the amount of accurate information should increase to the extent that networks of parents are outward looking and hence connected to diverse sources of information. Equivalently, net of the density of friendship networks, the density of parental networks across schools should be negatively associated with levels of commitment. Thus, turning things around, it is possible that the stochastic decision tree framework suggests a mechanism that explains why we observed that achievement gains in mathematics are highest in schools with dense student networks and sparse parent networks. Students in these optimally organized schools benefit from network configurations that ensure that the means of their belief distributions are relatively close to those that would be estimated from labor market data and that the variances of their belief distributions are relatively small.

6. In this section, I build directly on what is published in Morgan and Mehta (2004). Virtually all of the ideas in this section have been shaped by fruitful (and enjoyable) collaboration with Jal Mehta, and some of these ideas were developed simultaneously as we endeavored to secure publication for Morgan and Mehta (2004). I am therefore happy to acknowledge Jal's substantial input on all of the good ideas in this section, while absolving him of blame for all of the bad ones.

7. For sociologists, the usage of the term *disengagement* by Crocker et al. (1998) may be confusing because it refers to a social psychological state of mind—the dissociation of one's self-evaluations in a domain from external performance evaluations. Academic disengagement in the sociological literature is a behavioral

concept that refers to the withdrawal of commitment to schooling (i.e., doing homework, being attentive, coming to school; see Johnson, Crosnoe, and Elder 2001). Except where explicitly presenting Steele's ideas, I adopt the phrase "discounting of performance evaluations" instead of disengagement.

8. In more recent work, Steele and Aronson have revised their earlier emphasis on the inevitability of disidentification as a consequence of stereotype threat (Steele, Spencer, and Aronson 2002), taking note of an emerging psychological literature that suggests a variety of responses to stereotype threat (see also Major and Schmader 1998; Schmader, Major, and Gramzow 2001). However, these studies are generally restricted to laboratory conditions, and there is little work that examines how these processes play out in secondary schools in the United States.

9. The time points chosen for presentation correspond heuristically to the *NELS* data analyzed in Morgan and Mehta (2004), where $t = 1$ is 1988, $t = 3$ is 1990, and $t = 5$ is 1992.

10. The Ervin and Stryker article, however, is in no way a heretical departure from Rosenberg's research program, since the article is published in a recent Festschrift for Rosenberg (Owens, Stryker, and Goodman 2001).

11. Understanding when adolescent role behavior is consistent with student role behavior has been a major topic of analysis in the sociology of education. The literature on the student-athlete, for example, is well developed and demonstrates a case in which both roles can potentially reinforce each other in promoting academic achievement.

12. I see the disidentification process developed by Steele and his colleagues, drawing on James' and Rosenberg's notion of selective valuation, as generating alternative behavioral patterns that are measurable. In this sense, disidentification is similar at its core to the sociological literature that has sought to model race differences in achievement-oriented behavior and resulting patterns of academic achievement. What differs is simply the motivation for the relationships. Rather than rejecting achievement in school as "a white thing," in order to reinforce the fictive kinship supposedly at the core of the black identity, black students instead refrain from engaging in role choice behavior that is consistent with the student identity because they become frustrated with the evaluative procedures adopted by their teachers and by their lower-than-expected achievement.

13. One can develop many other elaborated models by placing restrictions on the parameters of these equations. For example, one could stipulate that $\alpha_t^{ID} - \alpha_t^{DIS}$ and/or that σ_t^2 are weakly increasing in t. Or one could pursue integration of these achievement equations with the self-esteem equations introduced later (i.e., by explicitly parameterizing $\alpha_t^{ID} - \alpha_t^{DIS}$ as a function of the difference between δ_t^{ID} and δ_t^{DIS}). Such modifications do not change the claims in the main text.

14. The variance terms for these equations could be further qualified. Self-esteem constructs have no inherent scale, and as a result the literature typically treats self-esteem as a standardized variable with unit variance. For this reason, I do not specify the variance terms of Equations 6.4a and 6.4b as precisely as I did

for Equations 6.3a and 6.3b. However, if the variance of self-esteem is stipulated to remain constant, then the variance of ψ_{it} must increase relative to the variance of η_{it} as the disidentification process unfolds. This would operationalize the selective valuation tenet of the disidentification explanation, where disidentified students find new sources for the regulation of their self-esteem.

15. Again, one could elaborate these models by placing further structure on the parameters. For example, one could stipulate that δ_t^{ID} is weakly increasing (and/or that δ_t^{DIS} is strongly decreasing) with the duration in the relevant state. In this case, the implied difference in the relationship between achievement and self-esteem would be even greater (and would not necessarily require an increased flow of additional disidentified students). In addition, one could allow self-esteem to be a function of lagged achievement shocks, ε_{it-1}, and so on. These modest changes would not affect the implications derived in the main text. (Changes that would affect the implications would have to be more considerable, such as allowing self-esteem to be a function of the achievement trends themselves, rather than just the normally distributed achievement variation around the trends defined by the disidentification process.)

16. There is a bedeviling intransitivity at the heart of the mixed results on the viability of the disidentification explanation offered in Morgan and Mehta (2004). Achievement differences appear to result in a different pattern of academic self-concept for blacks but not in a different pattern of self-esteem for blacks. Although entirely plausible, this apparent race difference in the construction of academic self-concept and self-esteem is not reflected in the relationship between the two, as reported in Table 3 of the article. That is, we were unable to detect any substantial black-white differences in the cross-sectional associations between academic self-concept and self-esteem, and hence concluded that the grounding of self-esteem on academic self-concept appeared to be the same for blacks and whites. This appears somewhat contradictory, given the conclusion that there is a race difference in how both self-concept and self-esteem are related to achievement. This complexity clearly deserves additional discussion and, likely, substantial follow-up research.

Notice first that the intransitivity is not as serious as it might appear. There is still a substantial relationship between academic self-concept and achievement for blacks. It is simply the case that the relationship is weaker. This difference suggests that the story lies in the heterogeneity of individuals, and in particular in a different pattern of heterogeneity of blacks. If this is the case, then there is a simple methodological explanation for the pattern, but one that is virtually impossible to confirm with the data. Transitivity is not a property that holds across covariances, since individuals who contribute relatively more to the strength of an association between one variable and another variable need not contribute the same amount to the association with a third variable (or even information in the same direction).

To see how this sort of pattern could generate a race difference, consider four white students and four black students. Among the four white students, there is a computer whiz who has a self-esteem, academic self-concept, and achievement triple of $(-1, .75, 0)$. The three remaining white students are an athlete $(1, 0, 0)$, an overachiever $(2, 2, 5)$, and a discouraged underachiever $(-1, -2, -1)$. The four black students are a disengaged but happy student $(2, 2, 0)$, a disengaged but unhappy student $(-2, -2, 0)$, a world-beater $(3, 2, 5)$, and a disengaged rebel who is depressed $(-5, 0, -5)$. For the white students, the correlation between self-esteem and both academic self-concept and achievement are high, at .67 and .82. And, the correlation between achievement and academic self-concept is even higher, at .83. Perhaps surprisingly, for the black students, the correlation between self-esteem and both academic self-concept and achievement are even higher than among the white students, at .71 and .88. And, yet, the correlation between academic self-concept and academic achievement is much lower for the black students, at only .43. Clearly, this is an entirely speculative exercise in the ambiguity of correlational data, but the patterns between the variables for these hypothetical eight students do match the broad pattern of results in Tables 2 through 4 of Morgan and Mehta (2004). There are obviously many more "types" of students and much less clear boundaries between them, but it is possible that this sort of pattern is driving the results.

17. Assuming an even higher value for the probability of becoming disidentified with achievement following the discounting of performance evaluations (e.g., .9 instead of .75) would increase the rate at which individuals fully disidentify with achievement and also produce a more extreme equilibrium distribution.

18. Notice, however, that these simulated students are not uniformly worse at eliminating extreme values from their belief distributions than fast Bayesian learners, as they are relatively swift in determining that a high school education alone does not pay off. That is, for this simulated group of students, I assume that the discounting of performance evaluations does not affect beliefs about the labor market for high school graduates. And, indeed, I stipulated that these students are actually quite well informed about this segment of the labor market. Assuming instead that they were slow learners about the labor market for high school graduates as well would simply have resulted in the same time path as for the slow Bayesian learners of Figure 5.2.

19. The results also show that any preparatory commitment shortfalls that may be evident for blacks are more likely to result from uncertainty of beliefs about the payoffs to alternative trajectories through the educational system rather than differences in beliefs about the probability of graduating from college.

20. Only if black students form beliefs that educational achievement is detrimental to their self-interest are they likely to have very low levels of prefigurative commitment to the decision "Go to college." In order to do so, it would seem that they would need to entirely reformulate their stochastic decision trees, focusing on final-stage lottery parameters for short-run hedonism. In this case, the resulting achievement declines would be severe.

CHAPTER SEVEN

A New Agenda for the Sociology of Educational Attainment

To enable breakthroughs in research on social stratification and in labor economics, to resolve unexplained empirical puzzles, and to develop more reliable policy guidance, the social sciences need a better model of educational attainment. The central claim of this book is that a new model can be built on a preparatory commitment framework, provided that the model is grounded on a sub-model for forward-looking assessments of alternative courses of future behavior and is responsive to belief formation processes that can destabilize these assessments in the interim. In this concluding chapter, I will recapitulate the main points of the argument as part of a general appeal for modeling belief formation processes in sociology and then lay out a new agenda for modeling educational attainment.

BELIEF FORMATION PROCESSES AND EDUCATIONAL ATTAINMENT

Early rational choice models of educational attainment assumed that individuals act in response to existing incentives (see Manski and Wise 1983; Willis and Rosen 1979). Maintaining this assumption, there is no need to specify in any explicit way the belief formation mechanisms that allow actors to recognize and respond to incentives. As a result, for noneconomists these early rational choice models of educational attainment remained unconvincing. Only in the 1990s were expectation formation processes given substantial attention within the economics of education. In perhaps the most influential piece, Manski (1993a) argued that knowledge of students' expectations of the payoff to educational investment could strengthen the explanatory power of decision-theoretic models, and he developed proposals for collecting new forms of subjective data (see Dominitz and Manski 1996, 1997). And yet, more than a decade later, models for the formation of the beliefs that are summarized in expected returns have received little attention, even though some intriguing treatments of social influence processes have been developed (see Manski 1993b). As a result, social scientists still do not know with any degree of depth how students and parents respond when incentives for pursuing education change.[1]

Sociologists of education have always maintained that belief formation processes are important. Status socialization models of educational attainment, as exemplified by the Wisconsin model of educational attainment discussed and reinterpreted in Chapter 2, are centered on a two-piece belief formation mechanism: (1) students' own expectations for future behavior are constructed through individual self-reflection and in response to the expectations of significant others, and (2) students' own expectations for future behavior cause future behavior. This two-part mechanism, although intriguing in its suggestion that educational attainment can be altered by simply changing one's own expectation of future behavior, is too coarse and incomplete to adequately characterize the observed relationships between respondent-reported educational expectations and subsequent educational attainment, as demonstrated in the empirical analyses of Chapter 3.

In the 1980s and 1990s, the literature on educational attainment in sociology headed in the wrong direction (based in part on evidence, as I also demonstrated in Chapter 3, that was ambiguous at best). Rather than redouble efforts to model the component beliefs that must underlie the Wisconsin model, and which generate the observed associations between expectations and attainment, the new mode of analysis placed measurable structural constraints at the core of all modeling efforts. And, in hindsight, these new models proved to be even less convincing (at least to some of us).

The new models, based on empirical analysis or simply written argumentation, generally maintained implicit additivity assumptions. When all constraints have additive effects on each other, the relaxation of a constraint on entry into a position in the educational system is assumed to result in an increased rate of entry to that position. Dropping the additivity assumption, the validity of this prediction then becomes contingent on students' beliefs about all existing constraints to each position, their predictions about how these constraints may change in the future, and their recognition of subsequent changes that do occur. Relaxing enrollment limits at four-year colleges, for example, does not on its own guarantee that substantially more high school graduates will enroll and then graduate from college, especially if some entry and graduation requirements remain stable. Moreover, if attainment is a function of preparatory commitment, then a shift in a constraint may have no effect whatsoever on eventual behavior, if the altered pattern of constraints becomes known long after many crucial preparatory commitment decisions have been made.

Sociological models that focused primarily on constraints acquired the same basic weakness of empirical applications of rational choice models. Without sub-models for how beliefs about opportunities and constraints affect short-run behavior, they became mechanical attempts to relate variation in educational attainment to variation in constraints and opportunities. Similar to modeling behavior only as a function of variation in costs and benefits, such a strategy allows for parsimonious explanations. But these explanations are not necessarily correct.[2] If they are to be believed, models of information processing and belief formation are needed to specify when and how individuals respond to such exogenous variation. Chapters 4 through 6 of this book outline one possible direction in which such modeling can proceed.

AN INTEGRATIVE MODELING AGENDA

It was once fashionable for sociologists to delineate their field from economics by claiming that: "Economics is about the choices people make while sociology is about the choices people don't get to make." Although perhaps rhetorically effective, such statements are unfair to both disciplines, for in almost every substantive area in which economics and sociology have been jointly engaged, the best research has always sought to find a middle ground, recognizing that distinctions between the cost-benefit duality and the constraint-opportunity duality are mostly a matter of semantics. For research on educational attainment, I have attempted in this book to organize the literature in this shared territory and then advance a set of modeling ideas to further cultivate it.

In pursuing this integrative agenda, I have developed a stochastic decision tree model for the regulation of preparatory commitment decisions, and I have suggested that it has the potential to improve the capacity to develop sufficiently complete explanations for patterns of educational attainment. Its adoption in sociology would allow for the formalization and empirical evaluation of ideas that have captivated the sociological imagination but that have been too vague to effectively specify in empirical research (see the quotations of Bourdieu and Willis in Chapters 1 and 3).[3] Its (partial) adoption in economics would help to develop a more flexible form of rational choice theory to overcome the limitations of discrete choice analysis and attendant reveal preference assumptions.

More generally, the framework can help to unite approaches to the study of educational attainment within sociology and economics, drawing on their appropriately complementary strengths. Sociologists have succeeded in delineating many of the potential mechanisms that generate the psychic costs and taste for education that economists often assume exist in order to help explain why college enrollment rates are lower than narrow cost and benefit calculations of tuition and labor market benefits would imply. However, economists have achieved a comparative advantage by deploying threshold-crossing models for instantaneous enrollment behavior, and the sociology of education could benefit from engaging these models more deeply. The stochastic decision tree model, by giving formal expression to sociological mechanisms of the past, has the potential to bring sociology into decision tree modeling and hence enable sociologists to join (or counter) economists in offering sharp policy-relevant predictions about enrollment behavior.

PRIMARY FEATURES OF THE NEW MODEL

In constructing the stochastic decision tree model, I borrow and then extend the strongest pieces of both status socialization and rational choice models of educational attainment. The key innovation of the framework is the specification of a simple decision tree with fundamentally stochastic parameters. When a simple, boundedly rational decision rule is invoked to specify the way in which individuals draw forecasts of future behavior from their stochastic decision trees, prefigurative commitment can be shown to be a function of the precision of one's beliefs about future courses of behavior. If, as assumed by status socialization theory, current behavior is a function of beliefs about the future, then everyday forecasts of future behavior, conceptualized as prefigurative commitment, will operate as self-fulfilling prophecies by regulating preparatory commitment in current behavior toward the course of behavior that is thought to be in one's best interest.

After specifying the core components of the stochastic decision tree framework in Chapter 4, I then introduced in Chapter 5 mechanisms of belief formation and belief revision for the parameters of the stochastic decision tree. I stipulated that Bayes' theorem is the proper starting point for modeling such processes, although I conceded that other mechanisms of belief revision may be shown to be more promising in future research.

Finally, in Chapter 6, I reintegrated normative and imitative sources of commitment into the framework, and I argued that, even if such processes are of independent importance (and I believe they will be shown to be so in subsequent research), such modeling is best pursued in tandem with models of purposive-prefigurative commitment centered on the evaluation of a stochastic decision tree. In the next section, I lay out a new agenda for the modeling of educational attainment with a stochastic decision tree model of commitment.

THE DIRECTION OF FUTURE RESEARCH

The argument of this book rests on the premise that sociologists are at a point in the study of educational attainment where little additional progress will be forthcoming if we do not push beyond the current frontiers of research capacity, devising new theory and data-gathering methodologies for the information and beliefs of prospective college students. If it is accepted that neither status socialization models nor rational choice models of educational attainment are satisfactory, then sociologists may proceed in two ways. The unproductive route is to follow the rhetoric of Pierre Bourdieu and embrace a non-positivist, anti-Cartesian stance in order to celebrate a dialectic of structural constraint and individual action.[4] It should be clear from the preceding chapters that I wholeheartedly reject this agenda, even though it should also be clear that I accept much of Bourdieu's criticism of the stream of sociology that culminated in the Wisconsin model. I see a larger and more promising role for unapologetic positivism, and I therefore support carefully defined and measurable concepts that through their predictive power and explanatory utility can trump poorly defined alternatives. One need not always accept the outcomes of a such an unabashed positivist agenda, but pursuing one, at least for models of educational attainment, seems the highest payoff agenda presently available.

Modeling Information and Beliefs

Throughout Chapters 4, 5, and 6, I discussed information as an abstract set of individual models regarded by students as realizations of an underlying process that they expect to navigate in their own futures. Clearly, this is an abstract representation of information, less so however than the notion of an information structure that is generally deployed in economics (see Hintikka 1962; Rubinstein 1998). It is unclear whether in practice something so simple will suffice for modeling educational attainment. More recent psychological research on stimulus and cue recognition progresses (see Goldstein and Hogarth 1997) and proposals for refinements to classic information structures in economics (for example, in Fudenberg and Levine 1998) have been advanced. But, this is clearly only the beginning, and one must assume that all such theorizing will founder if no one is willing to mount a positivist campaign to develop measures of information structures.

Sociology, by exploiting the middle ground between experimentally induced information recognition in psychology and abstract mathematical definitions of information in economics, has the potential to contribute to the development of a more useful framework for the representation of information. Perhaps surprisingly, however, there is at present little useful literature in the sociology of education on the modeling of information. Indeed, I can point to some of my own past research as an example where information is treated as important in the abstract and yet not given any useful definition (see Morgan and Sørensen 1999). And yet, this arises from a general limitation of the sociological literature, which is especially clear in social network analysis. Too much attention is devoted toward modeling the formation and dynamics of social connections, and too little attention is devoted toward modeling flows of information across social connections. As a result, sociology has an exploding number of published studies of social network patterns, and the processes that generate network structures, but precious few examples where the information that has flowed across networks has been shown convincingly to be consequential for outcomes of longstanding interest to sociologists, such as patterns of educational attainment.

Because processed information is a function of available information, researchers can learn something about available information from the beliefs that encode processed information. Thereafter, it may be possible to model available but unprocessed information. If this is the case, a productive starting point may be to develop better models of belief formation.

Collecting Data on Beliefs

For the construction of belief formation models for use in the study of educational attainment, sociology must first transcend coarse measurement techniques of the past that have yielded measures such as educational expectations. There is nothing wrong with posing questions such as "How far in school do you expect to get?" in large national surveys of high school students, but answers to these simple questions can only provide so much grist for the analytic wheel. We must go deeper. Small scale studies that deploy sophisticated data collection technologies, rather than massive fill-in-the-bubble paper surveys, have the most potential to yield new measurement techniques. Were such data collection efforts more widely appreciated in the social sciences, research might have long ago transcended the college plans questions that have been with us since the 1950s.

Three techniques for the measurement of beliefs should be further developed—scenario-based questioning, predictive elicitation, and graphical belief modeling. Especially in studies of prediction and decision making in medicine, scenario-based questioning has yielded considerable insight into how practitioners arrange and revise relevant information (see Bell et al. 1988, Chapters 26 to 29). Although there are qualitatively oriented and well-crafted studies of students' beliefs about their futures (for example, Schneider and Stevenson 1999), none of these studies seem to ask students to evaluate the permissibility of a series of hypothetical scenarios, either for themselves or for abstracted sets of actors. With relative ease, a researcher engaged in such a study could quickly determine whether scenario-based questioning yields insight into belief formation and belief revision processes. For example, the synopses in Chapter 6 of the mind-sets for hypothetical identified and disidentified students could be tailored to a survey-administration context. Knowing which description students see as most reflective of their own identity at different points in time would provide the information needed to estimate the transition rates for the Markov models of Chapter 6.

On a larger scale, a more demanding set of data collection techniques desperately needs to be attempted in studies of educational attainment: probability elicitation and graphical belief modeling. In Bayesian statistics, where the specification of a prior distribution of a parameter is necessary in order to compute a posterior distribution for subsequent inference, a literature exists on alternative methods to elicit the subjective probability distributions of non-statisticians (see Kadane and Wolfson 1998; O'Hagan 1998). To guide the development of a good elicitation scheme, Kadane and Wolfson (1998:2–4) write: "The goal of elicitation, as we see it, is to make it as easy as possible for subject-matter experts to tell us what they believe, in probabilistic terms, while reducing how much they need to know about probability theory to do so."

For *structural* elicitation methods, individuals are asked to directly assess the permissibility of alternative parameter values of a model. For structural elicitation of belief distributions for a stochastic decision tree, students would be asked to describe the probability distributions for a given stochastic decision tree (most likely a decision tree prespecified by the researcher). In the social sciences, the preliminary successes of Dominitz (1998) and Dominitz and Manski (1997) in eliciting distributions of individuals' earnings expectations are encouraging, especially since these studies generally utilize demanding elicitation schemes. And, as discussed in Chapter 2, Dominitz and Manski (1996) and Kane (2001) have shown that the elicitation of high school students' tuition and earnings expectations is both feasible and worthwhile.[5]

In order for structural elicitation of the parameters of a stochastic decision tree to be successful, most students would have to be taught some probability theory first (in contexts that are most intuitive for adolescents, such as sports and dating). And, it may be that a less demanding type of elicitation, generally labeled *predictive* elicitation, would work best. With this method, students would be asked to offer sets of predictions about the outcomes of a model, and then the researcher would induce a parameterization that is consistent with the predictions. For the stochastic decision tree model, a predictive elicitation scheme would require students to predict, for example, the number of n students similar to themselves who would obtain a very good position in life if they followed alternative trajectories through a decision tree.[6] Graphical encoding schemes, such as the probability wheel of Spetzler and Staël von Holstein (1975), can be used to further demystify the prediction exercise. And, as predictive elicitation schemes are elaborated, they approach the scenario-based questioning promoted earlier. A particularly effective belief elicitation scheme may begin with a set of scenarios, and then proceed from simple predictive elicitation exercises to a fully operative structural scheme, if possible.

Finally, a new strand of literature on eliciting beliefs has developed in computer science. Working broadly within the artificial intelligence tradition, computer scientists and applied engineers have invested in probabilistic modeling (see Jensen 1996; Pearl 2000) and in the development of decision support systems (see Dhar and Stein 1997).[7] Although the new literature has refined probability elicitation protocols (see Wang and Druzdzel 2000), and the relative effectiveness of some alternative methods has been established in some contexts (see Wang, Dash, and Druzdzel 2002), the main breakthrough has been in the elicitation of experts' implicit probabilistic models, rather than simply the elicitation of probability values for a prespecified model.

Well-developed and extensively tested computer packages now exist that pose sets of questions to actors as predictive exercises that are supplemented by graphical feedback. The goal of these programs is to uncover the probabilistic models that determine the outcomes of a system, starting entirely from scratch. It would therefore now be possible using these methods to determine whether students themselves would reveal the four lottery parameters specified for the stochastic decision tree in Chapter 4 as those that they see as most important for determining if further schooling is in their best interest.

With measures of beliefs and with new models of information, researchers can then determine how beliefs respond to changes in information and evaluate the tenability of Bayesian updating as a plausible model of belief revision.[8] And, with reliable explanations for prevalent patterns of belief formation and belief revision, we can then reintroduce exogenous constraints and opportunities into models of educational attainment.

The portrayal of educational attainment that I have constructed in prior chapters can be read as an extended but strategic evasion of the question that is the title of Diego Gambetta's 1987 book, *Were They Pushed or Did They Jump?*[9] From the perspective developed here, students simply wander through a series of daily decisions, adjusting current behavior to anticipation of future behavior. As a result, students can be analyzed as if they are pushed from the path to educational success or alternatively as if they choose to jump from it.

Although at present the promise of these two perspectives seems equally balanced, future empirical work on belief formation processes may tip the balance in favor of one. If belief formation is perfect and immediate, then individuals should be modeled as if they jump. If, as seems more likely, belief formation has its own inertia, is easily contaminated through social influence, and regulates current behavior, then students should be modeled as if they are pushed into specific decision contexts from which they make decisions about whether or not to jump. For now, it would seem best not to conceive of students as if they are standing on the edge of a cliff, contemplating whether to jump. It should suffice to see students as if they are on the edge of commitment to alternative futures.[10] This metaphor, although less dramatic, is enough to motivate the new generation of theoretically guided empirical analysis that is now needed.

NOTES

1. Studies such as Linsenmeier, Rosen, and Rouse (2002) do provide some additional information beyond the results of simple regression models, as they focus on known and targeted changes in financial aid packages (albeit at, presumably, one of the most elite colleges in the country). It is possible that if hundreds of such studies were available, researchers might be able to patch together enough knowledge about the full distribution of enrollment behavior in the specific time period considered. If so, then reliance on revealed preference models may be reasonable. But, until then, direct modeling of beliefs and enrollment responses will be needed. And, perhaps more worryingly, as soon as aggregate shocks to the cost-benefit decision emerge, the results from past revealed preference models of behavior may become entirely obsolete.

2. Or, even if they are judged correct in some sense, they are rarely sufficiently complete to foreclose further debate on alternative explanations.

3. Although I regard Bourdieu's ideas as amenable to explicit development, it is (again) important that I concede that his most ardent admirers probably disagree. These scholars wish to celebrate and preserve the most ambiguous components of his scholarship, which Wacquant, for example, celebrates as a bold attempt to "capture the intentionality without intention, the knowledge without cognitive intent, the prereflective, infraconscious mastery that agents acquire of their social world by way of durable immersion within it" (Bourdieu and Wacquant 1992:19).

4. For an example of how Bourdieu's admirers have adopted the rhetoric at the expense of the substance of his ideas, consider how Wacquant (Bourdieu and Wacquant 1992:16) defines Bourdieu's concepts of field and habitus: "A field consists of a set of objective, historical relations between positions anchored in certain forms of power (or capital), while habitus consists of a set of historical relations

'deposited' within individual bodies in the form of mental and corporeal schemata of perception, appreciation, and action." Although useful for further prosecuting classical antinomies, by my taste such reflexive posturing represents relatively fruitless scholastic celebration of conceptual tension. It does not move us forward by developing new ways for generating better explanations of the important social facts that demand our attention.

5. See also Rouse (2002).

6. Over a series of values of n, and invoking other methods of measurement such as average response time, implicit beta distribution for α, β, and γ could be derived. See Chaloner and Duncan (1983), who develop a method of predictive modal elicitation, inferring beta distributions from the predictions subjects offer for outcomes to binomial trials. Graphical interfaces would be optimal, especially if implemented with the knowledge of perceptual processes of graphs (see Hollands and Spence 1998, 2001).

7. Although the current literature is developing rapidly, and with an exciting "wild west" feel as new computing power is exploited, the general perspective has a relatively long tradition, stretching back to the 1950 and 1960s (see Ayyub 2001; Spetzler and Staël von Holstein 1975).

8. With access to new forms of data on students' beliefs, the evaluation of alternative belief formation and belief revision mechanisms will become tractable. The heterogeneous experimental findings on the tenability of Bayesian learning can be examined in a real-world context. If, through capable empirical analysis, Bayes' theorem fails to provide a solid foundation for belief revision mechanisms, other formal models of learning can then be examined. And, if so, then other ways of conceptualizing beliefs and their overlap can be determined, going as far back as the belief functions of Dempster (1966, 1967) and as recently as the membership functions from fuzzy logic (see Pedrycz and Gomide 1998).

9. For the record, Gambetta's response to his own question is less than declarative. His general position is that students decide whether to continue on to higher levels of education by developing preferences and life plans through rational evaluation of the costs and benefits of alternative choices. But, on deeper analysis, Gambetta (1987:186) argues: "Preferences and life-plans, though, are in turn 'distorted' by specific class biases which act as weights that subjects sub-intentionally apply to the elements of their rational evaluation. The formation of these class-specific preferences may be due to a variety of processes, such as a tendency to extremizing behaviour, a cautious 'view of the world' related to difficult past experiences, or normative effects of reference groups."

10. If I were asked to pick a topological metaphor that is consistent with this statement, I would resist because of the possibility of misinterpretation. If a reader then threatened to encapsulate my argument with his or her own metaphor, I would then offer the following as self-defense: Students enter adolescence on the knife's edge of commitment to alternative futures, as if they are beginning a hike on the

ridge of a mountain range. They walk along the ridge, calculating the payoff to alternative courses of descent. Unfortunately, the valleys below are shrouded in fog, and the paths to them are only partly in view. Some students never venture far from the edge of commitment, wandering along the entire ridge until it joins the horizon. Others quickly find a trail and walk down on switchbacks cut by their peers. But most students wander about, crossing the ridge several times while attempting to get beneath the fog. Eventually, all students arrive in valleys, which, in time, may reveal themselves to be the promised ones. But, on arrival, all that is clear is that climbing back up the mountain to look for an alternative is too costly to venture, as the paths traversed were jagged and perilous.

REFERENCES

Abelson, Robert P. 1964. "Mathematical Models of the Distribution of Attitudes under Controversy." Pp. 142–60 in *Contributions to Mathematical Psychology*, edited by N. Frederiksen, H. Gulliksen, and L. L. Thurstone. New York: Holt, Rinehart and Winston.

Ainsworth-Darnell, James W. and Douglas B. Downey. 1998. "Assessing Racial/Ethnic Differences in School Performance." *American Sociological Review* 63:536–53.

Alexander, Karl L. and Martha A. Cook. 1979. "The Motivational Relevance of Educational Plans: Questioning the Conventional Wisdom." *Social Psychology Quarterly* 42:202–13.

Alwin, Duane F. and Robert M. Hauser. 1975. "The Decomposition of Effects in Path Analysis." *American Sociological Review* 40:37–47.

Angrist, Joshua D. and Guido W. Imbens. 1995. "Two-Stage Least Squares Estimation of Average Causal Effects in Models with Variable Treatment Intensity." *Journal of the American Statistical Association* 90:431–42.

Angrist, Joshua D., Guido W. Imbens, and Donald B. Rubin. 1996. "Identification of Causal Effects Using Instrumental Variables." *Journal of the American Statistical Association* 87:328–36.

Arum, Richard. 1998. "Invested Dollars or Diverted Dreams: The Effect of Resources on Vocational Students' Educational Outcomes." *Sociology of Education* 71:130–51.

Ayyub, Bilal M. 2001. *Elicitation of Expert Opinions for Uncertainty and Risks*. Boca Raton, Fla.: CRC.

Becker, Gordon, Morris H. DeGroot, and Jacob Marschak. 1963. "Stochastic Models of Choice Behavior." *Behavioral Science* 8:41–55.

Bell, David E., Howard Raiffa, and Amos Tversky, eds. 1988. *Decision Making: Descriptive, Normative, and Prescriptive Interactions*. Cambridge: Cambridge University Press.

Berger, James O. 1985. *Statistical Decision Theory and Bayesian Analysis*. New York: Springer-Verlag.

Berk, Richard. 1988. "Causal Inference for Sociological Data." Pp. 155–72 in *Handbook of Sociology*, edited by N. J. Smelser. Newbury Park, Calif.: Sage.

Bielby, William T., Robert M. Hauser, and David L. Featherman. 1977. "Response Errors of Black and Nonblack Males in Models of the Intergenerational Transmission of Socioeconomic Status." *American Journal of Sociology* 82:1242–88.

Blau, Peter M. and Otis Dudley Duncan. 1967. *The American Occupational Structure*. New York: Wiley.

Bollen, Kenneth A. 1989. *Structural Equations with Latent Variables*. New York: Wiley.

Boudon, Raymond. 1974. *Education, Opportunity, and Social Inequality: Changing Prospects in Western Society*. New York: Wiley.

Bourdieu, Pierre. 1973. "Cultural Reproduction and Social Reproduction." Pp. 71–112 in *Knowledge, Education, and Cultural Change: Papers in the Sociology of Education*, edited by R. K. Brown. London: Tavistock.

Bourdieu, Pierre and Loïc J. D. Wacquant. 1992. *An Invitation to Reflexive Sociology*. Chicago: University of Chicago Press.

Breen, Richard. 1999. "Beliefs, Rational Choice, and Bayesian Learning." *Rationality and Society* 11:463–79.

Breen, Richard and John H. Goldthorpe. 1997. "Explaining Educational Differentials: Towards a Formal Rational Action Theory." *Rationality and Society* 9: 275–305.

Bush, Robert R. and Frederick Mosteller. 1955. *Stochastic Models for Learning*. New York: Wiley.

———. 1959. "A Comparison of Eight Models." Pp. 335–49 in *Studies in Mathematical Learning Theory*, edited by R. R. Bush and W. K. Estes. Stanford: Stanford University Press.

Camerer, Colin. 1995. "Individual Decision Making." Pp. 587–703 in *The Handbook of Experimental Economics*, edited by J. H. Kagel and A. E. Roth. Princeton: Princeton University Press.

Cameron, Stephen V. and James J. Heckman. 1999. "Can Tuition Combat Rising Wage Inequality?" Pp. 76–124 in *Financing College Tuition: Government Policies and Educational Priorities*, edited by M. H. Kosters. Washington, D.C.: AEI.

Carlin, Bradley P. and Thomas A. Louis. 1996. *Bayes and Empirical Bayes Methods for Data Analysis*. London: Chapman & Hall.

Carneiro, Pedro and James J. Heckman. 2002. "The Evidence on Credit Constraints in Post-Secondary Schooling." *The Economic Journal* 112:705–34.

Chaloner, Kathryn M. and George T. Duncan. 1983. "Assessment of a Beta Prior Distribution: PM Elicitation." *The Statistician* 32:174.

Chernoff, Herman and Lincoln E. Moses. 1959. *Elementary Decision Theory*. New York: Wiley.

Clemen, Robert T., Steven K. Jones, and Robert L. Winkler. 1996. "Aggregating

Forecasts: An Empirical Evaluation of Some Bayesian Methods." Pp. 3–13 in *Bayesian Analysis in Statistics and Econometrics: Essays in Honor of Arnold Zellner*, edited by D. A. Berry, K. M. Chaloner, J. K. Geweke, and A. Zellner. New York: Wiley.

Clogg, Clifford C. and Adamantios Haritou. 1997. "The Regression Method of Causal Inference and a Dilemma Confronting This Method." Pp. 83–112 in *Causality in Crisis? Statistical Methods and the Search for Causal Knowledge in the Social Sciences*, edited by V. R. McKim and S. P. Turner. Notre Dame: University of Notre Dame Press.

Cohen, Jere. 1983. "Peer Influence on College Aspirations with Initial Aspirations Controlled." *American Sociological Review* 48:728–34.

Coleman, James S. 1961. *The Adolescent Society: The Social Life of the Teenager and Its Impact on Education*. New York: Free Press.

———. 1964a. *Introduction to Mathematical Sociology*. New York: Free Press.

———. 1964b. *Models of Change and Response Uncertainty*. Englewood Cliffs, N.J.: Prentice Hall.

———. 1981. *Longitudinal Data Analysis*. New York: Basic Books.

Comay, Y., A. Melnik, and M. A. Pollatschek. 1973. "The Option Value of Education and the Optimal Path for Investment in Human Capital." *International Economic Review* 14:421–35.

Cook, Philip J. and Jens Ludwig. 1997. "Weighing the Burden of 'Acting White': Are There Race Differences in Attitudes toward Education?" *Journal of Policy Analysis and Management* 16:256–78.

Crocker, Jennifer, Brenda Major, and Claude Steele. 1998. "Social Stigma." Pp. 504–53 in *The Handbook of Social Psychology*, 4th Edition, vol. 2, edited by D. T. Gilbert, S. T. Fiske, and G. Lindzey. Boston: McGraw-Hill.

Davidson, Andrew R. 1995. "From Attitudes to Actions to Attitude Change: The Effects of Amount and Accuracy of Information." Pp. 315–36 in *Attitude Strength: Antecedents and Consequences*, edited by R. E. Petty and J. A. Krosnick. Mahwah, N.J.: Erlbaum.

Davies, Mark and Denise B. Kandel. 1981. "Parental and Peer Influences on Adolescents' Educational Plans: Some Further Evidence." *American Journal of Sociology* 87:363–87.

Davis, James A. 1985. *The Logic of Causal Order*. Newbury Park, Calif.: Sage.

DeGroot, Morris H. 1974. "Reaching a Consensus." *Journal of the American Statistical Association* 69:118–21.

Demo, David H. and Keith D. Parker. 1987. "Academic Achievement and Self-Esteem among Black and White College Students." *Journal of Social Psychology* 127:345–55.

Dempster, Arthur P. 1966. "New Methods for Reasoning Towards Posterior Distributions Based on Sample Data." *Annals of Mathematical Statistics* 37:355–74.

———. 1967. "Upper and Lower Probabilities Induced by a Multivalued Mapping." *Annals of Mathematical Statistics* 38:325–39.

Dhar, Vasant and Roger Stein. 1997. *Intelligent Decision Support Methods: The Science of Knowledge Work*. Upper Saddle River, N.J.: Prentice Hall.

Dominitz, Jeff. 1998. "Earnings Expectations, Revisions, and Realizations." *The Review of Economics and Statistics* 80:374–88.

Dominitz, Jeff and Charles F. Manski. 1996. "Eliciting Student Expectations of the Returns to Schooling." *The Journal of Human Resources* 31:1–26.

———. 1997. "Using Expectations Data to Study Subjective Income Expectations." *Journal of the American Statistical Association* 92:855–67.

Duncan, Greg J., Jeanne Brooks-Gunn, W. Jean Yeung, and Judith R. Smith. 1998. "How Much Does Childhood Poverty Affect the Life Chances of Children?" *American Sociological Review* 63:406–23.

Duncan, Otis Dudley. 1969. "Inheritance of Poverty or Inheritance of Race?" Pp. 85–110 in *On Understanding Poverty: Perspectives from the Social Sciences*, edited by D. P. Moynihan. New York: Basic Books.

———. 1975. *Introduction to Structural Equation Models*. New York: Academic Press.

Duncan, Otis Dudley, Archibald O. Haller, and Alejandro Portes. 1968. "Peer Influences on Aspirations: A Reinterpretation." *American Journal of Sociology* 74:119–37.

Eagley, Alice H. and Shelly Chaiken. 1998. "Attitude Structure and Function." Pp. 269–322 in *The Handbook of Social Psychology*, 4th Edition, vol. 1, edited by D. T. Gilbert, S. T. Fiske, and G. Lindzey. Boston: McGraw-Hill.

Educational Testing Service. 1957. *Background Factors Relating to College Plans and College Enrollment among Public High School Students*. Princeton: Educational Testing Service.

Edwards, Ward. 1968. "Conservatism in Human Information Processing." Pp. 17–52 in *Formal Representation of Human Judgment*, edited by B. Kleinmuntz and R. B. Cattell. New York: Wiley.

Ellwood, David T. and Thomas J. Kane. 2000. "Who Is Getting a College Education: Family Background and the Growing Gaps in Enrollment." Pp. 283–325 in *Securing the Future: Investing in Children from Birth to College*, edited by S. Danziger and J. Waldfogel. New York: Russell Sage Foundation.

Elster, Jon. 1984. *Ulysses and the Sirens: Studies in Rationality and Irrationality, Revised Edition*. Cambridge: Cambridge University Press.

———. 2000. *Ulysses Unbound: Studies in Rationality, Precommitment, and Constraints*. Cambridge: Cambridge University Press.

Ervin, Laurie H. and Sheldon Stryker. 2001. "Theorizing the Relationship between Self-Esteem and Identity." Pp. 29–55 in *Extending Self-Esteem Theory and Research: Sociological and Psychological Currents*, edited by T. J. Owens, S. Stryker, and N. Goodman. New York: Cambridge University Press.

Fordham, Signithia and John U. Ogbu. 1986. "Black Students' School Success: Coping with the Burden of 'Acting White.'" *The Urban Review* 18:176–206.

Friedkin, Noah E. and Eugene C. Johnsen. 1990. "Social Influence and Opinions." *Journal of Mathematical Sociology*, 15:193–205.

Fudenberg, Drew and David K. Levine. 1998. *The Theory of Learning in Games*. Cambridge: MIT Press.

Fuller, Wayne A. 1987. *Measurement Error Models*. New York: Wiley.

Gambetta, Diego. 1987. *Were They Pushed or Did They Jump? Individual Decision Mechanisms in Education*. Cambridge: Cambridge University Press.

———. 1998. "Concatenations of Mechanisms." Pp. 102–24 in *Social Mechanisms: An Analytical Approach to Social Theory*, edited by P. Hedström and R. Swedberg. Cambridge: Cambridge University Press.

Gamoran, Adam and Robert D. Mare. 1989. "Secondary School Tracking and Education Inequality: Compensation, Reinforcement, or Neutrality?" *American Journal of Sociology* 94:1146–83.

Gelman, Andrew, John B. Carlin, Hal S. Stern, and Donald B. Rubin. 1995. *Bayesian Data Analysis*. London: Chapman & Hall.

Giddens, Anthony. 1984. *The Constitution of Society: Outline of the Theory of Structuration*. Berkeley: Cambridge University Press.

Gigerenzer, Gerd and Reinhard Selten, eds. 2001. *Bounded Rationality: The Adaptive Toolbox*. Cambridge: MIT Press.

Goldstein, William M. and Robin M. Hogarth, eds. 1997. *Research on Judgment and Decision Making: Currents, Connections, and Controversies*. Cambridge: Cambridge University Press.

Goldthorpe, John H. 1996. "Class Analysis and the Reorientation of Class Theory: The Case of Persisting Differentials in Educational Attainment." *The British Journal of Sociology* 47:481–505.

———. 2000. *On Sociology: Numbers, Narratives, and the Integration of Research and Theory*. Oxford: Oxford University Press.

Greene, William H. 2000. *Econometric Analysis*, 4th Edition. Upper Saddle River, N.J.: Prentice Hall.

Haller, Archibald O. 1982. "Reflections on the Social Psychology of Status Attainment." P. 328 in *Social Structure and Behavior: Essays in Honor of William Hamilton Sewell*, edited by R. M. Hauser, D. Mechanic, A. O. Haller, and T. S. Hauser. New York: Academic Press.

Haller, Archibald O. and C. E. Butterworth. 1960. "Peer Influences on Levels of Occupational and Educational Aspiration." *Social Forces* 38:289–95.

Haller, Archibald O., Luther B. Otto, Robert F. Meier, and George W. Ohlendorf. 1974. "Level of Occupational Aspiration: An Empirical Analysis." *American Sociological Review* 39:113–21.

Haller, Archibald O. and Alejandro Portes. 1973. "Status Attainment Processes." *Sociology of Education* 46:51–91.

Hallinan, Maureen T. 2001. "Sociological Perspectives on Black-White Inequalities in American Schooling." *Sociology of Education* Extra Issue 2001:50–70.

Hallinan, Maureen T. and Richard A. Williams. 1990. "Students' Characteristics and the Peer-Influence Process." *Sociology of Education* 63:122–32.

Hanson, Sandra L. 1994. "Lost Talent: Unrealized Educational Aspirations and Expectations among U.S. Youths." *Sociology of Education* 67:159–83.

Hauser, Robert M. 1972. "Disaggregating a Social-Psychological Model of Educational Attainment." *Social Science Research* 1:159–88.

———. 1993a. "The Decline in College Entry among African Americans: Findings in Search of Explanations." Pp. 271–306 in *Prejudice, Politics, and the American Dilemma*, edited by P. M. Sniderman, P. E. Tetlock, and E. G. Carmines. Stanford: Stanford University Press.

———. 1993b. "Trends in College Entry among Whites, Blacks, and Hispanics." Pp. 61–104 in *Studies of Supply and Demand in Higher Education*, edited by C. T. Clotfelter and M. Rothschild. Chicago: University of Chicago Press.

Hauser, Robert M. and Douglas K. Anderson. 1991. "Post-High School Plans and Aspirations of Black and White High School Seniors, 1976–86." *Sociology of Education* 64:263–77.

Hauser, Robert M., Shu-Ling Tsai, and William H. Sewell. 1983. "A Model of Stratification with Response Error in Social and Psychological Variables." *Sociology of Education* 56:20–46.

Hedström, Peter and Richard Swedberg. 1998. *Social Mechanisms: An Analytical Approach to Social Theory*. Cambridge: Cambridge University Press.

Hey, John D. and Chris Orme. 1994. "Investigating Generalizations of Expected Utility Theory Using Experimental Data." *Econometrica* 62:1291–326.

Hintikka, Jaakko. 1962. *Knowledge and Belief: An Introduction to the Logic of the Two Notions*. Ithaca: Cornell University Press.

Hofferth, Sandra L., Johanne Boisjoly, and Greg J. Duncan. 1998. "Parents' Extra-familial Resources and Children's School Attainment." *Sociology of Education* 71:246–68.

Holland, Peter W. 1986. "Statistics and Causal Inference." *Journal of the American Statistical Association* 81:945–70.

Hollands, Justin G. and Ian Spence. 1998. "Judging Proportion with Graphs: The Summation Model." *Applied Cognitive Psychology* 12:173–90.

———. 2001. "The Discrimination of Graphical Elements." *Applied Cognitive Psychology* 15:413–31.

Hollingshead, August de Belmont. 1949. *Elmtown's Youth: The Impact of Social Classes on Adolescents*. New York: Wiley.

Hout, Michael and William R. Morgan. 1975. "Race and Sex Variations in the Causes of the Expected Attainments of High School Seniors." *American Journal of Sociology* 81:364–94.

Hyman, Herbert H. 1953. "The Value Systems of Different Classes: A Social Psychological Contribution to the Analysis of Stratification." Pp. 426–42 in *Class, Status, and Power: A Reader in Social Stratification*, edited by R. Bendix and S. M. Lipset. Glencoe, Ill.: Free Press.

Jencks, Christopher, James Crouse, and Peter Mueser. 1983. "The Wisconsin Model of Status Attainment: A National Replication with Improved Measures of Ability and Aspiration." *Sociology of Education* 56:3–19.

Jencks, Christopher, Lauri Perman, and Lee Rainwater. 1988. "What Is a Good Job? A New Measure of Labor-Market Success." *American Journal of Sociology* 93:1322–57.

Jencks, Christopher and Meredith Phillips, eds. 1998. *The Black-White Test Score Gap*. Washington, D.C.: Brookings.

Jensen, Finn V. 1996. *An Introduction to Bayesian Networks*. New York: Springer.

Johnson, Monica K., Robert Crosnoe, and Glen H. Elder Jr. 2001. "Students' Attachment and Academic Engagement: The Role of Race and Ethnicity." *Sociology of Education* 74:318–40.

Kadane, Joseph B. and Lara J. Wolfson. 1998. "Experiences in Elicitation." *The Statistician* 47:3–19.

Kahl, Joseph. 1953. "Educational and Occupational Aspirations of 'Common Man' Boys." *Harvard Educational Review* 23:186–203.

Kahneman, Daniel and Amos Tversky. 1972. "On Prediction and Judgment." *ORI Research Monograph* 12.

———. 1979. "Prospect Theory: An Analysis of Decision under Risk." *Econometrica* 47:263–91.

Kane, Thomas J. 1994. "College Entry by Blacks since 1970: The Role of College Costs, Family Background, and the Returns to Education." *Journal of Political Economy* 102:878–911.

———. 1999a. "Reforming Subsidies for Higher Education." Pp. 53–75 in *Financing College Tuition: Government Policies and Educational Priorities*, edited by M. H. Kosters. Washington, D.C.: AEI.

———. 1999b. *The Price of Admission: Rethinking How Americans Pay for College*. Washington, D.C.: Brookings.

———. 2001. "College-Going and Inequality: A Literature Review." *Working Paper*. New York: Russell Sage Foundation.

Keller, Suzanne and Marisa Zavalloni. 1964. "Ambition and Social Class: A Respecification." *Social Forces* 43:58–70.

Kerckhoff, Alan C. 1976. "The Status Attainment Process: Socialization or Allocation?" *Social Forces* 55:368–81.

Kerckhoff, Alan C. and Richard T. Campbell. 1977a. "Black-White Differences in the Educational Attainment Process." *Sociology of Education* 50:15–27.

———. 1977b. "Race and Social Status Differences in the Explanation of Educational Ambition." *Social Forces* 51:701–14.

Kosters, Marvin H., ed. 1999. *Financing College Tuition: Government Policies and Educational Priorities*. Washington, D.C.: AEI.

Kuo, Hsiang-Hui Daphne and Robert M. Hauser. 1995. "Trends in Family Effects on the Education of Black and White Brothers." *Sociology of Education* 68:136–60.

Lehmann, E. L. and George Casella. 1998. *Theory of Point Estimation*, 2nd Edition. New York: Springer.

Leonard, Thomas and John S. J. Hsu. 1999. *Bayesian Methods: An Analysis for Statisticians and Interdisciplinary Researchers*. Cambridge: Cambridge University Press.

Lewin, Kurt. 1999[1926]. "Intention, Will, and Need." Pp. 83–115 in *The Complete Social Scientist: A Kurt Lewin Reader*, edited by K. Lewin and M. Gold. Washington, D.C.: American Psychological Association.

Lewin, Kurt, Tamara Dembo, Leon Festinger, and Pauline Sears. 1944. "Level of Aspiration." Pp. 333–78 in *Personality and the Behavior Disorders: A Handbook Based on Experimental and Clinical Research*, vol. 1, edited by J. M. Hunt. New York: Ronald.

Liang, Kung-Yee and Scott. L. Zeger. 1986. "Longitudinal Analysis Using Generalized Linear Models." *Biometrika* 73:13–22.

Lieberson, Stanley. 1985. *Making It Count: The Improvement of Social Research and Theory*. Berkeley: University of California Press.

Lindley, D. V. 1985. "Reconciliation of Discrete Probability Distributions." In *Bayesian Statistics 2: Proceedings of the Second Valencia International Meeting, September 6–10, 1983*, edited by J. M. Bernardo, M. H. DeGroot, D. V. Lindley, and A. F. M. Smith. Amsterdam: North-Holland.

Linsenmeier, David M., Harvey S. Rosen, and Cecilia E. Rouse. 2002. "Financial Aid Packages and College Enrollment Decisions: An Econometric Case Study." *Working Paper 9228*. Cambridge: National Bureau of Economic Research.

Loomes, Graham and Robert Sugden. 1995. "Incorporating a Stochastic Element into Decision Theories." *European Economic Review* 39:641–48.

Machina, Mark J. 1985. "Stochastic Choice Functions Generated from Deterministic Preferences over Lotteries." *The Economic Journal* 95:575–94.

Major, Brenda and Toni Schmader. 1998. "Coping with Stigma through Psychological Disengagement." In *Coping with Stigma*, edited by J. K. Swim and C. Stangor. San Diego: Academic Press.

Manski, Charles F. 1989. "Schooling as Experimentation: A Reappraisal of the Postsecondary Dropout Phenomenon." *Economics of Education Review* 8:305–12.

———. 1990. "The Use of Intentions Data to Predict Behavior: A Best-Case Analysis." *Journal of the American Statistical Association* 85:934–40.

———. 1993a. "Adolescent Econometricians: How Do Youth Infer the Returns to Schooling?" in *Studies of Supply and Demand in Higher Education*, edited by C. T. Clotfelter and M. Rothschild. Chicago: University of Chicago Press.

———. 1993b. "Dynamic Choice in Social Settings: Learning from the Experiences of Others." *Journal of Econometrics* 58:121–36.

———. 1995. *Identification Problems in the Social Sciences*. Cambridge: Harvard University Press.

———. 1997. "Monotone Treatment Response." *Econometrica* 65:1311–34.

Manski, Charles F. and David A. Wise. 1983. *College Choice in America*. Cambridge: Harvard University Press.

Mare, Robert D. and Meei-Shenn Tzeng. 1989. "Fathers' Ages and the Social Stratification of Sons." *American Journal of Sociology* 95:108–31.

Marsden, Peter V. and Noah E. Friedkin. 1994. "Network Studies of Social Influence." Pp. 3–25 in *Advances in Social Network Analysis: Research in the Social and Behavioral Sciences*, edited by S. Wasserman and J. Galaskiewicz. Thousand Oaks, Calif.: Sage.

Mayer, Susan E. 1997. *What Money Can't Buy: Family Income and Children's Life Chances*. Cambridge: Harvard University Press.

McFadden, Daniel. 1999. "Rationality for Economists?" *Journal of Risk and Uncertainty* 10:73–105.

———. 2001. "Economic Choices." *American Economic Review* 91:351–78.

Mickelson, Roslyn A. 1990. "The Attitude-Achievement Paradox among Black Adolescents." *Sociology of Education* 63:44–61.

Mishel, Lawrence, Jared Bernstein, and John Schmitt. 2001. *The State of Working America 2000–2001*. Ithaca: Cornell University Press.

Morgan, Stephen L. 1996. "Trends in Black-White Differences in Educational Expectations: 1980–1992." *Sociology of Education* 69:308–19.

———. 1998. "Adolescent Educational Expectations: Rationalized, Fantasized, or Both?" *Rationality and Society* 10:131–62.

———. 2002. "Modeling Preparatory Commitment and Non-Repeatable Decisions: Information-Processing, Preference Formation and Educational Attainment." *Rationality and Society* 14:387–429.

———. 2004. Book review of *Causality: Models, Reasoning, and Inference* by Judea Pearl. *Sociological Methods and Research* 32:411–16.

Morgan, Stephen L. and Jal Mehta. 2004. "Beyond the Laboratory: Evaluating the Survey Evidence for the Disidentification Explanation of Black-White Differences in Achievement." *Sociology of Education* 77:82–101.

Morgan, Stephen L. and Aage B. Sørensen. 1999. "Parental Networks, Social Closure, and Mathematics Learning: A Test of Coleman's Social Capital Explanation of School Effects." *American Sociological Review* 64:661–81.

Nakao, Keiko and Judith Treas. 1992. "The 1989 Socioeconomic Index of Occupations: Construction from the 1989 Occupational Prestige Scores." *GSS Methodological Report*.

Norris, J. R. 1997. *Markov Chains*. Cambridge: Cambridge University Press.

O'Hagan, A. 1998. "Eliciting Expert Beliefs in Substantial Practical Applications." *The Statistician* 47:21–35.

Orfield, Gary. 1992. "Money, Equity, and College Access." *Harvard Educational Review* 62:337–72.

Orfield, Gary and Mindy L. Kornhaber. 2001. *Raising Standards or Raising Barriers? Inequality and High-Stakes Testing in Public Education*. New York: Century Foundation.

Oster, Sharon. 1980. "The Optimal Order for Submitting Manuscripts." *American Economic Review* 70:444–48.

Owens, Timothy J., Sheldon Stryker, and Norman Goodman. 2001. *Extending Self-Esteem Theory and Research: Sociological and Psychological Currents.* New York: Cambridge University Press.

Parsons, Talcott. 1951. *The Social System.* Glencoe, Ill.: Free Press.

———. 1953. "A Revised Analytical Approach to the Theory of Social Stratification." Pp. 92–128 in *Class, Status, and Power: A Reader in Social Stratification,* edited by R. Bendix and S. M. Lipset. Glencoe, Ill.: Free Press.

———. 1964[1959]. "The School Class as a Social System." Pp. 129–54 in *Social Structure and Personality,* edited by T. Parsons. New York: Free Press.

Pearl, Judea. 2000. *Causality: Models, Reasoning, and Inference.* Cambridge: Cambridge University Press.

Pedrycz, Witold and Fernando Gomide. 1998. *An Introduction to Fuzzy Sets: Analysis and Design.* Cambridge: MIT Press.

Petty, Richard E. and Jon A. Krosnick, eds. 1995. *Attitude Strength: Antecedents and Consequences.* Mahwah, N.J.: Erlbaum.

Pittman, Thane S. 1998. "Motivation." Pp. 549–90 in *The Handbook of Social Psychology,* 4th Edition, vol. 1, edited by D. T. Gilbert, S. T. Fiske, and G. Lindzey. Boston: McGraw-Hill.

Porter, Judith R. and Robert E. Washington. 1979. "Black Identity and Self-Esteem: A Review of Studies of Black Self-Concept, 1968–1978." *Annual Review of Sociology* 5:53–74.

———. 1993. "Minority Identity and Self-Esteem." *Annual Review of Sociology* 19:139–61.

Portes, Alejandro and Kenneth L. Wilson. 1976. "Black-White Differences in Educational Attainment." *American Sociological Review* 41:414–31.

Pratt, John W., Howard Raiffa, and Robert Schlaifer. 1995. *Introduction to Statistical Decision Theory.* Cambridge: MIT Press.

Raftery, Adrian E. and Michael Hout. 1993. "Maximally Maintained Inequality: Expansion, Reform, and Opportunity in Irish Education, 1921–75." *Sociology of Education* 66:41–62.

Rosenbaum, Paul R. and Donald B. Rubin. 1983. "The Central Role of the Propensity Score in Observational Studies for Causal Effects." *Biometrika* 70:41–55.

Rosenberg, Morris. 1979. *Conceiving the Self.* New York: Basic Books.

Rotter, Julian B. 1982[1966]. "Generalized Expectancies for Internal Versus External Control of Reinforcement." Pp. 171–214 in *The Development and Applications of Social Learning Theory: Selected Papers,* edited by J. B. Rotter. New York: Praeger.

Rouse, Cecilia. 2002. "Low Income Students and College Attendance: An Exploration of Income Expectations." Princeton University, July.

Rubinstein, Ariel. 1998. *Modeling Bounded Rationality.* Cambridge: MIT Press.

Savage, Leonard J. 1954. *The Foundations of Statistics*. New York: Wiley.

Schmader, Toni, Brenda Major, and Richard H. Gramzow. 2001. "Coping with Ethnic Stereotypes in the Academic Domain: Perceived Injustice and Psychological Disengagement." *Journal of Social Issues* 57:93–111.

Schneider, Barbara L. and David Stevenson. 1999. *The Ambitious Generation: America's Teenagers, Motivated but Directionless*. New Haven: Yale University Press.

Selten, Reinhard. 2001. "What Is Bounded Rationality?" Pp. 13–36 in *Bounded Rationality: The Adaptive Toolbox*, edited by G. Gigerenzer and R. Selten. Cambridge: MIT Press.

Sen, Amartya. 1982[1977]. "Rational Fools: A Critique of the Behavioural Foundations of Economic Theory." Pp. 84–106 in *Choice, Welfare and Measurement*, edited by A. Sen. Cambridge: MIT Press.

———. 1997. "Maximization and the Act of Choice." *Econometrica* 65:745–79.

Sewell, William H. 1964. "Community of Residence and College Plans." *American Sociological Review* 29:24–38.

———. 1971. "Inequality of Opportunity for Higher Education." *American Sociological Review* 36:793–809.

Sewell, William H., Archibald O. Haller, and George W. Ohlendorf. 1970. "The Educational and Early Occupational Status Attainment Process: Replication and Revision." *American Sociological Review* 35:1014–24.

Sewell, William H., Archibald O. Haller, and Alejandro Portes. 1969. "The Educational and Early Occupational Attainment Process." *American Sociological Review* 34:82–92.

Sewell, William H., Archibald O. Haller, and Murray A. Straus. 1957. "Social Status and Educational and Occupational Aspiration." *American Sociological Review* 22:67–73.

Sewell, William H. and Robert M. Hauser. 1980. "The Wisconsin Longitudinal Study of Social and Psychological Factors in Aspirations and Achievements." *Research in Sociology of Education and Socialization* 1:59–99.

———. 1992. "The Influence of the American Occupational Structure on the Wisconsin Model." *Contemporary Sociology* 21:598–602.

Sheffrin, Steven M. 1996. *Rational Expectations*, 2nd Edition. Cambridge: Cambridge University Press.

Simon, Herbert Alexander. 1996. *The Sciences of the Artificial*. Cambridge: MIT Press.

Sobel, Michael E. 1998. "Causal Inference in Statistical Models of the Process of Socioeconomic Achievement: A Case Study." *Sociological Methods and Research* 27:318–48.

Sørensen, Aage B. 1998. "Theoretical Mechanisms and the Empirical Study of Social Processes." Pp. 238–66 in *Social Mechanisms: An Analytical Approach to Social Theory*, edited by P. Hedström and R. Swedberg. Cambridge: Cambridge University Press.

Spenner, Kenneth I. and David L. Featherman. 1978. "Achievement Ambitions." *Annual Review of Sociology* 4:373–420.

Spetzler, Carl S. and Carl-Axel S. Staël von Holstein. 1975. "Probability Encoding in Decision Analysis." *Management Science* 22:340–58.

Spiegelhalter, David J. and Robert J. Cowell. 1992. "Learning in Probabilistic Expert Systems." Pp. 447–65 in *Bayesian Statistics 4: Proceedings of the Fourth Valencia International Meeting, April 15–20, 1991*, edited by J. O. Berger and M. H. DeGroot. Oxford: Oxford University Press.

Steele, Claude M. 1992. "Race and the Schooling of Black Americans." *Atlantic Monthly* 269:68–78.

Steele, Claude M. 1997. "A Threat in the Air: How Stereotypes Shape Intellectual Identity and Performance." *The American Psychologist* 52:613–29.

Steele, Claude M. and Joshua Aronson. 1995. "Stereotype Threat and the Intellectual Test Performance of African Americans." *Journal of Personality and Social Psychology* 69:797–811.

Steele, Claude M., Steven J. Spencer, and Joshua Aronson. 2002. "Contending with Group Image: The Psychology of Stereotype and Social Identity Threat." In *Advances in Experimental Social Psychology*, vol. 34, edited by M. P. Zanna. Amsterdam: Academic Press.

Stinchcombe, Arthur L. 1964. *Rebellion in a High School*. Chicago: Quadrangle.

Stryker, Sheldon and Peter J. Burke. 2000. "The Past, Present, and Future of an Identity Theory." *Social Psychology Quarterly* 63:284–97.

U.S. Dept. of Education, National Center for Education Statistics. 1995. *High School & Beyond 1992 (Restricted) Data File* [CD-ROM]. Washington, D.C.: Office of Educational Research and Improvement [producer, distributor].

———. 2002. *National Education Longitudinal Study: 1988–2000* [CD-ROM]. Washington, D.C.: Office of Educational Research and Improvement [producer, distributor].

Wang, Haiqin, Denver Dash, and Marek J. Druzdzel. 2002. "A Method for Evaluating Elicitation Schemes for Probabilistic Methods." *IEEE Transactions on Systems, Man, and Cybernetics. Part B, Cybernetics* 32:38–43.

Wang, Haiqin and Marek J. Druzdzel. 2000. "User Interface Tools for Navigation in Conditional Probability Tables and Graphical Elicitation of Probabilities in Bayesian Networks." Pp. 617–25 in *Uncertainty in Artificial Intelligence: Proceedings of the Sixteenth Conference (UAI-2000)*. San Francisco: Morgan Kaufmann.

Wasserman, Stanley and Katherine Faust. 1994. *Social Network Analysis: Methods and Applications*. Cambridge: Cambridge University Press.

Wegner, Daniel M. and John A. Bargh. 1998. "Control and Automaticity in Social Life." In *The Handbook of Social Psychology*, 4th Edition, vol. 2, edited by D. T. Gilbert, S. T. Fiske, and G. Lindzey. Boston: McGraw-Hill.

Weisbrod, Burton A. 1962. "Education and Investment in Human Capital." *Journal of Political Economy* 70:S106–S23.

West, Mike. 1988. "Modeling Expert Opinion." Pp. 493–508 in *Bayesian Statistics 3: Proceedings of the Third Valencia International Meeting, June 1–5, 1987*, edited by J. M. Bernardo, M. H. DeGroot, D. V. Lindley, and A. F. M. Smith. Oxford: Oxford University Press.

Willis, Paul E. 1977. *Learning to Labour: How Working Class Kids Get Working Class Jobs*. New York: Columbia University Press.

Willis, Robert and Sherwin Rosen. 1979. "Education and Self-Selection." *Journal of Political Economy* 87:S7–S35.

Winship, Christopher and Stephen L. Morgan. 1999. "The Estimation of Causal Effects from Observational Data." *Annual Review of Sociology* 25:659–706.

INDEX

naive estimates of average causal effect, 73

no-assumptions bounds on average causal effect, 73–76, 90–91

strong ignorability assumption, 77–78

Crocker, Jennifer, 186, 190, 191, 195

Current Population Surveys (CPS), 8, 28–29n6

data collection techniques, 213–16

decision trees, commitment-based model
simple decision tree, 104–12
stochastic decision tree, *see* stochastic decision tree

DeGoot, Morris H., 179–81

demographic models, 59

Department of Education, U.S.
Gear Up program evaluation, 17–18
national surveys conducted by, 5

discrete choice analysis, 104

disidentification explanation for racial achievement gap, 184–202, *see also* tables, charts, and figures
commitment model, implications for, 198–202
disengagement, 187, 203–4n7
identity theory, 192, 204n12
Markov model for evolution of disidentification, 187–90, 194–99
original model developed by Steele, 185–87
performance evaluations, discounting, 195–98
self-esteem levels, 185, 186, 205–6n16
stereotype threat, 82, 184–89, 192, 195, 204n8
structural model for evolution of achievement and self-esteem, 190–95

Duncan, Otis Dudley, 27

economics and sociology, integration of, 58, 209–10

Education Department, U.S.
Gear Up program evaluation, 17–18
national surveys conducted by, 5

educational expectations as predictor of educational attainment, 10–13, *see also* belief/expectation forma-tion mechanisms, and more specific entries
causal relationship, *see* causal relation-ship between expectations and attainment
core concept of status socialization the-ory and Wisconsin model, 35, 36, 45–47
future research directions, 211–16
mechanisms, need for, 19–20, 24, 26–27, 31n24
mode of theoretical development for new model of, 24–27
policymaking guidance, inadequacy of current models for, 15–20, 16–19
predictive factors, 6–13
reasons for needing new model of, 3–5
sociology's readiness to embrace new model for, 20–24

Educational Testing Service, 16

ethnic groups, *see* racial/ethnic groups

evidence and theory, relationship between, 25–26

exogenous impact of shifts in costs and benefits, 22

expectations, *see* belief/expectation for-mation mechanisms; educational expectations as predictor of educa-tional attainment

expected utility theory *vs.* prospect theory, 137n17

fairness and openness of educational sys-tem, beliefs about, 184

family background as predictor of educa-tional attainment, 9–11, 100, *see also* tables, charts, and figures
Cameron and Heckman's theory as to, 23–24
path-model estimates, racial differences in, 61, 62

fast learners and Bayesian theory, *see* Bayesian learning theory

father, *see* entries at parent

federal policymaking guidance, inade-quacy of current models for, 15–20

females, *see* gender groups

field theory, 41–44

functionalist sociology, origins of Wiscon-sin model in, 35, 38